Faith and Hope in a War-Torn Land: The US Army Chaplaincy in the Balkans, 1995–2005

CH (LTC) Kenneth E. Lawson

Combat Studies Institute Press
Fort Leavenworth, KS 66027

Library of Congress Cataloging-in-Publication Data

Lawson, Kenneth E., 1961-
  Faith and hope in a war-torn land : the U.S. Army chaplaincy in the Balkans, 1995-2005 / by Kenneth E. Lawson.
    p. cm.
  Includes bibliographical references and index.
  1. Bosnia and Hercegovina--History--1992- 2. Peacekeeping forces--Bosnia and Hercegovina. 3. Kosovo (Serbia)--History--1980- 4. Peacekeeping forces--Serbia and Montenegro--Kosovo (Serbia) 5. United States. Army. Chaplain Corps--History--20th century. 6. United States. Army. Chaplain Corps--History--21st century. 7. Lawson, Kenneth E., 1961- I. Title.

  DR1750.L39 2006
  949.703--dc22
  [B]

2006021509

For sale by the Superintendent of Documents, US Government Printing Office
Internet: bookstore.gpo.gov Phone: toll free (866) 512-1800; DC area (202) 512-1800
Fax: (202) 512-2250 Mail: Stop IDCC, Washington, DC 20402-0001

ISBN 0-16-076436-X

Foreword

In *Faith and Hope in a War-Torn Land: The US Army Chaplaincy in the Balkans, 1995–2005,* Chaplain (Lieutenant Colonel) Ken Lawson has provided the Army with an unusual and much needed perspective on its history. The Combat Studies Institute is proud to add this study from the US Army Chaplain Corps to our Special Studies series of publications.

The Chaplain Corps, with justifiable pride, has demonstrated in this study the key role played by the Reserve components (Army National Guard and Army Reserve) in providing religious support to the Army. While this has become routine today, it was certainly not the case in 1995. This is yet another step forward in the integration of the Active and Reserve components in the Army.

This study analyzes the planning, command and control, and operations of the Chaplain Corps, but its target audience should be much larger. Commanders and staff officers alike will gain a better appreciation for what it takes to implement an effective ministry program for their units by reading this study. They will also gain insights about the operational role that chaplains can play in the accomplishment of the Army's objectives in a theater of operations.

We believe this work will be a valuable addition to the Army's history. *CSI—The Past is Prologue!*

Timothy R. Reese
Colonel, Armor
Director, Combat Studies Institute

Foreword

Chaplain (Lieutenant Colonel) Ken Lawson has added a significant body of research to the Army Chaplaincy history with *Faith and Hope in a War-Torn Land: The US Army Chaplaincy in the Balkans, 1995–2005.* Thorough research with a blend of names and stories from those who served there provides a historical sketch that will enable interested parties to examine this oft-neglected period of chaplain history.

Chaplain Lawson's initial historical review of the Balkans provides the setting to help one understand what led to America's involvement in the region. He deftly works his way through the key points of a confusing history that ultimately leads to US and international engagement in the area. Later in the book, he provides an excellent summary of the Bosnia and Kosovo regions and the consequent US presence there. This background information is very helpful in understanding the crucial nature of chaplain ministry, because much of the Balkans conflict is related to religious issues.

Chaplain Lawson's use of personal Army chaplain and chaplain assistant accounts makes up the bulk of the work. His use of quotes, stories, written accounts, and personal observations provides a broad look at religious ministry in this relatively new Army environment—an environment of peacekeeping and multinational, joint-service coordination. He points out that the religious support in the Balkans conflict was also a period in which the Army had to use the Reserve components (Army National Guard and Army Reserve) in a significant way.

This excellent book provides a wealth of practical and timely information that will serve the Army chaplaincy well into the future. It should also prove to be a valuable addition to any study of this region and this period of history.

Chaplain (BG) Douglas E. Lee
Assistant Chief of Chaplains for
Mobilization and Readiness

Preface

This study of United States (US) Army chaplains and chaplain assistants serving in the Balkans would not have been possible without the support and cooperation of many of the Unit Ministry Team (UMT) members who were there and were willing to tell their stories. On completion, a tour of duty in the Balkans was almost universally considered inglorious duty. For those US Army troops who arrived in Bosnia in late 1995 and 1996, accommodations were miserable. Undeveloped base camps, miserable traveling conditions, inhospitable weather, and the ever-present threat from land mines and snipers made the early years of the US Army in Bosnia quite challenging. In 1999, Kosovo repeated the same scenario.

Initially, the US military involvement in the Balkans was predicted to last about 1 year. At the time of this writing, the US military has been in the Balkans for more than 10 years. Much of the US military presence in that region faded once missions were accomplished. Large numbers of base camps have closed or been turned over to European allies. Currently, the US Army has approximately 2,500 troops in Kosovo and about 250 in Bosnia,[1] these numbers being a fraction of the Army soldiers stationed in the Balkans several years earlier.

The entry of the US military into the Balkans in 1995 was not an attack on a nation that threatened the vital interests or national security of the United States. Essentially, the US military was sent to the Balkans on a humanitarian, peacemaking, and peacekeeping mission. As Yugoslavia imploded and civil tensions developed into ethnic cleansing (genocide), President Bill Clinton, for moral and humanitarian reasons, committed US troops to the area. This was a mission against an aggressive and illusive foe. The Army of Serbia was formidable for their region, but nowhere near the class of the juggernaut US military. As one author stated, "America has long been more powerful than all but a handful of countries, so the cost of intervention in small states has always been low. Or so it appeared before virtually every conflict; it did not always work out that way."[2]

Providing religious support to US soldiers in the Balkans was a challenge to Army chaplains. Beginning with minimal resources or supplies, chaplains met the religious needs of soldiers in both formal and informal settings. Chaplains conducted religious services, counseling, prayer meetings, family reunion meetings, and morale enhancing lectures in often austere and humble situations and circumstances. As the years went on, more and better chapels were constructed in the Balkans; these buildings became the focal point for religious activities for soldiers. Chaplains also led or participated in humanitarian or nation-building missions related to developing friendships with the local populations. Army chaplains delivered huge amounts of donated supplies from religious and other groups in the United States to the destitute of the Balkans. Further, Army chaplains led the way in creating opportunities for discussion of religious and social issues with indigenous clergy, these groups often composed of Muslim, Roman Catholic, and Orthodox Christian groups that have been antagonists for centuries.[3]

My personal experiences in the Balkans were in the years 2002 and 2003. While assigned as an Army chaplain with the 7th Army Reserve Command (ARCOM) in Heidelberg, Germany, I was able to make five short ministry trips to various sites in the Balkans. Small numbers of soldiers from my Army Reserve unit mobilized and deployed to locations in Bosnia, Kosovo, Hungary, and Macedonia. I also went to the Balkans with the approval of the US Army Europe (USAREUR) chaplain and my commander at the 7th ARCOM, Brigadier General (BG) David Zabecki, to troubleshoot integration issues between Reserve component chaplains and Active Duty chaplains.

These trips, 5 to 10 days each, were to soldiers stationed far away from home. It was a rewarding experience for me. By 2002–2003, the major security risk for US soldiers in the Balkans was past. Nevertheless, the physical destruction was still evident in many places. Burned out and bombed buildings were common, while in small villages and in cities like Pristina there were still bullet holes in numerous buildings, demolished structures, and bomb craters. Driving in a small convoy from Sarajevo to Tuzla in Bosnia revealed numerous signs of military destruction. The road from Pristina Airport near Camp Bondsteel in Kosovo south to Camp Able Sentry near Skopje in Macedonia was treacherous itself, even without the malicious looks from the local populous. In Bosnia, I stood and prayed at the killing fields in Srebrenica, where Serbian troops murdered several thousand Muslim men and boys while people in nearby villages heard random gunfire at night.

I will always have fond memories of ministering to soldiers in the Balkans as they performed their missions in a hostile fire zone. Although there were no US casualties as a direct result of combat with enemy forces, there were numerous fatalities from land mines, malfunctioning or mishandled weapons, traffic accidents, aircraft crashes, and suicides. In these instances of death, grief, loss, frustration, and pain, there were Army chaplains to minister to those in need of spiritual or emotional strength. Chaplains also conducted more routine chapel-based ministries such as religious services, holiday celebrations, family reunion lectures, Bible studies, tours of local religious sites, and similar things. Chaplain David Zalis recalled:

> I was the first KFOR Chaplain. There was always a sense of danger in Kosovo in 1999. We had good military intelligence that told us when civilian riots were happening and we avoided those areas at those times. There was a lot of hate in the people's faces, toward each other and toward the NATO troops in their country. The US and NATO troops did a remarkable job of peacekeeping and were very restrained in dealing with the ethnic and religious hatred in the region.[4]

I wish to express my appreciation to Dr. John Brinsfield, US Army Chaplain Corps Historian, for his encouragement and guidance throughout this project. The librarians at the US Army Chaplain Center and School provided me invaluable assistance in gathering resources for this work. I take full responsibility for any mistakes in the text.

Chaplain (LTC) Kenneth E. Lawson
US Army, 2006

Notes

1. *Army Times*, 17 October 2005, 7.

2. Max Boot, *The Savage Wars of Peace: Small Wars and the Rise of American Power* (New York: Perseus Books, 2002), xx.

3. Ronald L. Cobb, *Memories of Bosnia: The 35th Division's SFOR 13 NATO Peacekeeping Mission* (Bloomington, IN: AuthorHouse Publishers, 2004), 183–279. While in Bosnia, Chaplain (COL) Cobb was the Command Chaplain for the 35th Infantry Division, Kansas Army National Guard.

4. Chaplain (BG) David Zalis, interview by author, 4 May 2005.

Contents

Maps

Figures

Chapter 1

Introduction

At the time of this writing, the US Army operations in the Balkans are only a fraction of what they were 10 years ago. The term "Balkans" is a common way of describing the geographic region composed of the peninsula-shaped land mass between Italy and Turkey in Eastern Europe. The etymology of the word "Balkan" comes from the Turkish word for mountain or a highland slope.[1] Noting the divisive and fragmented civil history of this region, in the English language the word "balkanize" has come to mean "to divide (a country, territory, etc.) into small, often quarrelsome states."[2] Modern nations that fall in the geographic region of the Balkans are Albania, Bulgaria, Greece, Rumania, and European Turkey; and the states spawned from the collapsed nation of Yugoslavia, namely Bosnia-Herzegovina, Croatia, Macedonia, and Slovenia. What is left of the former Yugoslavia is now called the Federal Republic of Yugoslavia (Serbia and Montenegro). Sometimes Hungary is considered a Balkans nation and sometimes it is excluded.

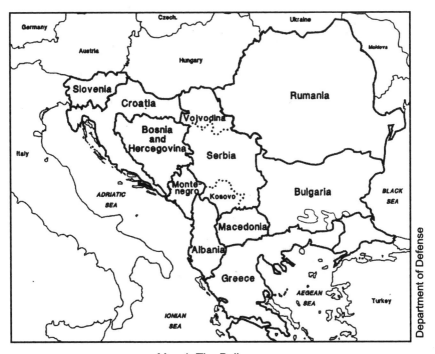

Map 1. The Balkans.

President Bill Clinton's administration was initially reluctant to fully engage and confront the civil, military, and cultural turmoil of this region. Many perceived the internal strife of the Balkans as a black hole, a hopeless religious and cultural quagmire best avoided by the US military. Clinton remarked in 1992 that he was 100 days into office and was frustrated over the US policy in the Balkans. Clinton criticized his predecessor's role in allowing Bosnia to dissolve into a civil war, stating that peace in the Balkans was "a long way from a solution." He further described the handling of the situation by the United Nations (UN) and the North Atlantic Treaty Organization (NATO) as a "long, torturous process."[3]

Initially, there were many reasons the United States expressed reluctance to get involved in a Balkans war. The three basic reasons were:

- The long and desperate history of warfare and ethnic hatred in that region.
- The confusion related to the rules of engagement and chain of command between NATO, the US military, the European Union (EU), and the role of the US president in tactical decisions.
- The reluctance of the Clinton administration to commit ground troops into a military quagmire reminiscent of Vietnam.

Understanding what was going on in the US government and in the military in the 1980s and 1990s helps to explain why the United States was slow to respond militarily in the Balkans. Perhaps no other person was more qualified to speak about the diverse political and military strains on the United States during this period than former Ambassador to the United Nations and later Secretary of State Madeline Albright. Before Secretary Albright was in office in the 1980s, there were the successful United States military operations in Grenada and Panama. In 1990–91, the United States was at war with Iraq, a quick-ending conflict that resulted in a decisive US victory. Albright was quite perceptive in her comments related to the pressures on the US government in the 1990s and the final decision to commit the use of military force in the Balkans.

> Early critics of the Clinton administration's foreign policy questioned the president's wisdom in focusing so much attention on parts of the world that were not central to America's strategic interests, but this was unfair and hardly his choice. The new administration was deeply involved in strengthening ties to our European and Asian allies, fashioning a new relationship with Russia, seeking peace in the Middle East, winning support for a free-trade agreement with Canada and Mexico, and dealing

with other 'big ticket' items. The Clinton team could hardly overlook the fact that, early in his term, a civil war was under way in Bosnia, more than 20,000 US troops were busy saving lives in Somalia, ethnic tensions would explode in the Central African nation of Rwanda, and thousands of desperate migrants were fleeing a cruel and illegitimate regime in Haiti. . . . In Rwanda, we did too little. In Haiti and Bosnia, after false starts, we eventually got it right.[4]

While serving at the United Nations in 1994, Albright commented on the world situation:

At the time, there were clashes or extreme tensions in Bosnia, Somalia, Haiti, Georgia, Azerbaijan, Armenia, Angola, Liberia, Mozambique, Sudan, Cambodia, Afghanistan, and Tajikistan, as well as ongoing defiance of Security Council resolutions by Saddam Hussein's Iraq. . . . Since 1994, new and frightening dangers have arisen that also compete for their [the UN's] attention. There are no grounds for confidence that the next intimations of genocide will be detected in time or that there would be volunteers for the job of preventing wide-scale killing once it got under way.[5]

Religiously, the Balkans has been an area of tension for many centuries. Located at the junction of Asia and Europe, the Balkans has served as a buffer zone and a place of tension between various and alien cultures, languages, and beliefs. It is not as simple as stating that the Balkans is a Muslim versus Christian region of the world. Each religion has militant and nonmilitant followers. Each group has those who are belligerent and those who seek reconciliation with their neighbors. Some Muslims are mostly secular while others are devout. For those with Christian traditions, there have been centuries of rivalry and tension between Roman Catholics and Eastern Orthodox or Serbian Orthodox adherents. In this capacity, US Army chaplains would provide invaluable service to their commanders and to other soldiers related to the religious issues that still divide the Balkans today.

General John M. Shalikashvili served from June 1992 through October 1993 as Supreme Allied Commander, Europe (SACEUR) and Commander of the US European Command (EUCOM). As pressure for US military involvement in the volatile Balkans was increasing, Shalikashvili retained the Clinton administration's attitude of passive US and international pressure to encourage the cessation of hostilities. Commenting on the behavior of the Serbians as the enemy, the general remarked that if humanitarian aid could be brought to the suffering and if water, electricity, and other modern necessities could be returned to the people, the United States would not intervene militarily. Shalikashvili commented that the US intent toward the Serbians was "to persuade them to modify their behavior." Seemingly unconcerned with the power of centuries of ethnic and religious hatred, the United States' passive and nonmilitary persuasion efforts failed. Shalikashvili further showed the naïve perspective of the US senior leadership toward the Balkan powder keg when he remarked that the civil war within the former Yugoslavia was a "senseless struggle."[6] Certainly the centuries of religious and ethnic hatred made sense to the Balkans population. As inhumane and cruel as they were to each other, the issues related to ethnic and religious hatred were historically verifiable.

The delicate balance of religion, politics, and ethnicity in the Balkans is vital to peace in Europe and elsewhere. As was predicted by Serbian Orthodox Priest Father Sava Janjic in the late 1990s, civil war in the Balkans could easily engulf the entire region, including Greece and Turkey, and could develop into a contest between European Christendom and the Muslim world.[7] Thankfully that did not happen, in part because NATO and the United States became involved at a point where military intervention produced a cease-fire and ongoing peacekeeping and nation-building operations have been successful. As the delicate balance of peace in the Balkans became unsettled in the early 1990s, Albright assessed the world situation and the role of the United States as peacekeepers as follows:

> The early 1990s were a time of experimenting and learning hard lessons about the potential and limits of multilateral peacekeeping. One of the most basic lessons taught by our experience in Somalia, Rwanda, and Haiti was that an arbitrarily rigid or cookie cutter approach would not work. Each situation was different, with a unique blend of history, personality, culture, and politics. To me, however, the overriding lesson was clear. The international community, through the UN or other means, had a responsibility to help societies endangered by natural or human caused catastrophe. It was in America's interest to ensure that this responsibility was fulfilled because it would make the world more stable and peaceful, and because it was right.[8]

Notes

1. Andrew Wheatcroft, *Infidels: A History of the Conflict Between Christendom and Islam* (New York: Random House Publishers, 2003), 214.

2. *Webster's Random House Dictionary* (1999 edition), 102.

3. Bill Clinton, *My Life* (New York: Alfred A. Knopf Publisher, 2005), 424, 508, 510, 513, 534.

4. Madeline Albright, *Madam Secretary: A Memoir* (New York: Miramax Books, 2003), 177–178.

5. Ibid., 187, 195.

6. "Announcement by President Clinton of His Nomination of General John M. Shalikashvili to be Chairman of the Joint Chiefs of Staff, the White House, Washington, DC, 11 August 1993." Quoted from John M. Shalikashvili, *Selected Speeches, Testimony and Interviews by General John M. Shalikashvili, Chairman of the Joint Chiefs of Staff* (Washington, DC: US Government Printing Office, 1998), 1–2.

7. Michael A. Sells, *The Bridge Betrayed: Religion and Genocide in Bosnia* (Berkeley: University of California Press, 1998), xvii–xviii.

8. Albright, *Madam Secretary*, 202–203.

Chapter 2

Background: A War-torn Region of the World

The Balkans has a tortured history. The ancient Greeks attempted to spread civilization north into the Balkans region by force and were largely successful. When the Romans came, the region was still volatile, a haven for Asian nomads and Slavic peasants who resisted Roman rule. At the beginning of the Christian era, the Apostle Paul and others attempted numerous missionary trips into this area, achieving various degrees of success. During the decline of the Roman Empire, hordes of so-called barbarians came through the Balkans area to attack the declining power of Rome. Throughout later church history, this region became a point of contention between Roman Catholic and Eastern Orthodox missions. Then, with the intervention of Islam in the region, hatred of various religious and ethnic groups intensified. Simply stated, this part of the world has been politically unstable for millenniums.

The turmoil in the Balkans is a direct result of centuries of religious and political unrest. Contemporary atrocities are the result of past prejudices and violence coming to fruition. People of the Balkans have long memories, and events that took place years or centuries ago are considered modern injustices to be rectified with a vengeance. As one author stated, "Today, it is a war fanned by vivid religious memories of the past and a desire to get revenge at any cost. This is evident in the population cleansing that is currently taking place. It is not just ethnic cleansing; it is religious and the intent is to inflict as much pain and suffering as possible."[1]

It is inappropriate solely to base the cause of unrest in the Balkans on the introduction of Islam. Certainly, the spread of Islam exasperated an already tense political and cultural region of the world. From 700 to 1100, Islam was a distant threat to the Balkans; from 1100 to 1300, Islam became a severe threat. By 1300 to 1500, Islam was an urgent threat, with the fall of Constantinople in 1453 signaling the defeat of the Christian Byzantine Empire and the triumph of the Muslim world. Nevertheless, within the Balkans themselves, while still under the Christian Byzantine Empire, ethnic tensions and political rivalries severely fractured social and civil harmony in the region. The introduction of Islam into the Balkans only further divided the territory.

Religion has always played a major role in Yugoslavian cultural and ethnic identity and has been, on many occasions, the cause for major or local conflicts. From the earliest Christian times, the southern part of this region was thoroughly evangelized. Yet the penetration of the Christian faith into the more northern Balkan states did not occur until centuries later. At the rise of the bishopric of Rome in the sixth century, there was little support in the Balkans for this Latin prelate. Allegiance for Eastern European Christians was toward Alexandria, Antioch, Jerusalem, and Constantinople. When the first three of these cities fell early to Muslims, Constantinople became the sole location for the senior bishop of Eastern European Christianity. The Balkans region was on the border between Roman Catholic Latin Christianity and primarily Greek speaking Eastern Orthodox Christianity. A unified Christian voice has never sounded from the Balkans. The three major religious groups in the Balkans have been Eastern Orthodox Christianity, Roman Catholic Christianity, and Islam.

The most severe threat by Islam to the Balkans came under the expanding Ottoman Empire. From the 13th through the 18th centuries, Ottoman Muslims made an attempt at regional if not world supremacy. Muslim armies expanded their influence across the Bosporus into the Balkans, ultimately desiring to bring all of Europe under Islam. When initially Constantinople would not fall, the Muslims simply bypassed the fortified city and pillaged throughout the Balkan Peninsula. In 1389, Serbian, Albanian, Montenegrin, and Bosnian armies under the command of Serbian Prince Lazar were defeated at the Battle of Kosovo. This was the beginning of the Muslim Ottoman rule and Christian persecution in what would become Yugoslavia. Ruthless vengeance by Muslims on infidel Christians resulted in a Balkans bloodbath, as complete Christian villages were systematically massacred, enslaved, tortured, and looted. Common practices of death on the Christian Balkans people were impaling, beheading, and dismembering of men, women, and children. Every 4 years the most talented and athletic Christian boys were taken from their parents, coerced to convert to Islam, and forced into service for the Ottoman Empire as special combat troops.[2]

During the subsequent few hundred years of direct Muslim control, various ethnic groups under Ottoman rule had diverse experiences in the Balkans. In the northern Balkans regions, which would eventually become the countries of Hungary, Romania, Czechoslovakia, and Moldavia, total Muslim control was fleeting. Local Christian armies from these regions resisted domination by the Ottomans and became only vassal states. Muslim control above the Danube River was always tenuous. By the 1600s, Muslim influence in the northern Balkans region was in rapid decline.

Bosnia and Herzegovina had a large-scale conversion to Islam both in the rural and urban populations. Those who converted received free land. Christians and others who did not convert were either killed or subjected to oppressive rule. From 1463 through 1878, Bosnia and Herzegovina were under Ottoman rule. While many converted to Islam, many did not, with one account stating that about 50 percent of the Bosnian population remained Christians.[3] Christians were harassed, persecuted, and murdered. It was these Christians and their continual rebellion against Muslim rulers that for centuries irritated the Ottoman rulers and eventually led, with European help, to the expulsion of Ottoman Muslims from the region. Local converts to Islam remained behind at their own peril.

Muslim rule in Serbia was not so oppressive. As long as the Christians paid taxes and did not proselytize, they were permitted to live according to Serbian customs and to govern their own local affairs. Most Muslims in Serbia from the 14th through the 18th centuries were tolerant of their Christian subjects. However, the wealth and the hierarchy of the Serbian Orthodox Church were particularly dismantled by the Ottomans, with the clergy assuming more local civil responsibilities. Tension was always present. The clergy are credited with preserving the Serbian culture through Muslim rule, thus elevating them in the minds of the people.[4] Nationalistic pride became synonymous with the Serbian Orthodox Church. In the late 17th century, Serb peasants, encouraged by Serb clergy, supported several attempts by the Roman Catholic European Hapsburg armies to overthrow the Muslims, all unsuccessfully.

Montenegro, a tiny region located between Bosnia-Herzegovina and Albania, through evasion and guerrilla warfare was able to avoid being conquered by the Ottomans. Using the inhospitable mountainous terrain to their advantage, the overextended Muslim armies could not defeat the Montenegrin forces in open combat. While their neighboring kingdoms fell to the Muslims, Montenegrin Prince Ivan Crnojevic moved his capital from Zabljak on Lake Skadar into the highland valley of Lovcenski Dolac (precursor to the capital Cetinje) under Mount Lovcen in 1482. This event conventionally marks the beginning of the history of Montenegro and its capital, Cetinje, built around the Cetinje monastery. As the influence of the Ottoman Muslims waned in the 19th century, Montenegrin troops often assisted their neighbors in expelling the Muslims.

The Croats along the Dalmatian coast joined with the Hungarians in fighting the Turks for about 60 years after the fall of Bosnia in 1463. The defeat of the Hungarian army in 1526 forced the Croats to turn to the Roman Catholic Hapsburg emperors for protection. By the end of the 16th century, the Muslims had conquered most of Croatia, their main years of domination being from 1526 to 1699. The Austrian armies of the Hapsburg emperors continually fought small skirmishes with Ottoman forces west of the Drina River. After the Muslims lost control of Croatia around 1700, the Hapsburg armies shared the gains with the Roman Catholic Austrian soldiers as spoils of war, to the neglect and frustration of the Croatian people.

Albania was captured relatively late by Ottoman armies as they controlled the Albanian region from 1482 through 1912. Conversion of the Albanians to Islam was widespread, so much so that the predominate religion today in Albania is a Balkan-style form of Islam. Feuding Albanian armies were no match for the Ottoman Empire. Five centuries of Ottoman rule fractured the Albanian people along religious, tribal, and regional lines, with even the Muslim converts dividing into rival sects. Both Roman Catholic and Eastern Orthodox Albanians converted to Islam, with many only outwardly professing faith in Islam. During the centuries of Ottoman rule, the Albanian region remained one of Europe's most backward areas.[5]

During the 15th through the 18th centuries, Christian Orthodox Russia was a major player in the religious and political tensions in the Balkans. Expanding Russian influences consistently threatened Ottoman control above the Danube River and around the Black Sea. Religiously, the Russian Orthodox Church and the Serbian Orthodox Church were similar in liturgy and Slavic culture and developed a close bond. Russia was very interested in stopping the Ottoman influence along its southern borders. Beginning in the late 1400s, Russian armies fought Ottoman Muslims along the northern and northwestern shores of the Black Sea. By 1475, the lands directly above the Black Sea became an Ottoman vassal area, while 50 years later the region of the modern nation of Moldavia came under direct Ottoman control. By 1800, Russia had mostly expelled the Ottoman Muslims from these regions north and northwest of the Black Sea. The Russian royal family longed for the fall of Istanbul and the restarting of orthodoxy in what was Constantinople—a goal they never were able to achieve.[6]

The collapse of the Ottoman Empire created chaos in the Balkans. Orthodox and Roman Catholic Christians persecuted those who sided with the Ottoman Muslims. Large groups of Muslims migrated to regions within the Balkans where they were tolerated, primarily Kosovo and Albania. Fighting and atrocities between villages were common. By the late 1800s, as the Ottomans departed the Balkan Peninsula, the Austrian Hapsburg Empire and the Russians sought greater influence. This outside desire for expansion and influence in the Balkans was often resisted with as much local vigor and passion as the Muslim Ottomans had been resisted. Having survived centuries of Ottoman rule, ethnic principalities of Serbs, Montenegrins, Kosovars, Bulgars, Slavs, Croats, and others did not want another foreign sovereign to rule over them. Muslims who remained in their villages were often harassed and persecuted, but in many cases, they simply were left alone resulting in a tense peace between neighbors.

The departure of the Ottomans from the Balkans left a political vacuum in the region. From the early 19th century on, the Balkan wars of liberation have been complex mixtures of emancipation from Ottoman rule, manifestation of Balkan unity, and rebellion against outside Christian and Muslim administrators.[7] This political vacuum was first evident in the Macedonian Struggle, which lasted from the late 1870s until the Balkan Wars of 1912–13.

In the Macedonian Struggle, there was a competition for the region of Macedonia between Greek, Serbian, and Bulgarian interests, with an element of native Macedonians calling for independent nation status. Later, Romanian and Ottoman military forces added confusion to this scenario. That which began as a propaganda campaign between rival factions, developed into roving bands of paramilitary thugs creating violence and deprecations throughout the region. The Balkan Wars of 1912–13 absorbed this military and political unrest. These wars were fought primarily in Thrace (in the east) and in Macedonia (in the west) and were major armed conflicts between the remnants of the Ottoman Empire against primarily Bulgarian, Serbian, Montenegrin, and Greek forces. Armies on each side numbered in the hundreds of thousands. Balkan armies had a decided artillery advantage over the less sophisticated artillery of the Ottoman Turks. As the Ottomans were withdrawing, the Bulgarians, sensing a possibility to acquire more land and influence, fought against Serbian and Greek forces. Romania then declared war against Bulgaria. In the midst of another escalating Balkans civil war, a sudden cease-fire was called on 30 July 1913.

On 28 June 1914, Archduke Francis Ferdinand, heir to the Austrian throne, was assassinated as he and his wife drove through the streets of Sarajevo, Bosnia. His assassin was a student from a secret terrorist organization in Serbia, which had protested against Austria's annexation of Bosnia and Herzegovina. At first, the European powers hoped this conflict of interests would not escalate. On 28 July 1914, Austria rejected an attempt at reconciliation with Belgrade, the capital of Serbia, and declared war. Russia, concerned for the welfare of fellow Slavs and their Christian Orthodox brethren, began a large mobilization of its military. On 1 August Germany, closely allied with Austria, declared war on Russia. France entered the war against Germany on 3 August. Germany invaded Belgium, forcing Great Britain into the war. Thus began, as one author stated, "one of the greatest catastrophes that have ever befallen the human race."[8]

During the early 20th century, Islam had declined in the Balkans to the point that Muslims were the recipients of the pain and persecution they had imposed on Christians under Islamic Ottoman rule. Muslims that did not congregate in larger groups remained rural, uneducated, and impoverished. Others were segregated into Muslim neighborhoods and remained isolated from non-Muslims. Muslims in the Balkans never regained their status in the upper echelons of Balkan society. At the turn of the century, Serbs perceived the Muslims as the chief impediment to creating a dominant Serbian culture in the reinvigorated and independent nation of Serbia.

During World War I, compared to central Europe the Balkans region was mostly an afterthought. The largest battles were fought far away in central Europe. Within the Balkans, there were divided loyalties and allegiances with some considerable but infrequent military activities. In 1914, the Austrians undertook three invasions of Serbia, all of which were repulsed. This front then remained inactive until 1915. After Bulgaria declared war on Serbia in October 1915, Allied troops advanced into Serbia. Bulgarian forces defeated a combined Serbian-British-French force, while the Germans launched a separate successful attack into Serbia through Austria-Hungary. By the end of 1915, the Central Powers had conquered all of Serbia and defeated the Serbian army. The surviving Serbian forces took refuge in Albania, Montenegro, and the Greek island of Corfu, with their British and French Allies taking refuge in the eastern Greek city of Salonika (Thessaloniki).[9]

Two periods of fighting took place in the Balkans in 1916. In August, a reconstituted Serbian army advanced with Russian and Italian allies against the Germans and Bulgarians near Salonika. After some initial success, a strong counterattack forced them back. On the other side of the Balkan Peninsula in October 1916, Allied forces began a large and successful offensive in Macedonia. On 19 November, the Allied troops captured Monastir and by the middle of December reached Lake Ohrid, on the border of Albania and Macedonia. Meanwhile, Austrian forces employed extensive repressive measures against the Bosnia Serbs. Over 5,000 Serbs were interred in horrific detention and torture camps where many starved to death. To cope with the almost continuous state of rebellion in the central Balkans, the Austrians deported or relocated thousands in a final futile effort to pacify the area.[10]

The years 1917 and 1918 saw the collapse of the German-Austrian-Hungarian-Bulgarian influence in the Balkans. In 1917, there were several inconclusive engagements between Serbian and Allied forces against the Central Powers near Monastir, at Lake Presba, and on the Vardar River.

The fighting in 1918 was disastrous for the Central Powers. In September, a huge force of about 700,000 troops consisting of French, British, Greeks, Italians, and the remnants of the Serbian army began a large-scale offensive against the German, Austrian, and Bulgarian troops in Serbia. The Allied offensive was so successful that the thoroughly defeated Bulgarians initiated an armistice with the Allies. Romania was invaded by the Allies and subsequently switched allegiance to the Allied cause, the Italians occupied Albania, and Serbian troops reoccupied much of their former territory and Belgrade.

The defeat of the Central Powers in the Balkans in 1918 led to the quick creation of a nation-state for the Czechs and Slovaks called Czechoslovakia. Shortly thereafter, the Slavic peoples in the region banded together to create what would eventually become Yugoslavia. In November 1918, the Hungarians established an independent government, while the last Hapsburg Emperor, Charles I, abdicated the throne as the Austrian Republic was formed.

As a tenuous peace settled over the post-World War I Balkans, deprecations by neighboring villages on each other were common. Those who fled their homes or were forcefully relocated returned to find their properties destroyed, looted, or occupied by strangers. One interesting result of World War I in the Balkans was the high esteem granted the Serbian people by Western nations. Seen as heroic resistors to outside aggressors, the Bosnian people proved a valuable friend to Allied forces.[11] What Western leaders did not notice was that Serbians were as guilty as the others were in their postwar revenge on civilians who supported the German, Bulgarian, or Austrian armies.

World War I devastated large sections of Serbia, Kosovo, Bosnia, Herzegovina, Albania, and Macedonia. There were dramatic consequences for the post-World War I Balkans. Serbia gained historic lands it had not possessed since medieval times. After the war, fear of an expansionist Italy inspired Serbian, Croatian, and Slovenian leaders to form the new federation known as Yugoslavia, "the land of the South Slavs." As early as July 1917 a vision for a united Serbian state was acknowledged in the Declaration of Corfu, which called for a union of Serbs, Croats, and Slovenes in one nation with a single democratic, constitutional, parliamentary system. Ethnic hatred, religious rivalry, language barriers, and cultural conflicts plagued the fledgling Kingdom of Yugoslavia. The question of centralization versus federalism bitterly divided the Serbs and Croats, democratic solutions were blocked, and a dictatorship appeared inevitable. Territorial disputes with Yugoslavia's neighbors complicated an already tense existence. Many people regarded the new attempts at self-government as alien, exploitative, and secondary to kinship loyalties, religious beliefs, and cultural traditions.[12] In deep respect for the courage and suffering of the Serbian people, President Woodrow Wilson on 28 July 1918 ordered the Serbian flag raised over the White House.

As World War II approached, the Balkans was essentially a rural, undeveloped region in a politically unstable situation. World War II began officially on 1 September 1939. The animosity from World War I toward Germany by Serbians, Kosovars, Bosnians, and others meant that Yugoslavia would naturally oppose Germany in the war. Almost immediately after the war started, Italy and Germany were active in the Balkan Peninsula. Berlin pressed the Balkan countries to sign the Tripartite Pact and align themselves with the Axis powers—Germany, Italy, and Japan. Romania signed in November 1940 and Bulgaria in March 1941. Italy and Germany became active in Greece. Now virtually surrounded by enemies, neutral Yugoslavia desperately sought allies, signing a nonaggression pact with the Soviet Union in 1941. Convinced that their situation was hopeless, Yugoslavia reluctantly signed a "protocol of adherence" to the Tripartite Pact on 25 March 1941. In return, Hitler guaranteed that Germany would not invade Yugoslavia or ask for military assistance. Two days later, the Yugoslavian military, with huge popular support, overthrew their compromising government in euphoria of anti-German sentiment. In response, on 6 April the German Luftwaffe bombed Belgrade, killing thousands of civilians. Axis forces then invaded, with Yugoslavia unconditionally surrendering on 17 April 1941.[13]

During World War II, Germany, Italy, and Bulgaria dismembered Yugoslavia. Germany occupied Serbia and the northern region of Vojvodina and created a puppet government in Croatia that included Bosnia-Herzegovina. Germany and Italy divided Slovenia while Italy focused its expansionist ideas on the Dalmatian coastline, Kosovo, and Albania. Hungary grabbed Yugoslavian territories along its border while Bulgaria took Macedonia and part of southern Serbia. Germany and Italy then began to exploit the natural resources of the region while unleashing a reign of terror.[14] In defiance of the cultural and religious sensitivities of the region, the Germans did mass deportations, looted and robbed civilians, and practiced genocide. German sponsored Croatian paramilitary forces, called the Ustase, eliminated two million Serbs, Jews, and Gypsies through concentration camps, deportations, forced conversions, torture, and murder. The Ustase were so vicious toward their Balkan neighbors that Germany and Italy had to introduce measures to minimize their horrific violence toward civilians.

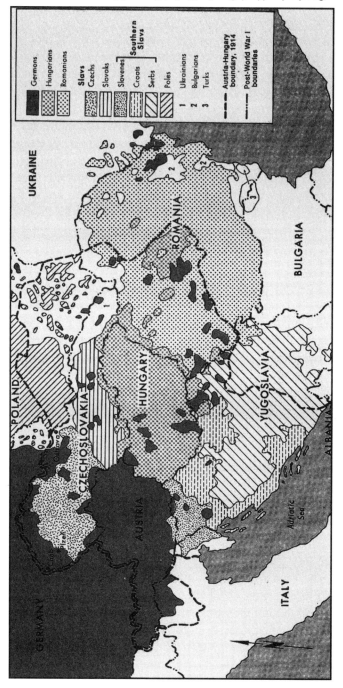

Map 2. Disintegration of Austria-Hungary, 1918.

Resistance in Yugoslavia to the Axis Powers came from two groups. One group was called Cetnic, from the Serbian word meaning detachment. The Cetnic were composed of fragments of the Yugoslavian army and Serbians fleeing genocide.[15] The second group to oppose the Axis forces in the Balkans was the communist-led Partisans. The leader of the Partisans was the dynamic Josip Broz Tito, a longtime communist who opposed the Tripartite Pact and sought to unify fragments of the old Yugoslavia against the Axis occupation forces. Tito's motto, "Death to Fascism, Freedom to the People" rallied various ethnic and religious groups to join his resistance movement. Beginning in July 1941, the Cetnic and Partisans fought a guerrilla war primarily against the occupying Germans. The multitude of skirmishes and small battles fought throughout the Balkans were savage encounters between hated enemies. Civilians on each side were massacred in the thousands. Then Cetnic forces and Partisans began fighting each other as the Balkans degenerated into total chaos, with the Partisans becoming the force supported by the western Allies.

Some sense of order came to the Balkans after the September 1944 arrival of the Soviet Union army at the Romanian-Yugoslavian border. It was clear who was fighting whom at this point. Soviet troops crossed the border on 1 October and a joint Soviet-Partisan force liberated Belgrade on 20 October. The Partisans with Allied support then concentrated on crushing the remaining German, Ustase, and Cetnic forces. When the Partisans entered Croatia, some of the most ruthless and savage fighting of the entire war developed. Meanwhile, Muslims in Albania and Kosovo made a brief attempt at a nationalistic revolt, but were crushed by the Partisans.[16]

World War II claimed 1.7 million Yugoslav lives, about 11 percent of the entire prewar population. The survival of the Serbian people within Yugoslavia was considered heroic and courageous against overwhelming odds. Fellow Yugoslavians killed about 1 million of the Yugoslav dead, an example of the horrid effects of historic ethnic and religious hatreds resurfacing in brutal form. The country's major cities, production centers, and communication and transportation systems were in shambles, with starvation widespread.[17]

Organized Muslim forces played only a minor role in the World War II Balkans. With the earlier unification of Yugoslavia in 1918–19, there emerged three distinct Muslim communities in Serbia, Bosnia, and Albania. These three communities under Yugoslav control had political unity but religious and cultural diversity. It was not until 1930 that all three branches of Yugoslavian Islam accepted the authority of a single Ulama. The Ulama was a religious leader who was responsible for enforcing the

Islamic religious and cultural code and administering the affairs of the Muslim community. While individuals or small groups of Muslims occasionally acted with great cruelty toward their Roman Catholic or Eastern Orthodox neighbors, this was typically in response to deprecation performed on Muslims. The Ulama and most Muslims kept a low profile during World War II. During the war, authorities tried and sentenced to death a local Muslim religious leader in Zagreb on charges of inciting Muslims to riot and murder Serbs. Aside from this incident, Muslims did not have nearly the amount of clergy moral scandals for wartime deviant behavior as did Roman Catholic or Serbian Orthodox clergy.

In the ruins of post-World War II, Tito (1892–1980) became predominant. Tito was born in northwestern Croatia and left school as a teenager to work. He soon became aware of communist labor movements and in 1910, at the age of 18, joined the Social Democratic Party of Croatia and Slavonia. He was a veteran of World War I and a former prisoner of war in a Russian prison camp. He then enlisted in the Soviet army in Siberia and in 1918 applied for membership in the Russian Communist Party. In 1920, he returned to the Balkans and became a member of the Communist Party of Yugoslavia, rising in leadership positions through the 1930s. After Axis forces invaded Yugoslavia in April 1941, the communists were among the first to organize a resistance movement. Tito was quickly named Chief of the Military Committee and a few weeks later became the Supreme Commander of the People's Liberation Army of Yugoslavia and Partisan Detachments. As Tito's guerrilla forces liberated villages, he imposed his communist agenda to willing recipients. As early as November 1942, Tito became head of the post-World War II Yugoslavian government.[18]

The post-World War II rise of communist Tito ended the dream of a unified Serb homeland. In 1945, the state headed by Tito proclaimed that Yugoslavia was to display the "brotherhood and unity of the peoples of Yugoslavia." Macedonians and Bosnians were recognized as national groups within the country. Serbs had to share their political identity with Croats, Slovenes, Macedonians, Bosnians, Kosovars, and others. As one writer stated, "Tito's answer to the problems of majorities and minorities was to abolish the very concept. All were equal within a people's democracy."[19] Initially, life under Tito's communist leadership was brutal, as Cetnic and Ustase remnants were put on mock trial and executed en mass. All resistance to this totalitarian communist rule was mercilessly squashed through espionage and assassinations. For the next few decades, Yugoslavia became stable and calm, as a ruthless but efficient dictator forced the diverse ethnic and religious groups to live together peacefully.

Longstanding nationalistic tendencies within the diverse Yugoslav people were suppressed by the higher goal of national Yugoslav unity.[20]

This supranational Yugoslav identity did not survive for long after Tito's death in 1980. A committee composed of the presidents of the six republics and two autonomous regions, with members taking turns as federal president, ruled for the next decade as Yugoslavia unsuccessfully attempted to govern itself. By the end of the 1980s, communism as an ideology and state system was coming undone throughout the entire region. Nationalism was resurrected to fill the ideological void, as each of Yugoslavia's member republics sought to make its own way. The first breakaway territory was Slovenia, which after a brief period of conflict broke away from Yugoslavia in June 1991.

Map 3. The Administrative Divisions of Yugoslavia, 1990.

Macedonia followed its other federation partners and declared independence from Yugoslavia in late 1991. The new Macedonian constitution took effect on 20 November 1991 and called for a system of government based on a parliamentary democracy. Prime Minister Branko Crvenkovski led the first democratically elected coalition government of the Social Democratic Union of Macedonia (SDSM) and included the ethnic Albanian Party for Democratic Prosperity (PDP). Kiro Gligorov became the first president of an independent Macedonia.

The 1991 secession of Macedonia from the former Yugoslavia was not clouded by ethnic or other armed conflict. During the Yugoslav period, Macedonian ethnic identity exhibited itself. Most of Macedonia's Slavic population identified themselves as Macedonians, while several minority groups, in particular ethnic Albanians, sought to retain their own distinct political culture and language. Although interethnic tensions simmered under Yugoslav authority and during the first decade of its independence, the country avoided ethnically motivated conflict incited by Serbia until several years after its independence.

In 1990, Croatia held its first multiparty elections since World War II. Long-time Croatian nationalist Franjo Tudjman was elected president, and 1 year later, Croatians declared independence from Yugoslavia. Savage fighting ensued. Conflict between Serbs and Croats in Croatia escalated, and 1 month after Croatia declared independence, war erupted between Croatia and Yugoslavia. Yugoslav Serbians practiced what would later be called "ethnic cleansing" on Croats in conquered areas. Genocide of entire villages was common. Serbian brutality toward Croats was justified in their minds from political and ethnic tensions from World War II, but such tension was prevalent since the time of the Ottomans.[21]

The United Nations mediated a cease-fire in January 1992; hostilities resumed the next year when Croatia fought to regain one-third of the territory lost the previous year. A second cease-fire was enacted in May 1993, followed by a joint declaration the next January between Croatia and Yugoslavia. However, in September 1993, the Croatian army led an offensive against the Serb-held Republic of Krajina. A third cease-fire was called in March 1994, but it, too, was broken in May and August 1995 after Croatian forces regained large portions of Krajina, prompting an exodus of Serbs from this area. In November 1995, Croatia agreed to reintegrate Eastern Slavonia, Baranja, and Western Dirmium peacefully under terms of the Erdut Agreement. In December 1995, Croatia signed the Dayton Peace Accords, committing itself to a permanent cease-fire and the return of all refugees.

The breakup of the Yugoslav federation after 1989 left Montenegro in a precarious position. The first multiparty elections in 1990 showed public support for the League of Communists, confirming Montenegrin support for the federation. Montenegro joined Serbian efforts to preserve the federation in the form of a Third Yugoslavia in 1992. Though Montenegro reaffirmed its political attachment to Serbia, a sense of a distinct Montenegrin identity continued to thrive. Outspoken criticism of Serbian conduct of the 1992–95 war in Bosnia and Herzegovina boosted the continuing strength of Montenegrin distinctiveness. Both the people and the government of Montenegro were critical of Yugoslav President Slobodan Milosevic's 1998–99 campaign in Kosovo, and the ruling coalition parties boycotted the September 2000 federal elections, which led to the eventual overthrow of Milosevic's regime. The Belgrade Agreement of March 2002, signed by the heads of the federal and republican governments, set forth the parameters for a redefinition of Montenegro's relationship with Serbia in a joint state. On 4 February 2003, the parliament of the Federal Republic of Yugoslavia ratified the Constitutional Charter, which established a new state union and changed the name of the country from Yugoslavia to Serbia and Montenegro.

The rise to power of Milosevic as president of the Serbian Republic and his embrace of an extreme Serb nationalist agenda hastened the dissolution of federal Yugoslavia. That agenda called for a solution of the "national question" by the creation of a Greater Serbia, uniting all Serbs in a single state; in 1986, it was endorsed by the Serbian Academy of Arts and Sciences. The following year, Milosevic and his hard-line faction gained power within the Serbian League of Communists, in large part by playing the nationalist card—appealing to the Serbian sense of grievance at having been deprived of a leadership role in Tito's Yugoslavia and at being outstripped by some other republics economically. Under Milosevic's leadership, the Serb possession of Bosnia-Herzegovina meant the forceful and often brutal elimination of all who would be dissidents in the new Serbian state.[22]

In 1989, seizing on the patriotic fervor surrounding a historic anniversary, Milosevic initiated a crackdown on Serbia's ethnic Albanians who formed 90 percent of the population in the country's southern autonomous province of Kosovo. In the romantic imagery of Serbian nationalism, Kosovo represents both Serbia's past greatness and its humiliation at the hands of Muslims. The continued presence of a large and politically assertive Muslim Albanian population in Kosovo was perceived as an intolerable affront to this nationalist vision of Serbia. Expressing violent ethno nationalism—the pursuit of ethnic national superiority to the disdain of all others—Serbian forces destabilized Bosnia-Herzegovina, attempting to force all non-Serbs out of the region by persuasion or by gunpoint, with numerous accounts of vicious brutality toward civilians.[23]

Following international recognition of Croatian and Slovene independence (January 1992) and news that Macedonia's secession was imminent, the elected government of Bosnia-Herzegovina found itself faced with an impossible choice. The prospect of remaining part of a rump Yugoslavia dominated by Milosevic was clearly unacceptable to the majority of Bosnia's population, while Bosnian independence was anathema to Serb nationalists both in Bosnia and in Serbia. In February 1992, 70 percent of Bosnian voters (including many Bosnian Serbs) turned out to cast their votes for independence.

On 5 April 1992, following the declaration of independence by Bosnia's parliament, there was a mass multiethnic demonstration by citizens of Sarajevo calling for peace among Bosnia's three major communities (Eastern Orthodox Serbs, Roman Catholic Croats, and Muslims). Yugoslav national army snipers and Serb nationalist militants hidden on surrounding rooftops opened fire on the crowd killing and wounding scores of unarmed citizens. The following day, Serbian units began to shell Sarajevo from prepared positions on the hillsides overlooking the city, and columns of troops and tanks crossed the Drina River from Serbia into eastern Bosnia. Initially armed only with police side arms and hunting rifles, later with captured and smuggled weapons, Bosnians tried to defend their newly independent country against the onslaught of the Serb nationalist forces unleashed by Milosevic.

Notes

1. David Peterson, "Memorandum on Religious Conflict in Yugoslavia," 30 December 1994, 1.

2. Lord Kindross, *The Ottoman Centuries: The Rise and Fall of the Turkish Empire* (New York: HarperCollins Publishers, 2002), 53–60.

3. Ninian Smart, ed., *Atlas of the World's Religions* (Oxford: Oxford University Press, 1999), 183.

4. Peterson, "Memorandum on Religious Conflict," 3.

5. Raymond Zickel and Walter R. Iwaskiw, eds., *Albania: A Country Study* (Washington, DC: GPO for the Library of Congress, 1992), 9–15.

6. Andrew Wheatcroft, *Infidels: A History of the Conflict Between Christendom and Islam* (New York: Random House Publishers, 2003), 217–218.

7. Andre Gerolymatos, *The Balkan Wars* (New York: Basic Books, 2002), 132.

8. Kindross, *The Ottoman Centuries*, 602–603.

9. Tim Judah, *The Serbs: History, Myth, and the Destruction of Yugoslavia* (New London: Yale University Press, 2000), 97–104.

10. Robert J. Donia and John V.A. Fine, Jr., *Bosnia and Herzegovina: A Tradition Betrayed* (New York: Columbia University Press, 1994), 117–119.

11. Judah, *The Serbs,* 90.

12. Glenn E. Curtis, ed., *Yugoslavia: A Country Study* (Washington, DC: GPO for the Library of Congress, 1992), 26–30.

13. Ibid., 36–37.

14. Donia and Fine, *Bosnia and Herzegovina*, 11.

15. Judah, *The Serbs*, 117.

16. Curtis, *Yugoslavia*, 42.

17. Ibid., 42–43.

18. Phyllis Auty, *Tito: A Biography* (New York: McGraw-Hill Book Company, 1970), 217–234.

19. Wheatcroft, *Infidels,* 251.

20. Josef Korbel, *Tito's Communism* (Denver: University of Denver Press, 1951), 159–171.

21. Alek N. Dragnich, *Serbs and Croats: The Struggle for Yugoslavia* (San Diego: Harvest Books, 1992), 170–172.

22. Stella Gresham, *The Bosnia Files: An Intimate Portrait of Life Behind the Lines* (Bristol, IN: Wyndham Hall Press, 1996), 1.

23. Francine Friedman, *The Bosnian Muslims* (Boulder, CO: Westview Press, 1996), 206.

Chapter 3

The Bosnia Theater of Operations

Events Leading to US Military Activity in Bosnia

By 7 April 1992, the United States and most European countries officially recognized Bosnia-Herzegovina's independence. On 22 May 1992, the United Nations admitted Bosnia-Herzegovina as a full member. An arms embargo, imposed on all of the former Yugoslavia by the United Nations in 1991 (requested by the Belgrade government and maintained at the insistence of the United States and its Western European Allies), had in effect barred the internationally recognized Bosnian government from acquiring the means to exercise its right to self-defense guaranteed under the UN Charter. In the summer of 1992, President Clinton stated that the United States would take an active military role in Bosnia. The United States began to airdrop supplies to beleaguered civilians under attack by the Serbs while simultaneously enforcing a no-fly zone. The no-fly zone helped to prevent the Yugoslav and Serb forces from massacring civilians.[1]

Meanwhile, Milosevic and Serb nationalist forces in Bosnia had at their disposal the resources of the Yugoslav national army, including the fourth largest arsenal in Cold War Europe. They used these weapons to lethal effect in their assault on Bosnia's cities, towns, and villages. Over a million people were bombed and driven from their homes; hundreds of thousands of civilians were killed and wounded. Serb nationalist forces overran 70 percent of Bosnia's territory, "cleansing" conquered areas by driving out or killing the non-Serb inhabitants in acts of genocide. As US Ambassador Albright stated, "Day after day the world witnessed the murder of civilians, the burning of villages, the shelling of apartments, the destruction of churches and mosques, and reports of mass rape."[2] Among the methods of "ethnic cleansing" employed by the Serb forces were the selective killing of the non-Serb community's civic, religious, and intellectual leaders; the confinement of all males of military age in concentration camps; and the use of mass rape as a weapon of terror and abasement. Nationalist forces throughout the area torched, dynamited, and bulldozed historic mosques, churches, and synagogues as well as national libraries, archives, and museums.

In anticipation of the coming flood of Bosnian refugees, ministers of Western European countries held a meeting at the beginning of June 1993 to coordinate tighter restrictions on asylum and immigration. Later the siege of the city of Sarajevo outraged many Western leaders, as Serb artillery stationed at elevated positions around the city cut off escape routes and began indiscriminately shelling the city. As Albright summarized, the United States sought to lift the UN arms embargo but did not initially have enough votes in the Security Council to do so. Endorsing a permanent cease-fire was also not an issue because such an agreement would be condescension to Serbian ethnic cleansing and resettlement of captured areas. Finally, a sudden military assault by US forces and NATO troops would inevitably result in a massive hostage-taking maneuver by Serbs against UN peacekeepers throughout the area.[3]

Throughout 1994, tension and random violence remained constant within Bosnia-Herzegovina. During the winter of 1994–95, a tenuous cease-fire was agreed on, and a tense peace permeated the Balkans. Seemingly endless and unproductive bureaucratic negotiations that winter appeared to go nowhere. In the spring of 1995, horrific violence was unleashed in numerous areas throughout Bosnia. The Bosnian Serbs celebrated the end of the winter cease-fire by unleashing the worst shelling Sarajevo had received in months. The UN peacekeeping force requested air strikes, a request that was initially refused based on the clumsy "dual-key" system that required both UN and NATO approval. After a second request for air strikes was approved, NATO planes successfully bombed Serbian targets, with many US pilots flying their F-16 aircraft under NATO control. The Serbs responded to the bombing campaign by shelling Muslim safe havens in Bosnia and taking about 300 UN peacekeepers hostage. Meanwhile, as General Wesley Clark, then working as Director for Strategic Plans and Policy for the Joint Staff at the Pentagon, remarked, "We held our breaths on Srebrenica. Then Srebrenica fell. There were rumors and then confirmation of a huge massacre, and international outrage grew."[4]

The United Nations created six safe areas in 1993, including Srebrenica. The intention was to stabilize the map of Bosnia, pursuant to a negotiated peace that would determine the layout of postwar Bosnia. However, in agreeing to protect the Srebrenica enclave, the United Nations established a fatal contradiction that would doom the safe areas. The UN mandate in Bosnia required its troops to act with neutrality. In reality, the UN Protection Force (UNPROFOR) was protecting aid deliveries, not local residents. Its freedom of movement was at the mercy of the stronger belligerent, and in eastern Bosnia, this meant the Serb forces. As a result, the Dutch battalion's ability to protect, or at least feed, the inhabitants of Srebrenica depended on the cooperation of the Serbs. This cooperation was generally bought with bribes, usually consisting of aid intended for the enclave. Whenever it suited the strategic needs of the Serb forces, the cooperation disappeared. The final offensive on Srebrenica began in early

July 1995 with a troop buildup around the enclave and the heaviest bombing in 2 years. By 7 July the Serbs were disarming Dutch observation posts and forcing them to withdraw, giving them the choice of either going into Srebrenica or leaving the area altogether via the nearby Serb-controlled Bratunac. The Serbs then captured approximately 30 Dutch soldiers from one outpost and held them hostage.

In Potocari, thousands of refugees who had fled Srebrenica entered the UN base. When approximately 5,000 had entered, the Dutch declared the base full and halted entrance. Around 20,000 more people gathered outside the base, sitting down in streets and nearby fields. The next day Serb soldiers began the evacuation of Potocari. The Dutch forces did not intervene. In some cases, they even helped the Serbs load people onto the buses in an orderly way. During the evacuation, Serbs were secretly taking men into the woods near the UN base and shooting them. Hundreds of Serbs were involved in the final "cleansing" of Srebrenica. Many of these men were from neighboring towns between Visegrad and Zvornik, but others were from deep within Serbia. As thousands of Srebrenicans fled to Potocari, another column of people was heading for the woods. Serb soldiers claimed to have killed between 10,000 to 15,000 military-age men. However, the number of missing Srebrenicans reported by the Red Cross is approximately 7,500.[5]

The massacre at Srebrenica moved Clinton to support increased air strikes in Bosnia; to endorse negotiations between Bosnian, Serbian, and Croatian leaders; and to make a decisive commitment to send US ground troops to fight the Serbians.

Srebrenica was the most extensive post-World War II genocide incident and helped to awaken the Western community. Clark was actively involved in planning a potential US and NATO invasion of Bosnia to subdue forcefully the Serbian army and its vicious paramilitary supporters. An offer to NATO of 25,000 US ground forces was developed.[6] While the air campaign against Serbian interests and troops was ongoing and successful, months of negotiations continued between Bosnia's neighbors, NATO, and US representatives. Throughout the summer and fall of 1995, negotiations continued while Serbian forces sought to avoid NATO bombings and at the same time continued to abuse non-Serbian civilians in Bosnia-Herzegovina. Finally, on 5 October 1995, all parties agreed to a nationwide cease-fire with peace talks to begin in Dayton, Ohio.

The warring factions flew their representatives to Wright Patterson Air Force Base near Dayton, Ohio, and started their main negotiations on 1 November 1995. The peace talks almost broke down several times as old animosities evidenced themselves through last minute attempts at land grabbing by each party. Nevertheless, US Secretary of State Warren Christopher and his team pushed through a compromise the Serbs, Croats, and Bosnians could all agree to sign. This document, commonly called the Dayton Peace Accords, was signed on 21 November. Needing verification from each party's political leadership, the peace accords called for a NATO-led political and military effort to stop the bloodshed in the former Yugoslavia. A diverse military force called the Implementation Force (IFOR) was the main thrust of the plan. According to US Secretary of Defense William J. Perry, military aspects of the peace agreement included the "cessation of hostilities, withdrawal to agreed lines, creation of a zone of separation, return of troops and weapons to cantonments, and, of course, IFOR will be responsible for its own self-defense and freedom of movement."[7]

Albright clearly stated the reasons why the Serbian aggression in Bosnia ultimately failed and why the Dayton Peace Accords was successful.

> Three factors ended the Bosnian War. The first was over-reaching on the part of the Bosnian Serbs. For years, they had bet successfully on the fecklessness of the West, but they didn't know when to fold their hands. The second was the changing military situation. In early August, Croatia launched an offensive to reclaim territory seized by ethnic Serbs. The offense quickly succeeded, sending a message to the Bosnian Serbs that they weren't invincible and could not, in a crisis, count on help from Milosevic. The third factor was Bill Clinton's willingness to lead. . . . After Srebrenica, the President's frustration had boiled over.[8]

The December 1995 Dayton Peace Accords called for 60,000 NATO troops (20,000 Americans) to be stationed throughout Bosnia and adjoining areas. The IFOR was an armed peacemaking and peacekeeping force. Operation JOINT ENDEAVOR was the United States' part of IFOR. Numerous problems confronted the first US troops to land on the ground in the Balkans. Peacekeepers would be deployed in six republics with five languages. About 25,000 Bosnians were missing and presumed dead. There remained over 4,000 minefields with a combined million or so landmines. Ethnic hatreds were seething throughout the region, and the ravages of war created huge unemployment. In many cases, Serbs would not move out, destroyed the homes, or reluctantly departed homes owned by Muslims. The same tensions existed between Croats and Serbs in the north.

Looking at this chaotic and potentially escalating situation, Clark stated that he wanted to minimize the US involvement in what could be another Vietnam-type quagmire. He spoke of Bosnia as a "seemingly intractable problem" and was reluctant to project the image of the United States as policemen of the world. Further, Clark made some tough remarks that could not be readily answered. He stated, "It seemed difficult to define the objectives, strategies, and means of Bosnia policy. Of course, we wanted the fighting stopped. But on what conditions, and at what price?"[9]

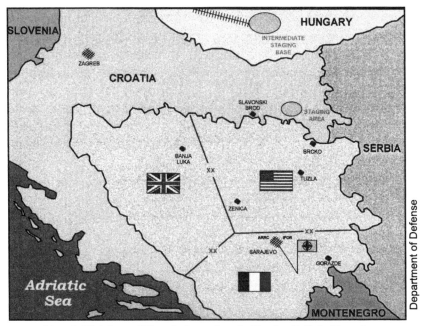

Map 4. Divisions of Bosnia in sectors led by the British, French, and United States.

Preparations for the First US Army Chaplains to Arrive in Bosnia, 1995

Throughout 1995, NATO air assets bombed Serbian troops, munitions, and supply elements. UN peacekeepers were in consistently vulnerable positions, as their presence on the ground did nothing to deter Serb aggression. NATO troops replaced UN peacekeepers in Bosnia, and the arms embargo against the Bosnians was lifted allowing them to fight for themselves against Serb aggressors. A humanitarian disaster of epic proportions was developing with tens of thousands of homeless and unemployed refugees seeking vengeance on their Serbian antagonists. Atrocities were performed by both sides, with it difficult at times to identify the good guy from the bad guy. US Ambassador Albright remarked that parts of Bosnia had become "a shooting gallery"; mass graves were being discovered, and those responsible for the murders should be held responsible.[10] Three and a half years of civil war in Bosnia and surrounding areas produced 3 million homeless people; there were 12,000 dead in Sarajevo alone with about 200,000 total dead in Bosnia. There was an estimate of 20,000 reported "policy rapes," the intentional forced impregnation of non-Serbian women by Serbs to sway the population demographics.

Exhaustive and detailed planning throughout 1995 called for an IFOR of 60,000 personnel, more than double the strength the UNPROFOR had in Bosnia in 1993–94. The American component of IFOR included 20,000 ground troops in Bosnia-Herzegovina, composed mostly of the US Army's 1st Armored Division. Chaplains from the 1st Armored Division would be busy meeting the religious needs of soldiers in a hostile fire zone while providing their commanders religious and cultural guidance on the volatile ethnic divisions in the area. Other IFOR participants came from NATO and non-NATO countries, with 27 total nations represented in the IFOR. The USAREUR set up support elements in the countries adjoining Bosnia to facilitate supply and transportation missions. For example, 5,000 soldiers were sent to Croatia while 7,000 more were deployed to Hungary and Italy. Eventually smaller numbers of US troops would be sent to Albania, Macedonia, and a few other temporary locations.[11]

Figure 1. UMT members (left to right) MSG Paul Wanshon, CH (CPT) Jamie MacLean, and CH (LTC) Scott McChrystal, Eagle Base, Bosnia, 1995–96.

One of the senior Army chaplains in Europe in 1995 was Chaplain (Colonel [COL]) Henry Wake, assigned as the USAREUR chaplain. Wake served in this position from 1994 to 1997 and was a key player in coordinating chaplain support for US troops preparing to deploy to the Balkans. Following the chain of command, Wake worked closely with the V Corps chaplain, Chaplain (COL) Barry Lonigan, and the 1st Armored Division chaplain, Chaplain (Lieutenant Colonel [LTC]) Scott McChrystal. The 1st Armored Division would be the major unit deploying to the Balkans, having been assigned this mission from the USAREUR headquarters, then through the V Corps. Wake spoke of the training before deployment as follows: "When we started the buildup for Bosnia we did a lot of MOPP [mission oriented protective posture] drills, a lot of stuff, set up in parking lots, and lived out there . . . we had staff meetings every morning and every night . . . and we're on video teleconferencing with all these people downrange. . . ."[12]

The deployment of US ground troops to the Balkans was no surprise. Ongoing training with Army units in Germany lasted for months before the deployment. Chaplain Assistant Sergeant (SGT) Deborah Peek of the 16th Corps Support Group, Hanau, Germany, recalled that the time leading up to their deployment to the Balkans consisted of "long training days and an increase in the stress level."[13] Chaplain (Captain [CPT]) Marvin Luckie arrived in Bosnia in December 1995. Having served in Operation DESERT STORM and in Somalia, he was intently watching the news when the Dayton Peace Accords were signed, knowing that he would be deployed. While working in Bosnia in a US and NATO Joint Psychological Operations Task Force, Luckie bemoaned the fact that prior to his deployment he had not received any training in joint operations.[14]

In summary of the extensive preparations for deploying into Bosnia, McChrystal of the 1st Armored Division stated:

> There are ways to plan deployment and ways not to. We did it the hard way. Nothing we could do to control it. . . . Most of the train up lasted from the spring, early summer 1995 well into October. And you remember what vacillating was going on. We couldn't decode as a nation whether we were going in or not. The UN wasn't doing anything. . . . Going through those times of training tends to be harder than the exercise, the real thing itself, because there is so much uncertainty built into it. So, then, back and forth. 1st Armored Division back and forth to Grafenwehr. . . . So, once it was determined that I was going to be the 1st

AD chaplain, and I probably knew 2 months prior to taking over, I arranged to go down to Grafenwehr and meet [Division Commander] William Nash where he made an official offer.[15]

While Army units and their chaplains prepared to deploy to the Balkans, the American news media was relentless in its questioning of the validity of this mission and speculating that sending US troops on the ground in the Balkans could have catastrophic consequences. In the 27 November 1995 edition of *TIME Magazine*, statements were made about the US "fecklessness on foreign policy" and that the American people, "are actively hostile to the notion of American leadership [in the Balkans] if it requires risking American lives. . . . They are not convinced that their sons and daughters should die for the sake of Sarajevo."[16] In speaking of the Dayton Peace Accords, one media outlet stated that unity and reconciliation in the Balkans would be "largely in vain," stating "The accord calls for reconciliation—fat chance." The article also stated that only 38 percent of Americans believed sending US troops to the Balkans was the right thing to do.[17]

After several months of intense training, the 40th Engineer Group with Chaplain (CPT) Jeff Giannola arrived on 3 January 1996 in Bosnia. The preparation for the deployment was a rich time of ministry, Giannola stated, with many soldiers and family members becoming serious about their relationship with God.[18] Others were not able to train with their units before deployment. For example, Chaplain Assistant Private First Class (PFC) Dae Lee was straight out of training when he joined the 47th Forward Support Battalion in Baumholder, Germany. When he arrived, the unit had already trained and deployed, it taking him a month to join his unit in Bosnia.[19] A similar situation occurred with Chaplain (CPT) Brent Causey of the 212th Mobile Army Surgical Hospital (MASH), who came from another assignment and met the unit and other UMT members in Bosnia.[20]

Preparations for the Army Reserve and its chaplains to support missions in the Balkans began in the summer of 1995. Specifically, chaplain backfill by mostly US Army Reserve chaplains and chaplain assistants was necessary so Active Duty chaplains could deploy to the Balkans with their units. The Office of the Chief of Chaplains contacted USAREUR Chaplain Wake and asked what type of chaplain backfill would be necessary once Active Army units deployed to the Balkans. Wake anticipated the need for 20 to 25 Reserve chaplains to backfill, mostly in Germany. Standing operating procedures for this type of mission were that Army Personnel Center (ARPERCEN) would solicit volunteer Reserve chaplains to meet this requirement. The Chief, Army Reserve had another plan in mind. He ordered the US Army Reserve Command (USARC) to create an over-strength derivative unit to fulfill this backfill requirement. This mission was assigned to the Army Reserve 131st Chaplain Support Team (CST) out of Fort Belvoir, Virginia. In the coming months, this two-person unit would expand to 40 chaplains and chaplain assistants [21]

Figure 2. USAREUR CH (COL) Henry Wake (far right) visits UMTs in Bosnia.

Throughout the fall of 1995 and beyond, Chaplain (COL) James Hoke of the 7th ARCOM in Germany functioned in two capacities. The 7th ARCOM became the USAREUR Mobilization Station, meaning that US Army Reserve units from Europe and some from the United States inprocessed through this headquarters. In this capacity, Hoke provided pastoral care and counseling to incoming soldiers, their chaplains, and the inprocessing personnel team. Hoke also functioned as a chaplain to the soldiers of the 7th ARCOM who were mobilizing and deploying with their parent 1st Armored Division headquarters to such diverse Balkans locations as Kaposvar, Hungary; Zagreb, Croatia; and Zupanja, Croatia. The 7th ARCOM units deployed to these remote locations contained small numbers of soldiers. In addition to his other duties, Hoke made periodic visits to these soldiers deployed throughout the Balkans.

The Dayton Peace Accords brought a momentary peace to most of Bosnia. In late December 1995, advanced units of the US and NATO peacekeeping force were deployed throughout Bosnia and surrounding areas, familiarizing themselves with Bosnia's physical and political distinctiveness. Although not opposed by military force, these initial peacekeepers faced a potentially volatile situation while furious and frustrated people of various ethnic groups adjusted to their presence. Demonstrations arose where flags from the United States were trampled and burned, revealing that the implementation of the Dayton Peace Accords would be a difficult task.[22]

Chaplain (Major [MAJ]) Chester H. Lanious was assigned as the Division Support Command (DISCOM) chaplain attached to the 1st Armored Division. He recalled his training in Germany before deploying to Bosnia as a series of false starts, slow downs, then restarts. In the late fall of 1995, his unit had the mission of organizing and transporting huge amounts of equipment to staging areas throughout the Balkans. Lanious remarked, "Our mission was to conquer a logistical nightmare. In December, we had to deal with poor roads, antique railways, swollen rivers, underdeveloped airfields, and horrible weather. The cold, damp, foggy weather with almost daily snow and poor visibility made our transportation missions both grueling and dangerous."[23]

The initial major thrust of the US military in Bosnia came with the construction and the 31 December 1995 crossing of the Sava River Bridge. To enter the country, the 1st Armored Division had to bridge the Sava River, which marked the border with Croatia. Army engineers under difficult weather conditions conducted this mission—the construction of the longest assault bridge in modern history—with no casualties or serious injuries. Melting snow caused deep mud and flooded the river. Nevertheless, the construction of the bridge was completed, the bridging of the Sava River being the first of a number of successful operations by US troops and NATO personnel.[24]

Before crossing the Sava River Bridge into Bosnia, Peek and her 16th Corps Support Group languished in Croatia. She stated, "Facilities in Croatia were very dumpy. We lived in freezing cold train cars that sat in the mud. For the first 30 days, there were no showers, and then we were able to get showers twice a week about 30 miles away. We could hear rounds going off at night very close by. We were on constant alert. Lots of guard duty. There were civilian buildings on fire or smoldering in our area. We were happy to leave Croatia and enter Bosnia."[25]

On 14 December 1995, the 1st Armored Division was ordered to Bosnia-Herzegovina as part of Operation JOINT ENDEAVOR. This task force, known as Task Force *Eagle*, did a 20 December transfer of authority ceremony with UN forces at Eagle Base, Tuzla. After the historic crossing of the Sava River on 31 December, the 1st Armored Division, with supporting Army units from V Corps and Army Reserve units from the 7th ARCOM, was joined by Nordic-Polish, Turkish, and Russian brigades. McChrystal, the first Task Force *Eagle* chaplain, described his view of the US Army's entrance into Bosnia:

So, as we came down most of us came by rail from Germany down through Hungary. Well, I flew . . . a lot of people came down. They went to Slavonski Brod and then we just started infiltrating into this whole sector, and the first people in country flew down to Tuzla, Bosnia. That was an old Yugoslavian Air Base and believe me, there were few buildings, a lot of land mines, and an airfield. And so, we started from there with the advanced party of about 20 people. . . .

It wasn't like we were getting in an assembly line and it was really going to be, I think, probably the hardest thing a division equivalent chaplain has had to do, and I'm including everything up to the day because we didn't know what we were wanting to do. Six million unexploded land mines, we just didn't know if we could keep the factions separated . . . a preponderance of the population of military folks in the task force were going to drive across the Sava River and infiltrate south. . . .[26]

Those US soldiers who flew or drove into Bosnia in late December 1995 as well as those Special Forces soldiers who were already in the

Army Art Collection, National Museum of the US Army

Figure 3. *Engineering Excellence,* a painting by Christopher Thiel showing the US Army crossing the Sava River.

area were about to observe the Christian holiday of Christmas. Organizing Christmas church services for these newly deployed and widely scattered soldiers throughout Bosnia was not an easy task. These few thousand soldiers received Christmas Eve and Christmas Day religious services from two Air Force Protestant chaplains and a Roman Catholic chaplain who were earlier deployed to the region. McChrystal coordinated the efforts of these chaplains, saying that clear-cut planning was essential and only performing denominational services for a select group of people at this point in the mission was not an option.[27]

Chaplain (CPT) David Brown of the 1st Squadron, 4th Cavalry arrived in the Balkans shortly after Christmas 1995. The months prior to deployment were spent in the field doing gunnery training at Hoensfels and Grafenwehr, Germany. In mid-December, his unit was bused from Germany to Taszar, Hungary, to organize and inventory new equipment. David Brown commented, "The unit was in an intense training mode, as our mission was changed at the last minute from a peacekeeping mission to a peace-enforcement mission. Apprehension grew as we knew we were going into a potentially volatile area." David Brown and his unit then drove military vehicles from Taszar to a final staging area in Croatia. In describing Croatia, David Brown stated, "There were select areas that were decimated. It was obvious that a very select targeting of certain areas has occurred." He further recalled, "My unit and I traveled from Croatia and crossed the Sava River Bridge in the last days of December 1995. The weather was cold, snowy, and foggy. We could hear gunfire in the distance, some of it from automatic weapons. We never got off the main roads since we all knew that there were millions of land mines throughout the area. As we drove over the Sava River Bridge listening to gunfire I thought, what in the world are we getting into?"[28]

Initial Chaplain Activities and Ministries in Bosnia, 1996

Chaplains who deployed into Bosnia and other Balkans sites in 1996 were part of a 12-nation peacemaking and peacekeeping force divided into three brigades from the nations of Denmark, Estonia, Finland, Iceland, Latvia, Lithuania, Norway, Poland, Russia, Sweden, Turkey, and the United States. Task Force *Eagle* enforced the cease-fire, supervised the marking of boundaries and the zone of separation between the former warring factions, enforced withdrawal of the combatants, and coordinated the movement of heavy weapons to designated storage sites. Task Force *Eagle* also supported the Organization for Security and Cooperation in Europe

(OSCE) in their efforts to administer the country's first-ever democratic national elections.

On 9 January 1996, Chaplain Lanious of the 1st Armored Division departed Germany by bus with elements of his unit for a staging area at

Figure 4. Sketch by Gary N. Cassidy of the US Army staging base in Taszar, Hungary.

Taszar, Hungary. They stayed at this austere location for 6 days while matching specific units with predelivered equipment. This area, over the course of a few days, became a bustling but crude US Army staging area. Living conditions were miserable in the middle of a Balkan winter, causing numerous vehicle crashes and other accidents. Soldiers shivered in tents, ate in filth, and worked in mud. Lanious' unit then moved to an unnamed rural pasture in Croatia and for 3 days awaited orders for permission to deploy in convoy to Bosnia.

In convoy, Lanious and his chaplain assistant drove the 6-to-8-hour trip from their location in Croatia to the border of Bosnia. While he noticed minimal signs of war destruction during this convoy, the evidence of war drastically changed once they entered Bosnia. He stated:

> We saw minimal war damage from artillery in Croatia. When we entered Bosnia territory that all changed. Burned and demolished buildings were everywhere. Then we reached the Sava River. We crossed on the US Army bridge just built by the Engineers. It was very narrow and hazardous. My chaplain assistant was driving and she was noticeably nervous about driving on this bridge. The weather was terrible and visibility was poor. But at that time I was able to sense the historic nature of this river crossing, as we entered Bosnia as peacekeepers or peace enforcers.[29]

US Army soldiers entering Bosnia for the first time had various impressions of their surroundings. Chaplain Assistant PFC Dae Lee arrived in Bosnia in January 1996 as part of the 47th Forward Support Battalion. Dae Lee stated, "Civilian destruction was very evident due to lots of ruins around the villages and the town I saw. Many homes and buildings were torn apart or had significant signs of battle around their homes. I had seen many bullet holes and structure of their homes broken off."[30] On entering Bosnia in early January 1996, Lanious recalled, "Our destination was Lukvac. In this area, we saw lots of decommissioned soldiers sitting around with nothing to do. They sat around all day drinking coffee and smoking cigarettes and looking at us menacingly. They wore their military uniforms since it was winter and that clothing was warm." Lanious further commented, "Since the Dayton Peace Accords were signed and we entered this area, the military forces in the region were either decommissioned or began covert training operations. We saw men in fields with no weapons rehearsing military squad level tactics, they waited for us to depart so they could continue their rage." In noticing the large number of children in the area, Lanious remarked, "The children were all over us, very friendly, some spoke English. They were curious, begging, and seemed to be relieved that we were there. It was easy to see the natural physical beauty of this place in spite of the ravages of war."[31]

As 1996 began, extensive news reports covered the deployment of American soldiers throughout Bosnia and neighboring nations and raised political and policy issues for Americans to consider. In a 1 January 1996 interview in the *Army Times*, Clinton stated he deployed US troops to Bosnia "to stop slaughter," and that the Bosnia mission is "the first significant military test of Cold War policy" in which the US military joins with allies to try to prevent wars and "stand against chaos." Clinton further commented, "Our leadership in NATO and our ability to lead the world toward peace and democracy are very much tied to our willingness to assume a leadership role in the Bosnia mission."[32] A few weeks earlier in a speech to the 1st Armored Division, Secretary of Defense Perry stated:

> For the first time in nearly 4 years, we face the promise of lasting peace in Bosnia. It is clear from my discussions with the negotiators in Dayton, and my talks with the leaders throughout Europe—including Russia—that this peace agreement could not have been reached without American leadership, nor can it be implemented without American participation in the peace Implementation Force (IFOR). The alternative to peace is clear: more killing, beyond the 200,000 already dead; more ethnic cleansing; more refugees beyond the more than two million who have already fled their homes flooding nearby countries; and more instability in Europe.[33]

Soldiers deploying into Bosnia in winter conditions and in a hostile fire zone would inevitably suffer injuries or casualties. In the extensive 1995 buildup for deployment in the Balkans, the US Army Combat Readiness Center (USACRC) reported only one aviation injury (a soldier was hurt from shifting cargo as a plane landed in Hungary) and eight various accidents that caused injuries. These eight 1995 injuries all occurred at or near staging areas in Hungary and were either traffic related or occurred while setting up equipment. One of these soldiers received a permanent partial disability. In 1996, the numbers of injured US Army personnel increased, as 20 recorded incidents resulted in various injuries to soldiers. For example, these 1996 injuries were received from operating vehicles, handling heavy equipment, traffic accidents, or from horseplay.[34] In 1996 there was a death of a US soldier. As one report stated:

A US soldier from Houston [was] killed in a truck crash in Bosnia-Herzegovina. . . . Pfc. Floyd E. Bright, Jr., 19, was killed and another soldier injured when their truck ran off a temporary bridge and overturned while on a supply run Friday night. Bright was the passenger. . . . Bright was sent to Bosnia in January. . . .

Clouds gathered and a chill filled the air Saturday as Bright's comrades in Bosnia-Herzegovina bid him farewell on his final journey home. Bright was the second American soldier killed in Bosnia during the NATO-led mission to safeguard peace.

Soldiers from Russia, Poland, Norway, Sweden, Denmark, Turkey, and Britain, as well as the United States, were among those forming a 22-person honor guard for Bright's casket. An Army Humvee carrying the body drove slowly to the flight line at Tuzla Air Base, the headquarters of the US forces in Bosnia. Six pallbearers lifted the container case and stood for just a few moments at the head of the honor guard.

The chaplain, LTC Scott McChrystal, read from the 23d Psalm. The commander of the US peacekeepers, Maj. Gen. William L. Nash, stood at attention in front of the honor guard. The pallbearers then marched through the two-column honor guard. The soldiers presented their arms in tribute as the container passed and was loaded on a plane that would take the body to Ramstein, Germany, before heading home.

Pfc. Bright was assigned to the headquarters of the Army's 2/678 Armored Battalion. . . . The first American GI killed in the mission was Army Sgt. Donald A. Dugan, who died in a land mine accident on Feb 3.[35]

Chaplains arriving in Bosnia in early 1996 had initial issues related to coordination with other chaplains and reporting to supervisory chaplains. Simply put, the lack of infrastructure and inaccessibility of many locations combined with the rapid buildup of US forces made chaplain coordination and cooperation an initial challenge. As the task force chaplain, McChrystal explained, "I learned that in attempting to lead chaplains a collegial approach works fine." He asked chaplains as they came to Bosnia or neighboring countries to report to him for coordination, accountability, and resourcing. He stated to incoming chaplains, "Just let me know where you were so we got everybody's name and UMTs . . . they did all I asked. They called in and told me where they were and of course, we had none of these base camps. Everyone was living in mud; it was cold and miserable. And of course, there was a lot of area in our sector that we were just so careful not to get off the main roads because we did not know the safety factor."[36]

Chaplains assigned to Special Forces units in Bosnia in 1996 had diverse and challenging ministries to soldiers in small groups who were often in potential danger in isolated communities. The mission of the US Army Special Forces in Bosnia was to find weapons storage areas and confiscate or destroy them; to gather intelligence related to armed or potentially armed factions that would not support the Dayton Peace Accords; to locate and apprehend those accused of war crimes; and to enforce peace by separating belligerent factions within Bosnia. Chaplain (MAJ) Jay Hartranft of the 10th Special Forces was in Bosnia at this time. He stated, "I had soldiers scattered in 25 locations around Bosnia. They were working with Romanian, Russian, Hungarian, and other international military units as advisors. My colonel wanted me to be a circuit preacher. So, I traveled as best I could from site to site, all by ground transportation. I sure saw a lot of that war-torn country."[37] Hartranft elaborated, "I served specifically as the JSOTF [Joint Special Operations Task Force] chaplain and worked almost exclusively with Special Forces chaplains. They included Chaplain Mark Jones . . . and Chaplain Mike Brainerd. . . . Since only one SF battalion was employed at a time, we did not work together but rotated in and out as the battalions did."[38]

Figure 5. Army Chief of Chaplains (MG) Donald Shea visits with Task Force *Eagle* soldiers in Bosnia, 1996.

As crude living conditions slowly improved into what would become base camps, the construction of chapels in locations throughout Bosnia became a high priority for chaplains. Soldiers leaving the relative safety of the fledgling base camps for missions in dangerous areas needed a place of spiritual and emotional support. McChrystal stated that the chaplains made a "great effort" to get chapels constructed. He stated that by mid-1996 there were 21 chapels built in Bosnia, with construction of several chapels at one time in various base camps being common. McChrystal stated, "You talk about the chapel building program . . . it really took well into May to dig ourselves out of the mud, get up and running, and it was interesting to see."[39]

While the vast majority of religious services performed by Army chaplains in Bosnia in 1996 were in small groups in outside areas, the rapid construction of chapels helped to provide a quiet, dignified setting for spiritual and emotional renewal. Two interesting stories related to the construction of chapels in Bosnia in 1996 deserve special attention.

The first chapel construction story relates to an advanced party of soldiers entering Bosnia and, with the supervision of two Air Force chaplains, renovating a building to be a chapel. The problem was the location was poor and they did not receive prior permission from the officer in charge (OIC) of that area. The Air Force chaplains did not support the decision to move the chapel they had renovated, and they did not appreciate McChrystal as the task force chaplain telling them the chapel had to be moved. One of the Air Force chaplains spoke to the media about this scenario and there quickly appeared headlines in newspapers throughout the United States and Europe that "Jesus had been kicked out of Tuzla." Seeking to avoid a public relations nightmare, the Commander, General William Nash, publicly invited Jesus back to Tuzla. McChrystal remembered these events as follows:

> Within a week of me getting there [Bosnia], it was in the headlines in major papers across the world that we'd kicked Jesus out of Tuzla. That's exactly what the headline said. . . . So we kicked Jesus out of Tuzla and General Nash showed some, not only sense of humor, but some wisdom that was just incredible. He invited me up to this big battle update brief where we had routinely 150—sometimes more than that—all of these people because there were five brigade sectors. . . . So we had all these people and he told me to get up there and say a prayer and invite Jesus back to Tuzla. And that was one time, knowing who was out there

[in the audience] I said . . . I'm going to say this prayer in Jesus' name, with your permission. And we did and that was the end of it. So that was an interesting start.[40]

The second unique chapel construction story related to the interdenominational use of all military chapels. As explained by USAREUR Chaplain Wake, civilian construction workers were happy and eager to build military chapels in Bosnia. In one case, the enthusiastic construction workers wanted to erect a large wooden cross in front of the new chapel. This seemingly innocuous gesture did not take into consideration that Jewish and Muslim soldiers and others would be sharing the chapel schedule with Protestant and Roman Catholic services. Some soldiers, Wake stated, would feel like the Christian symbol of the cross did not represent their faith traditions and was showing favoritism. While Wake suggested that the cross be mounted on some type of mobile apparatus, the civilian construction workers were uninformed about the religious sensitivities of the Balkans and the diverse religious composition of the NATO forces.[41] Wake stated that there was to be no favoritism toward Christians and that in the construction of all chapels in the Balkans there should be an emphasis on the religious neutrality of the building, which could be decorated by various religious groups to their own preferences.

US troops in the early months of 1996 in Bosnia had a wide array of considerations that formed the parameters of their peacekeeping mission. Within the anarchy and chaos of the collapsed former Yugoslavia there remained strong ethnic identities, weak political institutions, fervent nationalism, failed economics, volatile local fiefdoms, bands of vigilantes, and religious hatred. The IFOR intended to do four major things: to create self-determination, to enforce peace, to provide justice, and to restore territorial integrity. The key factor in this ambitious agenda was to create and enforce the zone of separation (ZOS) and then to monitor and enforce compliance. Then the IFOR would conduct peacekeeping or peace-enforcing missions while assisting UN humanitarian efforts in the area.

While American and other NATO leaders wondered if Serbian leader Slobodan Milosevic and his cronies would obey the Dayton Peace Accords and cooperate with NATO troops in Bosnia, the US troops and their allies were authorized to take such actions as required to fulfill their orders, including the use of necessary force. As McChrystal stated of these tense early months, "We basically postured ourselves, establishing the ZOS, the zone of separation, and so basically we just occupied and, throughout the whole time I was there, we were just gradually sort of crawling out as we were able to clear the roads, clear the land, and make sure we were not going to lose people." In speaking of peacekeeping and then nation-building missions, McChrystal remarked, "That did not kick in for 6 months. In that time there was still hostile fire. Drive-by shootings, mines on roads, there was definitely that and there was always the threat we would have these joint military commission meetings and you just haven't lived until you've sat around or shaken hands with some of those thugs."[42]

On 12 February 1997, Shalikashvili, Chairman of the Joint Chiefs of Staff, summarized the 1996 US and NATO entry into Bosnia and their initial successes as follows:

> Fifteen months ago in many Bosnian towns and cities, artillery fire was killing men and women in their homes and snipers shot children playing in the streets. Atrocities were nearly a daily occurrence. US forces went into Bosnia with the Implementation Force (IFOR), the NATO force tasked to accomplish the military tasks assigned in the Dayton Accords. It was a heavy force, involving nearly 20,000 US military members who participated in keeping the factions separated, demobilizing forces, and achieving the other military goals of the Dayton Accords.
>
> The situation has changed dramatically since then. Today there are no weapons firing into towns, and children once again play in the streets. The absence of war brought by IFOR offers a ray of hope for the future. . . .[43]

Developing Chaplain Ministries in Bosnia, 1996

The US and NATO forces that sought to stabilize Bosnia throughout 1996 faced numerous obstacles and setbacks. The US news media extensively covered the attempts at peace enforcement and peacekeeping by the newly arrived US troops. A *Washington Post* front page story stated, "The Bosnia Serbs' military commander [General Ratko Mladic] announced today that he has ordered his troops to suspend contacts with NATO peacekeeping forces in retaliation for the Bosnian government's detention of eight Serb soldiers and officers suspected of war crimes."[44] An article in the 9 February 1996 *European Stars & Stripes* reported a weather related vehicle accident in which three soldiers were injured, one seriously and the others with bruises and small cuts. The accident occurred near Tuzla with the soldiers evacuated to a nearby field hospital.[45] An editorial in the *Wall Street Journal* tersely stated, "Why does Clinton seem prepared to risk the lives of 20,000 American soldiers and to make a deal with the devil (i.e., Slobodan Milosevic . . . who could perhaps drag US officials down with them if they told the whole truth)?"[46] Clearly in 1996 there was no unanimity from the United States related to the validity of the peacekeeping mission in Bosnia, its chances of success, or the role of the United States in the internal affairs of the sovereign nation of Yugoslavia.

Figure 6. Winter/spring 1996 home of CH (CPT) Yarmen and CA SPC McAniff in Bosnia.

The peacemaking and peacekeeping missions of the US forces in Bosnia were missions unfamiliar to most of the Army's leadership at that time. Senior soldiers used to training on large and deadly weapon systems on an open battlefield found themselves in urban areas or rural villages interacting with locals who may or may not be hostile to the United States and NATO. Friend from foe could not be readily determined. Skills of diplomacy took priority over combative skills. As one news report stated:

> Long schooled in the traditional art of fighting war, American commanders now find themselves grappling with political, diplomatic and military demands that go far beyond the martial skills they were taught.
>
> They are warriors without a war, and, for many, the soldiering business has never been more difficult or more removed from their orthodox notions of command. Yet

Bosnia is recognized as a likely paradigm for future military actions: a multinational peacekeeping deployment to a place that is neither benign nor wholly hostile, under circumstances in which vital American interests are peripheral at best.

Commanders are expected to retain their prowess for the brand of high intensity warfare unleashed during the Persian Gulf War, but also to become masters of negotiation, arbitration, bluff and restraint—all within a framework of a shrinking US military that has gone through the most radical restructuring in a generation.

'I've trained for 30 years to read a battlefield. Now you're asking me to read a peace field,' said Maj. Gen. William L. Nash, Commander of US forces in Bosnia. 'It doesn't come easy. It ain't natural; it ain't intuitive. They don't teach this stuff at Fort Leavenworth. . . . It's an inner ear problem. No one feels completely balanced.'[47]

In this scenario of uncertainty, danger, and political turmoil, US Army chaplains placed themselves in harm's way to minister to soldiers. An example of ministry in 1996 in Bosnia is provided by Chaplain (CPT) Jeff Giannola assigned to the 40th Engineer Group. When Giannola arrived in Bosnia on 3 January 1996, there was no infrastructure to support the troops. They had to sleep in or under vehicles, eat unpopular meals, ready to eat (MREs), and build their own housing compound. Giannola was located near Vlasenica for most of his tour. He recalled, "Life was primarily lived behind barbed wire. Soldiers were always heavily armed. Mines were always on everyone's mind. One soldier in my unit lost his foot on a mine. Another soldier from a nearby unit was killed by one." Giannola remembered his first church service in Bosnia as "a time of prayer and preaching outside behind a vehicle." He stated, "Most services were held in a dining tent. I preached firmly to soldiers of all religious backgrounds and was well accepted. I built a relationship with them so each company I visited provided a tent for services."[48]

For the 10 plus months that Giannola was in Bosnia, life was a constant series of adjustments. Initial rumors of snipers, minefields, and ambushes gave way to the monotony of living humbly in the mud and snow. He stated, "After we got all set up, we were taken care of well—food, housing, a real bed, and heat in our tents. It was a big improvement." Ministry for Giannola consisted primarily of providing religious services and counseling to the widely scattered Engineer company soldiers within his battalion. He recalled, "We always had to travel according to the four-vehicle convoy rule. The men were always heavily armed. These were special times from the Lord. A sovereign God blessed me with a supportive commander and the full support of the men. How many became Christians I do not know. It was a blessing to preach and be so well received." Giannola admitted, "An actual combat zone ministry was an exhilarating experience, doing real ministry under pressure." He recalled how proud he was of his soldiers when "they showed an awesome amount of self-discipline when spit on by a mob during a riot control mission. They were great." He further stated, "My wife and I grew closer through the deployment. I appreciated my family more. Even though I was away, it was an opportunity for God to bless."[49]

Chaplains who remained in the rear while small elements of their units deployed to the Balkans had viable and rewarding ministries. Massachusetts Army National Guard Chaplain (CPT) Kenneth Lawson of the 42d Infantry Division Artillery serves as an example of providing chaplain support to small numbers of separated soldiers and family members from the rear area while loved ones were deployed to Bosnia. From April to July 1996, Lawson ministered to 45 Fire Support Team (FIST) soldiers and their families through a number of premobilization briefings, family activities, and church services. Lawson had many private prayer and counseling sessions that were less visible than the public rallies and departure ceremonies. On 11 July 1996, Lawson led a gathering of several hundred supporters in public prayer as 45 soldiers prepared to get on buses and begin their deployment.

By February 1997, the 45 FIST soldiers from Lawson's unit were due home in a few months. As he maintained contact with family members and continued to support them through counseling, family support group meetings, and crisis intervention, another element of his 42d Division Artillery unit received orders for a 180-day tour in Bosnia. The 87 men that composed the target acquisition battery (TAB) had a few months before they were due to rotate into Bosnia. One unit prepared to return home while another was preparing to deploy, making this an extremely busy time for Lawson, who had to balance his full-time civilian ministry with his ever-demanding part-time military ministry. As one report stated, "February through April 1997 was an extremely busy time for Chaplain Lawson, as he counseled soldiers and their families both as they were returning home from deployment and as others prepared to leave. Hundreds of gospel tracts were given out, in addition to the Bibles that he made available to every single soldier who had deployed or redeployed home."[50]

Chaplains and chaplain assistants serving in Bosnia and in neighboring regions in 1996 and 1997 had numerous unique and challenging ministry experiences. From January through May 1996, Chaplain (CPT) Marvin Luckie of the 4th Psychological Operations (PSYOP) Battalion was on the road often visiting 4th PSYOPs soldiers throughout the area of operations. In this itinerant ministry capacity, he conducted numerous religious services for isolated soldiers and counseled soldiers dealing with low intensity combat fatigue. After any major incident, Luckie performed serious incident stress debriefings, allowing the soldiers to speak of their experiences and feelings in a safe and structured atmosphere. Luckie stated, "While in convoys our peacekeepers faced some RPGs [rocket propelled grenades] and AK-47 rifle fire. Some Serbs were still shooting, and there was the constant threat of snipers and landmines. We saw many civilian men who would drink alcohol or coffee or both all day that looked dangerous. They had nothing to do since they were disarmed and we were now in the area. We always traveled in teams to be safe." Luckie further remarked, "It was profitable to work with the United Methodist Committee on Relief, and we worked well with multinational chaplains for Christmas and Easter services."[51]

Chaplain Assistant Peek departed Bosnia in September 1996. Assigned to the 16th Corps Support Group, she observed the local civilians who still feared for their lives—the horrors of ethnic cleansing deeply affecting them. She commented on the terrible destruction throughout Bosnia and the uncertainty as to who was friend or foe: "Conditions were very primitive. It was like the local people were living in the Stone Age. All their facilities were destroyed." Peek further commented, "We adopted a bombed-out school nearby. We got school supplies donated from our unit back in Germany. There was a great response to this, and we enjoyed delivering the school supplies to the local children." As far as ministries to soldiers at Camp Dallas, she stated that interest in religious services was good. There was a minor problem, she recalled, in that there was no wine for communion, making the Lutheran and Roman Catholic chaplains unhappy. One program that worked very well was the gospel service choir the unit sponsored back in Germany that was reassembled in Bosnia.[52]

The political situation in Bosnia in 1996 was unsettled. The year began with reports of Serbian slave-labor camps being hidden from NATO forces, with up to 1,000 Muslim prisoners enslaved and brutalized by their Serbian captors. Reports also stated that mass grave locations, sites where thousands of Muslims were massacred by Serbs, were being hidden.[53] American and NATO forces appeared to quickly side with the Bosnian Muslims against the Eastern Orthodox Serbs. Yet, further investigation showed that the Bosnian Muslims were themselves guilty of anti-Americanism, receiving funds and weapons and mercenaries from extremist Muslim countries. A report in the US House of Representatives by Ike Skelton of Missouri stated of Bosnia: "There is the enduring presence of Muslim extremists in that country." The report further said, "Recently the *Washington Post* reported that the United States had threatened to halt military and financial aid to the Muslim-led Bosnian government unless it expels Iranian guerrilla fighters who remain in the country in violation of the Dayton Accords." Some US officials accused Muslim leaders in Bosnia of playing a "double game by attempting to continue a military relationship with Iran even as they receive support from the United States."[54]

While politically Bosnia was in turmoil, life for US soldiers throughout 1996 began to settle into some semblance of routine. Base camps rose out of the mud and squalor and became humble but reasonably comfortable places to live. For most soldiers, sleeping conditions and bathing facilities remained basic, with even the simplest facilities being an improvement over conditions experienced on their arrival in Bosnia. Military chapels appeared on all major NATO facilities, and recreational activities sponsored by numerous organizations became popular. One unpopular decision hotly debated in the Pentagon was not to allow US soldiers in Bosnia to drink alcohol. Stating traditional Muslim sensitivities against alcohol use, US troops in Bosnia would not be allowed to drink alcohol at all, except when on leave in Hungary or Germany. Senior political and military leaders stated they were worried about Muslim sensitivities to Americans drinking alcohol and were concerned about mixing alcohol use with the heavy firepower and the permissive rules of engagement in place for US forces.[55]

Knowing that US and NATO troops had ample spare time in base camps between missions, McChrystal became concerned about the day-to-day spiritual and moral climate within each compound. As the senior chaplain for Task Force *Eagle*, McChrystal saw that the combination of high stress missions outside the camps combined with the boredom within the camps was a combination that could lead to deviant behavior, spiritual lethargy, and an overall melancholia within each base camp. At that time, a Christian musical group who desired to perform at numerous base camps throughout the region contacted McChrystal. After gaining the approval of the Task Force *Eagle* commander, McChrystal and the US Army Europe (Forward) Staff Chaplain (LTC) Daniel Paul coordinated with the music group to arrive in Hungary and then be sent to Bosnia. Becoming an official Department of Defense Overseas Touring Show, the musicians traveled throughout Bosnia according to the armed four-convoy rule, with gaining chaplains at each location doing the coordination. As one report stated, "Over the course of their 12 days on tour, the group performed at 20 different bases, making 28 separate appearances at concerts, worship services, and unit prayer breakfasts, to well over 1,500 IFOR personnel. . . . Inevitably after each concert, a cluster of soldiers would engulf the two singers with questions about their music and their Christian faith. . . . This ministry tour proved to be of great value within the command."[56]

Expanding Chaplain Ministries in Bosnia and Surrounding Areas, 1996–97

While life at base camps became more stable and comfortable, chaplain missions both within and outside the wire further developed. What began as a makeshift attempt at providing chaplain support developed quickly into an organized pattern of meeting the religious needs of soldiers in Bosnia.

Some of the frustrations or growing pains experienced by chaplains or chaplain assistants during these initial months in Bosnia are evident in the experiences of chaplain assistant PFC Dae Lee. Dae Lee was assigned to the 47th Forward Support Battalion (FSB) and was in Bosnia from January through October 1996. Dae Lee and Chaplain (CPT) Jerry Sieg were both new to the Army chaplaincy, and, as Dae Lee stated, "We were a little unsure of our roles but eventually got along excellently." Dae Lee also mentioned, "Once I arrived in Bosnia it took me several months to really understand why we were there." Dae Lee commented, "It took us a very long time to build our chapel. . . . Overall, we had a very hard time fitting into our unit. The unit at many times isolated the chaplain section. We had to make a double effort to fit in." A main reason they had difficulty fitting, according to Dae Lee, was the nonstop working conditions and the intense pace of operation in their FSB. The intense work environment produced exhaustion, low morale, and little interest in spiritual things. Dae Lee remarked, "My 10 months in Bosnia were very tough and hard working. I wish I and my chaplain would have been better prepared."[57]

Chaplain Assistant Specialist (SPC) Wyman Loveless of the 1st Squadron, 4th Cavalry Brigade had a positive experience in Bosnia. Serving in Bosnia from April through July 1996, he described his job as "Personal security for the battalion chaplain and battalion chaplain assistant." Loveless remarked that he and his chaplain, CPT David Brown, were well connected with the mental health professionals and the chain of command and that they participated in or attended many unit activities.

In commenting about the dangers that he and David Brown experienced, Loveless stated:

> We felt danger nightly as this was the time when aggressors would try to breach our perimeter or fire at patrols or at the base camp. Nationals would occasionally come in front of the gate and beg for food and shelter. They would also block convoys by standing in the road or by harassing drivers or passengers in vehicles.[58]

Jewish soldiers in Bosnia in 1996 experienced their holy days away from home. Seeing this need, USAREUR Chaplain Wake coordinated with the European Command (EUCOM) to allow a rabbi, Chaplain (COL) David Zalis, to go to Bosnia and meet the religious needs of Jewish soldiers, both American and others. Zalis' account of his ministry in Bosnia is as follows:

> In 1996 I served for 6 months as the EUCOM rear chaplain in Germany. My main job was to coordinate chaplains from various US forces as well as NATO chaplains. Our main focus was on Bosnia. I coordinated and administrated chaplains from numerous countries going to and coming from Bosnia.

> For 2 weeks during the 1996 Passover season I was sent to the Balkans to perform Jewish religious services. We flew by helicopter from Germany to Taszar, Hungary. After spending time there with soldiers and seeking out Jewish soldiers we flew by helicopter to Bosnia. While I traveled around Bosnia a lot to conduct Jewish religious services, I centered my activities out of Camp Bondsteel, Kosovo. Chaplain McChrystal was the senior chaplain there. I was assigned a driver and a bodyguard. There were signs of destruction all over the place. It was very tense. There was so much hatred in the faces of the people.

> I brought with me a large number of kosher MREs to distribute to Jewish soldiers during this holiday season. At Camp Bondsteel we had a large Passover celebration that was well attended and very popular. This was the time that US Secretary of Commerce Ron Brown was killed in a helicopter accident. My experience in Bosnia was very fulfilling. I was glad to meet the religious needs of Jewish soldiers in harms way as they performed a difficult and often thankless mission.[59]

Throughout 1996 and into 1997 the effectiveness of the United States and NATO intervention became apparent. A tense peace prevailed throughout Bosnia. Refugees returned to their looted homes, war criminals were pursued, relief agencies operated without interruption throughout Bosnia, and a gradual rebuilding program commenced. Many US troops rarely went outside the base perimeter, and with the no alcohol use policy for US troops, soldiers were safer, healthier, and less likely to be killed.[60]

For the first 6 months in Bosnia there were only three US soldiers killed—one by a landmine, one in a kitchen fire, and one in a truck accident. The number of US soldiers injured in accidents was also lower than the number of injuries in the Army as a whole, that being from the strict safety guidelines enforced throughout Bosnia. Throughout this same period, there were 62 pregnancies among the 2,000 or so US women stationed in Bosnia, a rate comparable to Army pregnancies worldwide. Nonserious injuries were frequent, caused mostly from vehicle maintenance, transportation accidents, sports injuries, or other routine factors. Serious injuries were so low that the large number of medical personnel deployed to Bosnia became obviously unnecessary, so doctors rotated from Bosnia back to Germany to keep their surgical skills sharp and then returned to Bosnia. This is not to say that duty in Bosnia was comfortable or hazard-free. What was most likely to injure a soldier was a road accident, and by mid-1996 there were 13 soldiers seriously injured in road accidents. Another cause for injuries was land mines, with two soldiers seriously wounded in mid-1996 from land mines. About the same time, there was a report that snipers wounded two US soldiers, with another soldier shot but not seriously wounded by someone trying to sneak into a base camp.[61]

Causey had an interesting and diverse ministry in Bosnia from June 1996 through January 1997. Assigned to the 212th Mobile Army Surgical Hospital (MASH) at Camp Bedrock, Bosnia, Causey was the base camp senior chaplain supervising two other chaplains. He described his job as follows:

> Provide religious support to MASH staff, soldiers, and patients. Provide worship services to the base camp, which were six weekly worship services and three Bible Studies. Member of the Critical Incident Stress Management Team. Advise the commander on local religious holidays and on the impact of moral, ethical, emotional, and spiritual issues.[62]

Causey further stated that he and his chaplain assistant were part of the first response team when injured or wounded soldiers came into their hospital. They would split up to provide religious support to as many soldiers at once as possible, with Causey being briefed by his chaplain assistant about those patients who needed to or requested to see the chaplain.[63]

Causey's medical unit performed various ministries outside their base camp at Camp Bedrock. He recalled:

> We did MEDFLAGs [medical training exercises] to local villages. This was a hospital mission and not a chaplain mission, although I went along to provide religious support to our soldiers and did some counseling when needed. Many of the main supply routes and alternative supply routes were mined. This caused a problem once when a convoy we were in got off the main road. We identified that the road we were on was mined.[64]

Chaplains, like Causey, and their assistants typically stated that their most harrowing experiences were from driving on pitiful roads in terrible weather conditions amidst a local populous in which antagonists of the United States were hidden. Chaplain Assistant SPC James Nelson summed up the view of chaplains and chaplain assistants in traveling on dangerous roads when he stated, "Most of the time when we would go on convoys we knew that there were numerous mines everywhere."[65]

Chaplain Assistant Nelson served with Chaplain (CPT) Glen McFarland with the 519th Military Police Battalion at Camp Colt, Bosnia. Nelson arrived in July 1996 and served through June 1997. Nelson remarked, "In addition to my other duties I assisted the Catholic priest, Chaplain Flock, when he did Catholic services for our unit. We worked directly together. I was an authorized 71M [chaplain assistant] providing religious assistance to my chaplain for the 519th MP Battalion." Nelson further stated, "With Chaplain McFarland we had prayer breakfasts every month and we would go out to different checkpoints where our MPs were. I did not notice anything that did not work well. We made sure that we were always where the soldiers were and I think that made the difference." Nelson recalled, "I was fairly new to the job and the Army so I had very little experience. But I was fortunate to have a chaplain who wasn't new and had a wealth of experience. We worked closely with Civil Affairs so we would take clothes and school supplies that had been donated to the local schools in our area."[66]

The fall of 1996 saw huge civilian political unrest in Bosnia. In late November, a crowd of 100,000 protestors gathered in Belgrade to oppose the policies of Serbian President Milosevic. What remained of the fractured Yugoslavia, namely Serbia and Montenegro, were ruled by Milosevic from Belgrade. Milosevic outmaneuvered his political opponents and maintained control despite economic ills and volatile ethnic tensions. He maintained his government with the reserved approval of NATO and the US. One news report stated:

> BELGRADE, Yugoslavia—In the largest protest ever against Slobodan Milosevic, more than 100,000 people marched through the capital yesterday, hurling eggs at government buildings and accusing the Serbian president of stealing municipal elections.
>
> People cheered from balconies as protesters coated the facades and windows of Milosevic's downtown office, City Hall, the state-run TV and the Politika newspaper in yellow. Huge columns of demonstrators stamped their feet and chanted, 'We will not give up our victory!'
>
> In the past, Milosevic has cracked down on such protests. . . . Milosevic, accused of instigating the Bosnian and Croatian wars, has used his control of the media and an ability to outmaneuver the fractured opposition. . . . He since has turned peacemaker, and the United States depends on him to keep far-right Bosnian Serbs from completely rejecting the year-old Dayton peace pact.[67]

While US and NATO troops in Bosnia performed their missions well, there was political and military disunity within the Clinton administration. This discord is especially evident in the memoirs of General Clark. Clark served as director of strategic plans and policy for the Joint Staff at the Pentagon from 1994 to 1996, then as the Supreme Allied Commander, Europe (SACEUR) from 1997 through 2000. Clark recalled the unpopular decision by the Clinton administration to allow homosexuals to serve in the military and an atmosphere in the administration that did not want people in uniform in the White House unless absolutely necessary. Further, Clark was repeatedly frustrated that Clinton made remarks to the media about troop movements and strength in the Balkans without consulting with his senior military advisers. The tension in the Clinton administration over strategy and policy in the Balkans is further illustrated in Clark's statement that he had "almost 2 years of tension" with Secretary of Defense William Cohen and the Chairman of the Joint Chiefs of Staff, Shalikashvili. As Clark stated, "the central problem [was] . . . trying to manage a limited war that wasn't the top Pentagon planning priority and hadn't received full national commitment and support." On a positive note, Clark did commend Clinton for his public remarks about removing

Milosevic from power and that the mission in the Balkans would be supported until complete.[68]

The disunity of the US position in the Balkans was even more complicated by the friction between the policies of the US government and the UN. US Ambassador Albright did not support the lackadaisical position on Bosnia held by Secretary General of the UN Boutros Boutros-Ghali. Albright called Secretary Boutros-Ghali's views on Bosnia "indefensible" while she was determined "to eliminate any danger of Bosnia erupting once again into flames." While Albright was perplexed by the Clinton administration's comments about the troops in Bosnia all being home within a year, she was fully impressed by the smooth deployment of troops into Bosnia and that "children reclaimed the streets from snipers, and reconstruction began." Like Clark, Albright was confused by the contradictory statements from the White House by Cohen and Clinton, making her job representing the United States at the United Nations that much more difficult.[69]

Chaplains serving soldiers in Bosnia were far removed from the political squabbles in Washington. Supporting chaplains in Bosnia from Germany was USAREUR Chaplain Wake. Wake spoke of the USAREUR Commander, General William W. Crouch, as a leader who had a high level of professionalism, commending Crouch for his seriousness in getting troops prepared to deploy to Bosnia in spite of political uncertainties at home. In speaking of the senior chaplain in Bosnia, Task Force *Eagle* Chaplain McChrystal, Wake remarked that anything McChrystal or his chaplains needed they would be sure to get. Speaking of the Reserve component chaplains who came to Europe for backfill to support deployed units, Wake stated that they were "unbelievably helpful" and "really great folks."[70] Wake visited Bosnia in the summer of 1996. He and his staff at USAREUR established a chaplain rotation policy, set guidelines for the distribution of donated supplies to charitable groups in Bosnia, provided UMT senior leadership, and resourced all chaplain missions in Bosnia.

Beginning in the late summer of 1996, Chaplain (COL) David Hicks was the V Corps Chaplain and was the senior chaplain between USAREUR Chaplain Wake and Task Force *Eagle* Chaplain McChrystal in Bosnia. In 1996 and 1997, many of the V Corps subordinate units were deployed to Hungary to administer the deployment, rest and recreation, and redeployment back to Germany for thousands of soldiers. Hicks balanced his time between Germany and Hungary with occasional visits to Bosnia. Most of the V Corps soldiers were stationed in Hungary at Slavgrad, Kasavar, or Taszar, sites frequently visited by Hicks. Traveling throughout the Balkans with his chaplain assistant, Sergeant Major (SGM) Mike Pukansky, Hicks encouraged UMTs, solved problems, inspected chapel programs, and lived for numerous brief periods in the mud of the Balkans. After May 1997, the deputy V Corps chaplain was LTC Phil Hill. Hill, like Hicks, was frequently on the road in Hungary and Bosnia, performing Roman Catholic services at key locations and times. In speaking of the living conditions in Bosnia in 1997, Hill said, "we were still up to our ankles in mud," living conditions were still terrible, and the chapels were humble but very adequate.[71]

As troop levels in Bosnia continued to rise, various short-lived US facilities appeared and then closed throughout the Balkans. These temporary facilities were used for transportation support and supply missions to facilitate the inflow of personnel, hardware, supplies, and weapons into Bosnia. One chaplain who visited several of these temporary locations was Chaplain (MAJ) Charles Howell. He stated,

> I was the 29th Support Group Brigade Chaplain (21st TAACOM) [Theater Army Area Command] from 24 June 1996 to August 1999.
>
> I deployed twice from Kaiserslautern to Taszar, Hungary, 4 July—30 August and 20 November—20 December 1996.
>
> From 1 February to 8 April 1999, I deployed to Rijeka, Croatia. My unit opened a sea port of embarkation (SPOE) to receive and send units in and out of the Balkans.
>
> From 20 June to 8 August 1999, I was deployed to Thessaloniki, Greece, to open a SPOE to receive and send units to Camp Bondsteel, Kosovo.[72]

While in Croatia, Howell was able to develop a close relationship with a Roman Catholic Croatian priest; this relationship provided Howell with valuable cultural, religious, and social-political information about his unit's local area of operation. Howell visited many places in the Balkans. He stated, "I was a brigade chaplain meaning at the time I had six battalions to cover in a host of countries. . . . I had overlapping coverage in Bosnia, Croatia, and Hungary, and so I had to be kind of a circuit rider. Each week I would move by helicopter from Bosnia to Croatia and then back to Hungary and then get in my hummer [military vehicle] and drive back to the support area." At the completion of the unit mission, a few company level units remained in Bosnia, Croatia, and Hungary, which allowed Howell to make additional visits to encourage and counsel soldiers.[73]

In his itinerant ministry, Howell addressed a large number of counseling issues with soldiers in diverse locations. Months away from home began to wear on families and soldiers, the emotional drain of separations creating numerous problems with deployed soldiers and their family members back home. Howell recalled, "Families were concerned and letters began to come up through the chain of command saying some of your soldiers are having problems, can you send somebody down to visit, and so my brigade commander said, 'Chaplain Howell, you're the guy.' So I went back down to see them." Howell faced numerous counseling issues. Some of the families from his unit lived in Germany while others returned to the United States for the length of the deployment, making family counseling difficult. The typical feelings of isolation and loneliness in the Balkans led to cases of marital infidelity in Army units. Spouses in Germany or in the United States had the same feelings of isolation and loneliness and some succumbed to the same type of temptations. US troops in Bosnia were not allowed alcohol, but soldiers stationed in Croatia or Hungary or other nearby places had easy access to alcohol. This meant that some soldiers drank heavily and lost inhibitions, resulting in a diverse number of discipline and moral problems that the command and the chaplain needed to address.[74]

One of the areas near Bosnia that was a key location for 1996–97 support missions in the Balkans was in nearby Hungary. As one news report stated, "The Hungarian towns of Taszar and Kaposvar are the major staging areas for 20,000 US troops heading for Bosnia. Hungary is contributing a 400-man contingent."[75] The vast majority of US soldiers in Hungary were very happy to be contributing to the greater cause of peace in the Balkans. Taszar became the most prominent US military facility, a virtual beehive of activity as new soldiers entered the Balkans and prepared for other missions, came to Taszar for rest and relaxation or to catch a flight back to Germany, or came to Taszar as a stop on their redeployment process at the end of their tour of duty.

In early 1997, about 25 percent of US troops in Hungary were from Reserve component units. Army National Guard Sergeant First Class (SFC) Melinda Early of Alabama looked at this peacekeeping mission as an opportunity to alleviate real suffering, saying, "When we came down here [to Tuzla] in that long convoy, there were elderly women along the street holding their hands up in peace signs. . . . I only wish we were here sooner." As one report stated, "Many Reservists consider Bosnia a good assignment. It's a humanitarian cause and it has been well received by most of the locals they've met." Army National Guard Chaplain (CPT) Steven Szasz of Idaho conducted numerous family reunion type briefings for soldiers stopping in Hungary on their way back home. Szasz commented that even though such briefings are not essential to the technical performance of the unit mission, these reunion briefings are something the Army does to help soldiers and their families. While the briefings are mandatory, Szasz stated the soldiers seem to appreciate that these briefings will help them reintegrate with their loved ones at home.[76]

Chaplain (CPT) Scott Sterling was assigned to the Taszar Airfield from 1 October through December 1996. Assigned to the 69th Air Defense Artillery, he did not deploy to Hungary with his battalion but rather in support of the larger brigade. Sterling was assigned as an OIC of a personnel verification team, a nontraditional chaplain assignment that he questioned through both command and chaplain channels. Because Sterling was given freedom to do hospital ministry, counseling, and other ministries as he wished, he decided to make the best of a difficult situation and complete his 90-day tour in this unique assignment. He stated, "I was encouraged to minister as creatively as I could under the circumstances. I was happy to be there with the troops, so I stayed the entire time."[77] Overlapping with Sterling in Taszar was Chaplain Assistant Loveless. Assigned to the USAREUR HQ but attached for duty in Hungary, Loveless was in Taszar from November 1996 through April 1997. Loveless enjoyed being a part of the numerous family reunion and reintegration briefings sponsored by the chaplains and was happy to be active in a "coffee house" ministry, as he and others provided a safe and wholesome place for soldiers to unwind and for chaplains to talk casually with the troops. The only time Loveless felt unsafe was when he was traveling on hazardous roads in war-torn areas with a Roman Catholic chaplain, going from Hungary to various locations in Croatia and then back, as he assisted the chaplain in Roman Catholic services.[78]

Chaplain Accounts of Ministry in Bosnia, 1997

In 1997, the US Army in Bosnia, past its initial growth pains of deployment, was settling down into its peacekeeping and nation-building missions. Structurally, the old IFOR was significantly downsized and was replaced by the Stabilization Force (SFOR). More than just a symbolic change of titles, the name change designated that stabilization of the area was the key concept and that NATO and the United States were determined to prevent a resurgence of violence in the Balkans. The senior Army chaplain in Bosnia had been McChrystal, Task Force *Eagle* chaplain. He was replaced in November 1996 by Chaplain (LTC) Donna Weddle of the 1st Infantry Division, the new Task Force *Eagle* chaplain. Hicks went from the V Corps chaplain position to the USAREUR chaplain assignment, replacing Wake. Other chaplains rotated in and out of assignments in Bosnia and throughout the Balkans. New chaplains throughout 1997 built on the initial ministries begun by their predecessors and continued to provide quality chaplain and chaplain assistant support to soldiers deployed throughout the Balkans.

The year 1997 began with Army news reports that troops in Europe were already feeling the strain from the Balkans rotations. Few soldiers who had seen the chaos in Bosnia took comfort in Secretary of Defense Cohen's comment that the United States would complete its mission and be out of Bosnia by 30 June 1998. Unquestionably, there was a strain placed on US Army troops because of the large-scale rotations into the Balkans. The Clinton administration was committed to downsizing the military. Debates waged about the US policy in the Balkans. As one writer stated, "On one issue, however, there is complete consensus; the Army in Europe is stretched thin by constant deployments to Bosnia and Macedonia and on numerous 'Partnership for Peace' missions in Eastern Europe." The article told of the more than 10,000 US troops in the Balkans in 1997 and that questions had arisen about the combat readiness of infantry and armor units sent to the Balkans for humanitarian and peacekeeping missions and not for conventional combat missions. Soldiers were not using the high power weapons they had trained on, and the fear was that combat skills would deteriorate. This fear, coupled with the strain on families from Balkans rotations and from fewer units available to deploy because of downsizing, created a pessimistic outlook for the US Army.[79]

Chairman of the Joint Chiefs of Staff, Shalikashvili, addressed the status of the US military in a 12 February 1997 speech to Congress. Shalikashvili spoke of the strain on soldiers from reductions in force and from deployments, and then addressed the good work he saw soldiers performing in the Balkans.

> One of the strategic consequences of the post-Cold War period is that the US has been able to reduce military force levels. Since 1989, the active all-volunteer force has been reduced by 700,000 people—about a third of the active force. . . . The force drawdown these past few years has not been an easy experience for military members. . . . America's military today is performing more missions, in more places than it did during the Cold War, and is doing so with significantly fewer personnel. Yet our men and women

have performed brilliantly from one end of the world to the other, with Bosnia standing as a prime example. . . .

SFOR continues to build on the successes of IFOR by providing time and an environment that will permit civilian initiatives to proceed. Up to approximately 8,500 US personnel in Bosnia and an additional 5,000 in neighboring countries are supporting the Stabilization Force. SFOR is a mobile force that will concentrate on providing a safe and secure environment for civilian implementation of Dayton Accords. The Commander, Stabilization Force (COMSFOR), is supported by an air operation built on the foundation of the successful Operation DENY FLIGHT; 1,800 US personnel are involved in this facet of operations.

Our forces will be in place for 18 months. Every 6 months, a review of the security situation and civil initiatives will be conducted with the goal of moving to a deterrent force of reduced size.

Equally important to regional stability in the Balkans was Operation ABLE SENTRY. ABLE SENTRY is the US contribution to the United Nations Preventative Deployment operation in Macedonia. 500 US personnel joined 500 troops from other nations to ensure containment of the crisis in Bosnia.[80]

The organization of chaplains coming and going into the Balkans and assigning them to the areas they were most needed was a complicated job. In 1997, much of the UMT coordination in the Balkans came from Chaplain (LTC) Hank Steinhilber of the USAREUR Chaplain's Office in Heidelberg, Germany. Steinhilber served briefly in the Balkans before becoming the assistant operations officer for the USAREUR chaplain. He stated, "I was assistant head of operations which meant we were in charge of the religious support for all of the down-range areas. We were to make sure coverage would come about either from organic units that flowed down or from Reserve units that came from the states. And also I had the responsibility to make sure that [rear area] religious coverage was still in Europe at the time." In 1997, Steinhilber had numerous opportunities to visit chaplains in the Balkans, observing that soldiers almost never went outside the base camp except on patrols. He said chaplains became essentially base camp ministers with little contact with locals outside the gate. This would change as the civilian areas stabilized, but early on in the IFOR and now the SFOR missions, soldiers mostly did their jobs inside the perimeter. Steinhilber concluded, "So they had a pretty good base camp ministry. I went to some of the base camps but I did a lot out of Tuzla. It was a base camp ministry, Bible Studies, the same that they did. Worship services, seeing the people, and a ministry of presence."[81]

From the summer of 1996 through the spring of 1997, Szasz was stationed briefly in Schweinfurt, Germany, and then at Taszar, Hungary. Later he would be stationed at Slavonski Brod, Croatia, near the Sava River. Born in Hungary and speaking the language, Szasz was thrilled at the opportunity to minister in his native land. Initially stationed at Taszar, Hungary, Szasz remarked:

> Taszar is a small town of about 1,200 people. But it's really known for the Hungarian Army Airfield. This is still an active airfield for the Hungarian military. . . . Within Taszar Air Base are several other work areas for our Armed Forces—IFOR/SFOR units. Our forces consist of Air Force, Army, Navy, and Marines numbering about 6,000. . . . I live and work in the Life Support Area (LSA). This LSA is really a glorified tent city or like an RV camp in the states. . . . I live in a tent with two others in our ministry team. We each have an 8'x8' section, enough room for a cot, a field desk or whatever one can creatively come up with. . . . I, along with our chaplain assistants conduct redeployment/reunion briefings. . . . The other half of my time is spent in leading Bible Studies and preaching on a rotating basis.[82]

Szasz elaborated on his ministries as they developed in Taszar. First, he stated that the reunion briefings were given to every soldier, sailor, airman, and Marine that departed his area. "The material we cover ranges from issues such as changes in one's self, challenges on arrival back home, marital issues, parental concerns and alcohol abuse." The second area Szasz narrated was his religious ministry. In this capacity, Szasz preached Sunday morning sermons, led Bible Studies, and performed ministerial counseling. The third aspect of his ministry in Taszar concerned translating. He stated, "This has been an unplanned blessing on two accounts. My Hungarian has improved immensely. Whereas when I arrived, I stumbled around mixing Hungarian and English. Now I can carry on a complete conversation in Hungarian. The Hungarians are truly amazed at my improvement. This has also benefited the chaplain corps here at Taszar. I have had numerous occasions for liaison with local clergy, Hungarian military chaplains, and assisting in the everyday ongoings of the ministry teams.[83] He further stated, "When the USAREUR Chaplain (COL) David Hicks spent time in Hungary I traveled with him as an unofficial translator. It was a fulfilling and interesting ministry."[84]

In March 1997, three chaplains reported for duty in Bosnia. Chaplain (MAJ) Michael Metcalf of the New York Army National Guard arrived on 7 March and was assigned to Camp Demi, Bosnia-Herzegovina. Around the same time Chaplain (CPT) Keith Belz of the 601st Aviation Support Battalion was assigned to Comanche Base near Tuzla. Joining Belz at Comanche Base was Chaplain (CPT) Patrick Appleget of the 1st Squadron, 229th Aviation Regiment. These three chaplains are representative of the several dozen chaplains that were in the Balkans throughout 1997, and their specific experiences are examples of the diverse and comprehensive religious support provided to soldiers in Bosnia.

Metcalf was assigned to the New York Army National Guard before he was mobilized and deployed to Bosnia. He was cross-leveled to fill a vacant chaplain position at Camp Demi. Metcalf stated, "I had limited contact with other chaplains due to the remoteness of my location. I had weekly contact with a Roman Catholic priest who flew or drove in for Sunday Mass. . . ." Stating that he did get periodic visits from supervisory chaplains, Metcalf continued: "I was a base camp chaplain serving as a type of installation chaplain for 750 to 1,200 US and coalition troops and Department of Defense civilians." He described his typical activities at Camp Demi as performing weekly worship services, scheduling biweekly chaplain visits to see soldiers at remote communication sites, and maintaining a Christian men's support group called Promise Keepers. Metcalf also performed ministry outside the fence of Camp Demi. He assisted the Civil Affairs soldiers in distributing school supplies to local children and advised a Civil Affairs team chief concerning interaction with the Serbian Orthodox priest of Srebrenica. While stating that he did not feel safe in convoy operations around local election times and during inspections of arms storage sites, Metcalf stated, "This was some of the most rewarding ministry of my chaplaincy career."[85]

Belz arrived at Comanche Base in March 1997. Sleeping on an Army cot in a sleeping bag in a tent with 20 other men, Belz used an Air Force tent for a chapel and built some offices and storage areas in the back of the tent. He was able to get a humble steeple to place in front of the tent and acquired hundreds of books to use as a lending library for the troops. Belz stated, "I conducted chapel services, Bible Studies, a Christian movie night, prayer breakfasts, a tract ministry, and a lot of counseling with soldiers. I also taught a lot of family reunion type classes." Belz remembered the time that an old hidden mine detonated within the camp, thankfully with no one injured, and that there were areas within the camp that still had active mines and were off limits to all personnel. As the chaplain, he addressed ethical and moral issues within the unit, like the fight he won not to house male and female soldiers in the same tents, and like his counseling related to six pregnant soldiers within the unit in the first 2 months of the deployment. He commented, "I had a great relationship with the 1st Armored Division chaplain who said we were the only other base that she never had to visit or worry about."[86]

Chaplain Appleget, like Metcalf and Belz, arrived in Bosnia in March 1997. While serving at Comanche Base as chaplain for the 1st Battalion, 229th Aviation Regiment, Appleget stated that as a battalion chaplain and as pastor of the Lutheran service he had a good relationship with other chaplains during the deployment. As far as his personal safety, Appleget commented, "Sometimes we would hear shots outside the camp. Once I found a dud rocket outside a tent that did not explode." At Camp Comanche there were traveling restrictions, meaning that Appleget maintained a base camp ministry and did not frequently travel outside the gate. He described his ministry as "visits to hangers, outposts, and later on firing ranges," and that he worked with Civil Affairs to locate volunteers through the chapel program to see if soldiers would be willing to volunteer their time at local orphanages near Tuzla. Appleget summarized, "We all were pretty restricted to the camps. Most of the ministry was with soldiers away from home with family issues. Some chapel programs grew."[87]

Politically, Bosnia in 1997 was unstable. On 10 February a procession of several hundred mostly middle-aged and elderly Muslims were attacked in Mostar, southern Bosnia. Animosity in Mostar between Muslims and Croatian Roman Catholics had kept the city divided since the 1995 cease-fire agreement. As one news report stated, "International investigators reported that the Croat police, in and out of uniform, first beat the marchers, then fired repeatedly at their backs as they tried to flee for safety. . . . Animosity between Muslims and Croats periodically bedevils efforts to reunify the city. . . . Although the Muslims and Croats were allies against the Serbs as the Bosnian war began, they started fighting each other in 1993." The specific incident on 10 February was related to Muslim mourners marching unarmed and peacefully to a cemetery to pay their respects to deceased loved ones. Croatian police and civilians attacked the crowd, killing at least one person and wounding many others. As a result, international police investigators condemned local Croat police and charged them with violations of international law in using "excessive force in beating marchers" and "unnecessary and disproportionate lethal force."

Fears spread throughout the Balkans that this incident could escalate and force NATO peacekeepers to become more involved in that region.[88]

The 28 August civilian assaults on US troops near McGovern Base, Bosnia, also illustrated the political instability in Bosnia in 1997. As US troops moved into an area at 0300 to secure a position, a civilian alarm was sounded. The media reported, "Hundreds of Bosnia Serb townspeople roused from their sleep by air-raid sirens pelted US peacekeeping troops with rocks early today, forcing them to retreat from positions around a police station. The incident represented one of the most serious challenges to NATO-led Stabilization Force troops since they took over peacekeeping in Bosnia in December [1995] under the terms of the Dayton Peace Accords."[89] Another news account provided more details stating, "Anti-NATO mobs . . . destroyed cars and wounded at least two US soldiers," and that "US soldiers in the NATO force fired tear gas and warning shots to fend off rock-hurling Serb mobs." Foreign media and international officials were also roughed up in this incident.[90] Having orders to use force if necessary to disperse the crowds, 18 American soldiers received recognition for their restraint because they did not fire on the mob even though they were injured by flying debris and physically assaulted.[91]

US Army chaplain assistants in Bosnia worked with their chaplains both outside the gate in the civilian community and inside the perimeter with US and NATO soldiers. In 1997, SFC Pamela Neal was the 1st Infantry Division chaplain assistant noncommissioned officer in charge (NCOIC). She served in Bosnia from 1 August through 30 October. She commented that she enjoyed being part of a UMT that provided assistance to wounded or distressed Serbians, the injured being victims of the ongoing tensions in Bosnia. She also enjoyed being part of a puppet ministry for local children, but stated that she did feel there was danger when she was part of convoys visiting other UMTs or civilian charitable groups throughout Bosnia. As a more senior chaplain assistant, she described her job responsibilities as "coordinating transportation via helicopter and convoy" and, "As the 1st Infantry Division NCOIC with temporary duty to Bosnia, I trained brigade and battalion chaplain assistants. I also coordinated religious activities in the area of operations."[92] Neal had additional duties related to ordering UMT supplies, information management, and coordinating security missions with other chaplain assistants. Her tour in Bosnia was successful and provided her a basis of knowledge for future missions.

In August 1997, Chaplain Assistant Sergeant (SGT) Yolanda Jackson came to Comanche Base as a member of the 2d Armored Calvary Regiment. In this capacity she worked with several chaplains, most notable for her were Chaplain (CPT) Dean Bonura and Chaplain (CPT) Timothy Vakoc. Yolanda Jackson assisted Bonura with coordinating weekly marriage and family classes for the soldiers, establishing a cycle of prayer breakfasts, and managing a chapel. She stated, "The special services and caroling and unique events we planned for Thanksgiving and Christmas in 1997 worked very well." Jackson also assisted the itinerant Roman Catholic chaplain in her area, Vakoc. With Vakoc she traveled by helicopter to various base camps in Bosnia to assist the chaplain in the set up, security, and recovery tasks related to conducting various Roman Catholic Masses in diverse locations. Jackson stated, "This was an interesting tour, to see how people in another part of the world lived. I saw a lot of the country by traveling on convoys. This was a highlight of my military career."[93]

Senior chaplains in Europe remained engaged with UMT activities in the Balkans. Chaplain (COL) Janet Horton followed Hicks as V Corps chaplain, based in Heidelberg, Germany. After beginning her new assignment at V Corps in June 1997, Janet Horton quickly went to the Balkans to see the structure of chaplain support and to meet the people on the ground. She stated that the Balkans mission at that time had succeeded in stopping the genocide and had transitioned to the sustainment phase. Janet Horton gave guidance as to how chaplains could relate to local indigenous religious leaders and helped set some standards about the role of the UMT in humanitarian operations. For example, as UMTs were overwhelmed with school supplies and clothing donations from the United States, it became apparent to Janet Horton that "We can't have the Unit Ministry Team being dedicated to the humanitarian operation at the expense of not getting the religious support mission done."[94] Chaplains thereafter had more guidance on how to balance their primary role as a chaplain to soldiers with other potential duties in humanitarian missions to the local population.

The year 1997 saw the further development and strengthening of chaplain missions throughout Bosnia and nearby areas. For example, as the year began Szasz saw his responsibilities in Hungary expand: he provided chaplain support to units as far north as the Hungarian Tank Gunnery Range at Taborfalva and as far south as Zagreb, Croatia.[95] In September 1997, Chaplain (CPT) Steven Firtko arrived at Camp Bedrock near Tuzla, Bosnia. Firtko was the only chaplain for the 2,000 personnel assigned at Camp Bedrock, a situation that meant he worked or was on call day and night for his 6-month tour in Bosnia. The highlights of his Bosnia tour, Firtko stated, were the Thanksgiving and Christmas 1997 services he performed. The Army Chief of Chaplains, Chaplain (MG) Donald Shea, did the Roman Catholic Christmas services and Firtko performed the Protestant services.

As far as dangerous situations, Firtko remarked, "I did a religious service on Hill 562—a radio tower taken by force and still disputed." Although the threat of Serbian snipers was real, the service was uninterrupted.[96] Firtko was an example of a stable base camp chaplain providing religious support to troops within his area of responsibility, a ministry in which he preached regularly and had daily contact with soldiers, this providing numerous counseling and one-on-one ministry opportunities.

The US Army Special Forces were active and engaged throughout Bosnia in 1997. One of the Special Forces chaplains who rotated in and out of Bosnia was Hartranft of the 10th Special Forces Group. Hartranft was deployed to Bosnia in December 1997 through April 1998. His Special Forces soldiers were divided into A-Teams and deployed to 26 locations throughout Bosnia for the purpose of enforcing peace, monitoring weapons turned in by various belligerents, gathering intelligence on small militant factions not supportive of the Dayton Peace Accords, and maintaining the cease-fire in potentially volatile areas. Hartranft stated, "As the chaplain, I traveled and did a service, or Bible Study (the choice of the A-Team), and did a lot of individual counseling. As far as facilities I used for religious services, I just used the A-Team's house. I traveled to each team house in a contracted local vehicle, a four wheeled Jeep-looking type vehicle." While conducting the 1997 Christmas services for Special Forces soldiers was a highlight of his ministry, he stated, "Counseling opportunities were endless. Since there were about 25 locations I got to every A-Team house only once a month. Every house had soldiers that wanted to speak to me. . . . I had several opportunities to counsel one on one. Other nonprivate conversations developed into impromptu Bible Studies."[97]

Overall, the year 1997 for the US Army in the Balkans was a time of stabilization, construction, and adjustments. Considered a hostile fire zone and not a combat zone, soldiers outside their base camps were still in constant danger from landmines, snipers, or angry mobs of civilians. Soldiers away from home for the holidays received religious support from UMTs, while thousands of schoolchildren wrote letters of encouragement and support to soldiers they had never met who were serving far from home.[98] Clinton spent the 1997 Christmas holiday in Bosnia. His bipartisan trip to support soldiers was very successful. Speaking to a large gathering of troops in Tuzla, Clinton stated:

> I don't think many Americans understand exactly how deep
> the burdens are on our men and women in uniform today.
> Because we have downsized the military in the aftermath
> of the Cold War, when we take on these responsibilities it

is very hard for a lot of people. We rotate these missions a little more rapidly than we would like to. We draw out Reservists and Guardsmen more often than we would like to. But you have always done what you were asked to do, and you have always delivered for America.

So, on this Christmas season, I ask the American people . . . to remember what we owe to the soldiers, the sailors, the airmen, the Marines of the Armed Forces at home and around the world, in the Persian Gulf, on the DMZ in Korea, here in Bosnia. . . .

I think that one of the things that you may wonder is whether people back home know you're here and appreciate what you're doing, since you've done it so well there aren't any visible problems, and you made it look easy.

I want you to know that, at this Christmas, you are in the hearts of the American people.[99]

Diverse Chaplain Ministries in Peacekeeping in Bosnia, 1998

The year 1998 began with the NATO and US mission in Bosnia coming under growing criticism. The 1995 promise of US troops being out of Bosnia in a year had obviously not come true. There was no end in sight to an often thankless and uneventful mission. While peace did prevail throughout the Balkans, there was a widespread assumption that as soon as the United States and NATO left the area, the fighting would resume. A large number of war criminals were still wandering and hiding throughout Bosnia, and the US and NATO policy of apprehending such criminals fueling this pessimistic attitude was seemingly ineffective. According to one account:

> The number of indicted war criminals wandering with impunity through Serb-controlled areas stands as a major barrier to a lasting peace that would allow the United States to complete its mission in Bosnia. . . .
>
> NATO's inaction on this front has stifled the reconstruction process, leaving precious little to show for 2 years and billions of dollars.
>
> Until war criminals are arrested and tried, refugees will feel unsafe in attempting to return home. Without the

return of refugees, the prospects for economic reconstruction will remain limited.[100]

As the mission in Bosnia and surrounding countries continued, the United States and NATO came to the conviction that much of the ongoing tension and uncertainty in Bosnia could be directly blamed on Milosevic. Secretary of State Albright saw Milosevic as a cunning and dishonest negotiator who, for example, in May 1998 posed for cameras during a peace conference while simultaneously having his troops wreck havoc in Kosovo and pillage Albanian villages. Albright spoke of Milosevic as a manipulator who ruthlessly played various Bosnian political and ethnic factions against each other to solidify his power. Albright bluntly stated, "I never trusted him. His ambitions were not the kind that could be satisfied except at great cost to others," and that Milosevic "invited destruction" and "was wrecking their [Bosnian] hopes for a peaceful and prosperous future."[101]

As far back as August 1997, reports stated Milosevic was meddling in the power struggle that has kept Bosnian Serbs divided.[102] Milosevic, as President of Yugoslavia, only had the territories of Serbia and Montenegro under his control, having lost Bosnia-Herzegovina as a result of the 1995 Dayton Peace Accords. Nevertheless, in 1998 cronies of Milosevic were still active in Bosnia disrupting the peace process, inciting Serbs to rebel, and hindering NATO and US efforts in the area, all the while seeking to gain further influence and power. Clark, the Supreme Allied Commander in Europe from 1997 to 2000, called Milosevic "a supremely manipulative liar and a bully," and one who was full of "self-interest and corruption" and "unscrupulous."[103]

Army chaplains and chaplain assistants in the Balkans in 1998 were fully engaged in religious support to their peacekeeping soldiers. A variety of religious and morale enhancing programs were developed that supported the religious and emotional needs of soldiers far away from home. Staff Sergeant (SSG) James Johnson of the 1st Battalion, 26th Infantry

Figure 7. General Wesley Clark, Supreme Allied Commander, Europe.

US Army

served at Camp Able Sentry, Macedonia, from February through July 1998. This facility, built in 1992 during the Bosnian War, functioned as a major logistical base for various Balkan, NATO, and US troops. James Johnson was active in supporting soldiers at Camp Able Sentry, Macedonia, by assisting chaplains with redeployment briefings; serving as a point of contact for the unit rear detachment; and participating in Bible Studies, worship services, and orphanage visits. James Johnson stated: "The only times I did not feel safe was when we went on chaplain visits to small observation posts close to the border." He helped coordinate a ministry retreat to Greece, and contracted with a local Roman Catholic Macedonian priest to help meet the needs of US and NATO Roman Catholic troops.[104]

Chaplain (MAJ) Jerry Moates was deployed to Taszar, Hungary, from March to July 1998 as an individual replacement and not with his unit from Germany. He commented:

> I took over for Chaplain JoAnne Knight, coordinated with her and with Chaplain Steinhilber at the USAREUR Chaplain's Office. I was responsible for coordinating and supervising four or five chaplains at one time, though other chaplains would come through Taszar on their way to Croatia or Bosnia. My position title was 'USAREUR Chaplain Forward.' The mission of our base in Taszar was to serve as a forward staging area and receiving area for missions in and out of Croatia and Bosnia. Vehicle convoys from Germany would stop here to load or unload supplies. Trains came and went loaded with equipment. And the airfield was busy with planes landing and taking off all the time. There were lots of ministry opportunities to soldiers who were awaiting transportation, and to soldiers who were loading or unloading equipment. Some were going to Bosnia or Croatia, and some were returning.

> The soldiers were very receptive to my ministry. We had three chapel locations in the Taszar area. One was at the main camp, another was at the LSA (Life Support Area) and one we opened while I was there, which was located at the airstrip. My predecessor, Chaplain JoAnne Knight, did most of the groundwork for opening this chapel and I was able to conduct a dedication ceremony with the USAREUR Chaplain (COL) David Hicks presiding.

> All troops coming through our area had to stop at the LSA for medical and personnel records updates. Here we

maintained a chapel tent, which was well used as a rest area, reading location, and a place for soldiers to watch videos and just relax. At the Jewish Passover celebration, I took three vans full of soldiers to a civilian synagogue in Budapest to celebrate Passover. Chapel services were regularly scheduled and as chaplains went on leave or TDY, I rotated the chaplains to the various chapels. We had a Roman Catholic priest who I made sure traveled around to conduct his denominational ministry. We Protestant chaplains frequently covered each other's chapels as needed. As soldiers arrived, we did chaplain orientation briefings. As soldiers redeployed out of Croatia and Bosnia, we conducted family reunion briefings.

While in Hungary I never felt I was in personal danger. But when we went on chaplain visits to see subordinate chaplains in units located in Croatia and Bosnia, it was different. There were many tense moments as we drove through areas with blown up buildings. Seeing structures covered with bullet holes was disturbing. In a few areas, you could still see the blood stained on the outside walls of dilapidated buildings. I traveled through these areas to attend civil events with the Hungarians as well as to do chaplain visits to subordinate units and to chaplains under my supervision.[105]

By 1998, the US Army's role as peacekeeper was under scrutiny. The initial Bosnian mission of stopping genocide and separating belligerent parties was a success. Rival factions were disarmed, arms cachets were destroyed, humanitarian aid poured into the area, and a tense calm pervaded the region. Yet many questions remained as to what exactly the role of the UN peacekeeping force was and how involved the United States should be with the United Nations, with NATO, and in the internal conflicts within Europe. These questions were more noticeable with the October 1998 celebration of the United Nations completing 50 years of global peacekeeping missions. Skeptics of the United Nations noted that the need for global peacekeeping operations has dramatically increased since 1998, primarily from the fallout of numerous failed states. The role of the United Nations to prevent the need for peacekeeping missions had not succeeded. While the United Nations improved at conducting peacekeeping missions, it nevertheless became in many parts of the world a token force, as one writer stated, "to provide a cloak of legitimacy and limited political oversight through small numbers of observers."[106] This was clearly the case in

Bosnia. Without question, the United States was the lead force in the Balkans, with significant contributions from Great Britain, France, Germany, Russia, and dozens of other nations.

In 1998, Steinhilber was serving under Hicks at the USAREUR Chaplain's Office, Heidelberg, Germany. Steinhilber was responsible for finding the right locations in the Balkans to deploy Reserve component and Active Army chaplains and for coordinating their comings and goings with the needs and locations of numerous units. When the need for an O6 chaplain opened at Sarajevo, Bosnia, Army Chief of Chaplains (MG) Don Shea selected Steinhilber to fill that assignment. Steinhilber recalled:

> We lived in a compound in Sarajevo. We had three old hotels that were down there. . . . The rooms of the hotel were all shot up. I could sit on my balcony and you could see the bullet holes where they went right across the top of it. But they got the lights going and the heat on and things were fine. . . . So I went down and spent 6 months. . . . I was primarily chaplain to the staff, although I did coordinate across the Balkans with the different chaplains. I was very fortunate; they gave me an assistant. . . .
>
> We had a vehicle; we had freedom to go wherever we wanted within the theater. We had no problems whatsoever, so we visited all the chaplains. I had over 50 chaplains when I started, representing 38 nations. They were broken up into what was called MD, multinational divisions. There were three of them: MD North, which had the Americans in charge, out of Tuzla; the Brits had MD Northwest, out of their headquarters; and then the French had MD Southeast, which was out of Sarajevo. So we had the French in charge of us. I had a bunch of chaplains in Sarajevo. There was a German hospital, which had two German chaplains. The head German chaplain, I found out, was also the assistant S4 chaplain, so he was in for 3 months and then another one came in. And they were great. When I was on the road, he took care of things there. In Sarajevo was the headquarters contingency, so there was a Dutch contingency of soldiers to take care of the Dutch soldiers out in the field, and all the supplies came through Sarajevo, and so there was a Dutch chaplain there. A variety of things made it pleasurable to be around. I traveled all over. We were out on the road almost all the time, visiting and coordinating. . . .

There were a lot of thugs and thievery and black market-
ing and you could be taunted by a crowd. . . . It was really
more bandits and thugs and black marketers that caused
more problems than anything else.[107]

Civil Affairs (CA) units of the US Army Reserve were active and
engaged with various missions throughout Bosnia. The 1993 version
of FM 41-10, *Civil Affairs Operations*, stated that "the CA mission
is to support the commander's relationship with civil authorities and
civilian populace, promote mission legitimacy and enhance military
effectiveness."[108] Operations in Bosnia showed that the CA mission was
critical to the success of the overall mission and that CA must be an integral
part of peacekeeping operations.[109] In Bosnia a typical CA unit performed
missions related to humanitarian assistance, military to civil coordination,
support to civil administrators, cooperation with NATO administrators,
and various benevolent projects. One chaplain assigned to a CA unit was
Chaplain (LTC) Frank Wismer.

Wismer of the US Army Reserve served with a Civil Affairs Special
Function Team in Bosnia from June 1998 through February 1999. He
stated:

I served as OIC [Officer in Charge] for a CA Special
Functions Team. On this team were a Slovakian major,
Frank Debnar, a US NCOIC, and a linguist, Besmir
Fedahic. We were to deal with issues throughout the coun-
try that involved Civil Military Operations. Occasionally
we did deal with some Military-to-Military Operations.
We conducted a seminar in CIMIC (Civil Military
Coordination) for the Turkish Brigade and once had an
interaction with the Federation [Yugoslavian] Military.
On Sundays, I assisted with the religious support program
at Eagle Base, Tuzla, Bosnia.

I did have the opportunity to work with civilians near
Eagle Base. Our team worked with Mustafa Turzic in the
institution and opening of the Tuzla International Airport;
with the Mayor of Dubrave in establishing sites for wells;
and with local beekeepers whose bee populations were
decreasing. We also assisted the British at Banja Luka
during the elections of October 1998. We also assisted
with providing toys and clothing to an orphanage in Tuzla
at Christmas.[110]

Wismer pointed out that technically chaplains do not serve as chaplains in Civil Affairs units, but as cultural affairs officers. In this capacity, chaplains perform religious worship services but their primary function is to serve as a CA officer while still advising the commander on any religious issues that may affect the mission of the larger unit. As Wismer remarked, "Even though I served as a CA officer, I did enjoy a healthy relationship with the chaplains at Eagle Base. We had good cooperation in conducting services and had a good working relationship with the Air Force chaplains who were stationed with the Air Force contingent at the airfield. I did have occasion to take services for the Air Force at their chapel at the airfield." On a negative note, Wismer stated, "Our unit was split between Sarajevo and Tuzla. The higher HQ lost all control over those of us assigned to MD North. Although they rated us, they had no command of us. And, although MD North commanded us, they did not rate us. . . . We also had some unit members at Camp McGovern. This created tension and a sense of 'us' and 'them.'"[111]

In May 1998, Chaplain (CPT) Lonnie Locke III arrived at Comanche Base near Tuzla as a member of the 485th Corps Support Battalion. He recalled, "There were three chaplains on Comanche Base, two Protestants and one Catholic. We all worked together great. I was the newest (youngest, rank-wise) chaplain of the three." He stated, "We were there at a time of transition from tents to hard-shelter dwellings. Everything worked well; it was just muddy and dirty most of the time." Locke mentioned, "My chaplain assistant SPC Dialetta Taylor and I worked very well as a ministry team," and that he ministered mostly at the flight line, the motor pool, and the chapel.[112] A chaplain who overlapped with Locke in Bosnia was Chaplain (CPT) Philip Smiley of the 2d Battalion, 5th Cavalry Regiment. Stationed at Camp Dobol and Camp Demi in Bosnia, Smiley coordinated or conducted numerous church services each week and especially enjoyed, as he stated, "special events, celebrating communion, Christmas tree lighting, Thanksgiving, Christmas song fest, and interaction with local clergy." He had difficulty with his chaplain assistant, who he stated "was not a self-starter, and just floated through his Army assignment."[113]

Throughout 1998, Taszar, Hungary, continued to be a key logistical and coordination center for United States and NATO forces in Bosnia and Croatia. Chaplain Assistant SFC Chris Patterson was assigned to the National Support Element (NSE) Tuzla from 1 June through 4 November. He commented, "The chaplains that I worked with were from the Army Reserve and the Army National Guard, while the chaplain assistants were from the Active component. This was a big benefit to all members of the UMT. . . ." Patterson described his daily responsibilities in Taszar as follows:

> Job Description: Coordinates comprehensive religious logistical support for four (4) Unit Ministry Teams (UMTs)

in Taszar, Hungary, and two (2) forward deployed UMTs, one in Zagreb, Croatia, and one in Sarajevo, Bosnia; supervises two Army chaplain assistants, one Air Force Chapel Programmer, and two Hungarian interpreters; manages training, rosters, local and USAREUR reports, property, appropriated and nonappropriated funds; organizes multi-faceted religious retreats; coordinates with NSE staff, DOD [Department of Defense] personnel, and civilian contractors.[114]

Patterson further stated that the only times he felt in danger was when a vehicle in a convoy he was in had an accident and a large local mob came on the scene. A second time of potential danger was when his convoy was diverted at night by local construction into the town of Banja Luka, a college town that overflowed with drunken young people. In both cases, violence was averted.[115]

Throughout 1998, chaplains from the Special Forces continued to rotate in and out of Bosnia in support of their soldiers. Chaplain Hartranft, in Bosnia from December 1997 through April 1998, described his unique ministry to Special Forces soldiers and their families as follows:

The command sent me home about 4 weeks prior to the redeployment of the soldiers. I conducted three reunion/homecoming briefings; one day, one night, and one weekend. Then I deployed again into theater and conducted redeployment briefings with each Team in their houses. I was able not only to give them the reunion brief, but inform them of some of the issues their spouses were experiencing and the trouble spots the soldiers should be prepared to face. The then Inspector General, LTG Jordan, was informed of this initiative by the Fort Carson installation chaplain, Chaplain (COL) Herb Kitchens, and wrote commendations about it to the Army Chief of Staff.[116]

Special Forces Chaplain (CPT) Steven Mark Jones also spent time in Bosnia in 1998. Specifically for that year, Jones deployed to Bosnia in September and then in November and December for holiday chaplain coverage. He remarked:

I had a very positive relationship with other chaplains during my 1998 deployments to Bosnia. Chaplain (CPT) Eric Albertson was a RC priest assigned to Eagle Base, and he supported my soldiers when I was not there. I had no problems coordinating religious support, both for the

HQ personnel at Eagle Base and for my Special Forces soldiers scattered in remote areas. Our SF soldiers in the field were in Team houses, such as A-Team, B-Team, etc. The SF soldiers in forward areas only wanted SF chaplains to visit them, as they were very picky as to whom they would welcome.

To visit my SF soldiers in remote locations I had to travel in an armed small convoy. At the Team houses, I did a lot of one-on-one ministry, conducted redeployment family briefings, and performed church services. I carried with me a flexible collection of relationship building type literature, which I would pick and choose from as needed. At each Team house, I also distributed religious literature, like daily devotional reading materials. . . .

When I held a religious service at a Team house, about 60 to 70 percent of the soldiers would attend. One Team house I visited during the day had an attack that evening, as they received small arms fire and a brief mortar attack. None of my troops were injured but they were shaken up. This was the only time in Bosnia that my soldiers took direct enemy fire. I returned to spend the next day with them and it was a profitable time of ministry. . . .

Anything I needed in Bosnia I got. The commander and other chaplains were very supportive. No problem getting religious supply items. I was always able to get where I needed to go, but our ground transportation had to follow the applicable convoy and weapons guidelines.[117]

Administratively, successive rotations of US soldiers into Bosnia received the designation of SFOR, with a numerical designation showing the specific rotation of US troops. For example, SFOR-1 was followed by SFOR-2 and then SFOR-3. In the summer of 1998, the SFOR-4 rotation entered Bosnia. Some of the challenges facing UMTs in SFOR-4 were as follows:

The chaplains and assistants experienced a new paradigm for ministry during OJF (Operation JOINT FORGE). Normal unit integrity was replaced by the "base camp" model. The Unit Ministry Teams (UMTs) quickly adapted to this model as they were required to provide religious support to all soldiers in the base camp, not just soldiers within their unit. Religious support includes religious services, Bible Studies, special events, holiday observances, counseling, and visitation. The battalion chaplain's challenge to work the varied chains of command for units represented in their respective areas of operation as well as the rear detachment at times took considerable effort. . . . Poor road or flying conditions often hampered religious support to remote sites. . . .

The overall theme for the SFOR-4 mission was "Poke Holes in the Darkness." Whether the loneliness of deployment, the personal crisis' in soldier's lives, or the long, cold nights in Bosnia brought darkness into soldier's lives, the ministry teams were to take every chance to lift the spirits of our soldiers through caring, visiting, worshiping, and supporting.[118]

As 1998 ended, there were various reports of military activity in nearby Kosovo, south of Bosnia. Rumors of ethnic cleansing in Kosovo were common. Having failed to unite Bosnia-Herzegovina under his control, it appeared that Milosevic was now focusing his territorial ambitions against the Kosovar people. Meanwhile, Bosnia enjoyed a relative peace.

Chaplain Duties in Maintaining the Peace in Bosnia, 1999–2000

In Bosnia 1999 began on a somber note. While trying to arrest Dragon Gagovic, a former Bosnian Serb police chief in Foca accused of raping and torturing Muslim women, NATO troops fatally shot him. Hundreds of Yugoslavian civilians daily stood in line at Western embassies in Sarajevo in hopes of obtaining a visa to depart their war-torn homeland. As tensions in nearby Kosovo developed into armed NATO intervention, the NATO and American focus on Bosnia depreciated. The Bosnian people in 1999 faced three enormous hurdles in their recovery effort: the problem of thousands of displaced refugees, the economic and political chaos that resulted in the decline of Milosevic's power, and the uncertainty of long-term humanitarian assistance from European and other allies.[119] In July 1999 there were 75,000 known refugees in Bosnia. The ethnic diversity of these despairing refugees created tensions to the point that they had to create ethnically specific refugee centers throughout the land. The Bosnian economy as a whole was in shambles. Infrastructures were destroyed or damaged, homes were looted or ruined, families were separated, and NATO investigators discovered evidence of war crimes and mass grave sites throughout Bosnia.

Chaplain (CPT) Alva R. Bennett was in Bosnia from September 1998 through March 1999. Assigned to the 20th Engineer Battalion under the 1st Cavalry Division, Bennett was stationed at Eagle Base, Bosnia. In referring to the devastation on the civilian population of Bosnia, he commented, "We delivered some humanitarian aid and took toys to an orphanage. My Engineer unit did several building projects to include constructing a bridge." On the danger of traveling throughout Bosnia, Bennett stated, "We always traveled in two-vehicle armed convoys. In the spring of 1999, we had tension raised in Bosnia from the pending NATO air campaign in nearby Kosovo. When my tour was over in March 1999, our airplane was the last to leave Sarajevo before the bombings in Kosovo began."[120]

In the summer of 1999, US Secretary of the Army Louis Caldera visited Eagle Base and predicted the Bosnian mission could exceed 5 more years in duration. A few days later, Clinton and 40 other world leaders met in Sarajevo to pledge for economic and political reforms throughout the Balkans. By 27 August, officials at Eagle Base reported it would take 250 years to rid Bosnia of its millions of land mines. On a more positive note, the fall of 1999 initiative to allow Bosnians voluntarily to disarm was in progress with favorable results.

American and NATO soldiers stationed in Bosnia in 1999 experienced both a downsizing of force structure and facilities while the remaining physical structures on NATO bases were improving. For example, in February a 10,000-square foot main exchange opened at Eagle Base, providing many of the comforts of home for shoppers. A few weeks later, Camp Bedrock in Bosnia closed and troops were realigned or redeployed. By the end of the year, Camp Demi also closed, while Eagle Base continued to develop as a huge and reasonably comfortable facility with a brand new movie theater. Also in 1999, the new Army Chief of Chaplains, Major General (MG) Gaylord Gunhus, made his first of several trips to the Balkans.

In March 1999, Chaplain (CPT) Peter Strong and SPC Phillip Fortner departed the closing Camp Demi, Bosnia. Before departing Bosnia, Strong wrote an after action review (AAR) of his tour. Excerpts from the lessons learned portion of that AAR are:

> a. Purchase of religious materials for deployment. We were allotted $1,500 less than 2 weeks before the loading of the military vans. This could have been planned out much sooner. The amount of money was just right for the development of outstanding ministry programs.

> b. Communication with unit in Bosnia. This was

very helpful. We did not know all the questions to ask but were given good 'heads up' in many areas. It would have been great to go on a recon mission prior to deployment but this was not seen as a priority.

c. Battle Book. The more you think ahead, the better. Bring only what you need for this mission. Find out about the history of Bosnia, know the camps in your AOR [Area of Responsibility], know the differences in the religious groups in Bosnia (Catholic Croats, Orthodox Serbs, Bosnian Muslims). Rough out a 6-month CMRP [Command Master Religious Program]. Bring phone numbers for POCs [points of contact] in the rear. Keep files from the rear on MASCAL [mass casualties], critical event debriefings, memorial services, suicide awareness, stress management, etc.

d. Humanitarian Aid. This is a very important part of the mission at the base camps. It gradually grew in importance. It is very important to know the relationship between Civil Affairs and the chaplain in this area.

e. Wholesome Spiritual Activities. This was accomplished by such events as distributing clothing and toys at refugee centers, allowing troops to get outside the wire and meet the local people. We also did a work project at a monastery, giving the soldiers a break out of the routine so they could do something different and worthwhile.

f. Transfer of Authority. Seven to 10 days is more than enough. The present chaplain should bow out as quickly as possible and let the new chaplain take over. . . . Get the new chaplain trained up as quickly as possible and let him/her start their program.[121]

The AAR of the Task Force *Eagle* chaplain, dated 15 May 1999, is a detailed eight page summary of UMT activities throughout Bosnia. Chaplain (MAJ) Erik Erkkinen narrated the religious activities at Eagle Base, as well as from Camp Comanche, Camp Demi, Camp Bedrock, Camp Dobol, and Camp McGovern. This report is interesting in how it describes the ongoing mission in Bosnia with the new name of Operation JOINT FORGE and with the US presence remaining focused on peacekeeping and nation building. Excerpts from this AAR are as follows:

a. Peacekeeping. Battalion, Brigade, and Division level: As the base camps settled into routines, the peacekeeping mission allowed ample opportunity for the battalion, brigade, and division level ministry teams to participate. When possible, the UMT would participate in various operations. Some ministry teams frequently assisted with humanitarian aid missions. Others visited orphanages and schools or accompanied routine patrols. Still others provided support for grave-site exhumations.

b. Thanksgiving/Christmas/Hanukkah: The Red Cross and MWR [Morale, Welfare, and Recreation] also supported holiday operations by providing assorted Thanksgiving and Christmas decorations, Christmas trees, and arranging special holiday functions and activities. Holiday worship schedules were planned and published well ahead of the holidays. . . . The Division UMT also arranged . . . to construct a large Menorah for a Hanukkah candle lighting ceremony. This was very much appreciated by Chaplain (MAJ) Ben Romer, a Rabbi and sponsor of the Jewish worshiping community.

Ramadan—A small population of Muslims was present as part of SFOR-4. As needed, a worship facility was made available for Muslim soldiers. An announcement was made for sensitivity to Muslim needs during Ramadan.

Easter/Passover—Celebration of these holidays were planned by SFOR-4 and revised and executed by SFOR-5 since the dates coincided with redeployment. Chaplain Rabbi Romer and Chaplain (CPT) Peter Baktis (Eastern Orthodox priest) from Central Region (Germany) came to Eagle Base to celebrate the holy days.

c. Chaplain (MG) Donald Shea: The Army Chief of Chaplains made one visit with the Army Chief of Staff, General Reimer. The Division UMT coordinated with USAREUR to establish an itinerary for his visit in December. . . . The Chief desired to conduct several Roman Catholic masses and visit soldiers of Task Force *Eagle*. Chaplain Shea was briefed on ministry operations of TF *Eagle* and flown to several base camps to meet with UMTs and soldiers. Chaplain (LTC) Dwight Jennings, the 1st Cavalry Division Chaplain, escorted Chaplain Shea.

d. Administration: many administrative actions

were required of the Division Ministry Team on a daily basis. Tracking and managing information, receiving weekly reports, coordinating religious support, and other significant staff actions were duties shared by the task force chaplain, the operations chaplain, and the NCOIC. Sharing information was critical to the success of the staff. Though infrequent, some of the issues that arose were: missed link-ups, schedule changes, Reserve component issues, lack of coordination, communication equipment failures, and time/manpower constraints.

    e.   Summary: Overall, the ministry teams performed magnificently during SFOR-4's mission. Highlights included worship and holiday activities, visits by senior leadership of the Army and the Army Chaplaincy, visits and shows by popular entertainers, opportunities for humanitarian assistance, interaction with partner nations, and many other great ministry opportunities. The UMTs, without exception, believed that we made a difference. Morale of the ministry teams was kept high through intentional monitoring and scheduling of events that would build team cohesiveness and esprit. Though visitation to base camps was hindered by poor visibility and road conditions, the Division UMT was able to keep in close contact with all the base camps and ministry teams.[122]

Chaplain (CPT) Brad Baumann of the 1st Battalion 10th Aviation Regiment from Fort Drum, New York, was assigned to Comanche Base, Bosnia, from September 1999 through March 2000. Before deployment, Baumann stated, "Morale was very good and soldiers were excited about the opportunity to experience a real-world mission." He elaborated, "During the deployment I was the Aviation Battalion Chaplain and also served as the Gospel Service Senior pastor. . . . My relationships with my battalion and brigade commanders were excellent." Baumann performed or provided some type of religious activity 6 nights a week at Comanche Base, and stated, "The only time I felt even remotely in danger was during our Staff Ride to Srebrenica. The male population made obscene gestures and acted as if they were shooting us. Other than that time I felt no danger at all."[123]

Inevitably, chaplains might experience friction or tension with other chaplains. Baumann stated, "The only 'slight' problem I had was with my brigade chaplain who was a Catholic priest. I felt he was jealous of my relationship with the brigade commander. The commander was Protestant and looked heavily to me for feedback. This caused some tension." One way to alleviate friction between UMTs was to have them participate in benevolent-type projects to the local civilians. Baumann remarked, "The battalion sponsored a small school in Tuzla, Bosnia. I was the project officer. We raised the money from the States and rebuilt the school (new roof, desks, floor, wood stove, chalkboard, paint, and we completely cleaned and cleared out the building being used). We also distributed clothing to a local orphanage throughout the rotation." In reflecting back several years later on his experience in Bosnia in 1999–2000, Baumann recalled, "My UMT experience was almost exclusively in a chapel setting. . . . God blessed my time during the rotation. We experienced growth each month with all of the programs we ran through both the unit and the base camp services. . . . I had a wonderful experience during my deployment with the battalion, Gospel congregation, and the Bosnians."[124]

The year 2000 began with Chaplain (CPT) Terrance Kesling already assigned to Camp McGovern, Bosnia. As a member of the 2d Battalion, 87th Infantry Regiment under the 10th Mountain Division, Kesling was the only chaplain at Camp McGovern. Kesling worked directly for the commander at Camp McGovern and was under the supervision of the 10th Mountain Division chaplain. The isolation of Camp McGovern meant that Kesling had little contact with other chaplains outside of preplanned UMT meetings. He stated, "My focus was on a base camp ministry. I operated a garrison-type chapel program." In addition to preaching and counseling at Camp McGovern, Kesling was able through the robust help of volunteers to renovate their chapel with fresh paint, new furniture, and new flooring. Due to guidance from the division chaplain, he did not engage in any humanitarian projects with the Bosnians.[125]

Roman Catholic chaplains in the US Army are frequently asked to develop an itinerant ministry, conducting services in numerous locations. The Bosnia ministry of Catholic Chaplain Rajmund Kopec was no exception. Kopec was in Bosnia from March through September 2000. He stated:

> I went to Bosnia with a lot of questions. I'm now speaking from a very personal perspective, because we'd been in Bosnia for a little while, and there was the discussion, well, maybe Europeans should make more effort to take care of that. Why do we have to go, it's a peacekeeping operation, so on and so. But over all, very quickly in that rotation I came to an understanding of why we were there,

that our soldiers were doing great jobs, good positive things happening in Bosnia, but even if we don't make any difference, by being involved with local communities and so on, there's one very important difference we make, by the fact that we are up there, those people don't kill each other. We stopped them from killing, and that's what I tried to relate to our soldiers. Yes, you wake up and every day is the same . . . even if this whole thing doesn't make sense to them, they need to keep in mind that the fact that we are here, those people don't kill each other. And how did I learn that? That's where knowing languages comes handy, because in the meantime I learned, in Bosnia and Croatia they are similar languages, and being from Poland and having a last name which some people thought I was Bosnian, I had an opportunity to talk to local people on a different level, I prefer to think. Several of them would say to me, you are one of ours. . . .[126]

Chaplain Assistant Neal, assigned to HQ EUCOM, deployed to Bosnia for specific missions in October 1999 and November 2000. In Bosnia, she acted as the NCOIC for the joint command chaplain, assigned to train US chaplain assistants from various service components on providing religious support. In this capacity, Neal served as primary trainer to chaplain assistants, organized an international chaplain's conference, and helped to provide religious support to troops in war-torn Sarajevo. One of the highlights of her Bosnia experiences was in helping other nations develop a chaplain assistant NCO corps. Difficulties in her Bosnian tours were from "language barriers and the translation of all classroom instruction" as well as from traveling on the unsafe roads around Sarajevo, Bosnia.[127]

In 2000, the chaplain for the 4th Squadron of the 3d Armored Cavalry Regiment (ACR) from Fort Carson, Colorado, was Chaplain (CPT) Joseph Blay. Deployed to Comanche Base, Tuzla, Bosnia, from February through September 2000, Blay stated that his unit was well prepared for the deployment and Family Support Groups were active and involved. In Bosnia, Blay served as chaplain to his unit as well as chaplain of the Gospel Congregation at Comanche Base. He also served as a liaison between his battalion and the Civil Affairs soldiers related to religious issues and interaction with the local Orthodox Church. Blay remarked that he never felt unsafe in Bosnia, preaching to soldiers was his greatest joy, and working with multinational chaplains did not work well because of language barriers and denominational constraints. A memorable experience for Blay was his ministry with local refugees. He stated:

We had a great opportunity for ministry to our soldiers and to local Bosnian nationals at nearby refugee camps. This camp was two buildings in the Tuzla suburbs in the woods. The people planted crops and raised chickens by a river. All the refugees were Muslims but they were secular. The soldiers adopted this refugee camp and distributed donated goods from US school children to these very needy people of all ages.[128]

Chaplain (MAJ) David Crary commented, "My deployment to Bosnia was one of the highlights of my military career." Crary was assigned to the 2d Brigade of the 3d Infantry Division, stationed at Eagle Base, Bosnia, from September 2000 through April 2001. He remarked, "My relationship with the commander was good. He was a strong supporter of chapel activities and attended chapel regularly." Crary continued, "One of the many positive experiences while in Bosnia was my relationship with two Air Force chaplains, both of whom were assigned to Eagle Base for 90 days consecutively. There was a great spirit of cooperation with never a hint of competition or rivalry."[129]

Crary spoke of his working relationship with Chaplain Assistant Veronica Todd:

During one visit to a predominantly Croat city we were briefed to be on guard because they were not particularly friendly to American forces. It was the first time I saw the chaplain assistant in action, as a bodyguard. I was impressed with their training and professionalism. . . . SSG Veronica Todd, now retired, was my chaplain assistant. She did a wonderful job of managing the chapel, supervising several junior chaplain assistants, and taking care of any and all that ventured through the chapel. The chapel was a real hub of the community, remaining open 24 hours a day. She was as much a mother to young soldiers as an NCO.[130]

As the year 2000 ended, the Pentagon announced a major shift in policy toward Bosnia. In a news headline stating "Army Will Give National Guard the Entire U.S. Role in Bosnia," the Pentagon announced the following:

WASHINGTON, Dec 4—The Army announced today that it would effectively turn over its mission in Bosnia to part-time National Guard soldiers, including troops from Kansas, Minnesota, Indiana, and New York, over the next two years.

The Army, like the other armed services, is increasingly relying on the Guard to supplement active-duty soldiers in military operations like the one in Bosnia. But the announcement today significantly expands the reliance upon the citizen soldiers.

Beginning this year, the Army has rotated command of the Bosnian mission between Active and Guard units, including the 49th Armor Division of the Texas National Guard. That unit oversaw the American sector in Bosnia for seven months, until the 3d Infantry Division, an Active Duty unit from Fort Stewart, Georgia, took over in October.

By late 2002, the peacekeeping mission is to be commanded exclusively in six-month rotations by troops from eight National Guard divisions. They include the 28th Infantry from Pennsylvania, the 35th from Kansas, the 34th from Minnesota, the 38th from Indiana, and the 42d from New York.[131]

Meanwhile, Active Duty Army UMTs in 2001 continued missions in Bosnia. Chaplain (CPT) Ronald Cooper of the 64th Armor Battalion, 3d Infantry Division, departed Bosnia in April 2001. Stationed at Camp Dobol, Cooper remarked, "I was a battalion chaplain with a base camp ministry for a community consisting of a BN TF [Battalion Task Force] plus contractors. The ministry was a base camp ministry. I oversaw the Gospel Congregation as well as leading the General Protestant service." Although "Bible Studies were a challenge due to patrols going out at various times of the day and night," Cooper had a unique and successful ministry to senior leaders at Camp Dobol. He explained: "We developed a 'Top Gun Leaders' ministry to commanders and staff officers. We studied together a leadership book each month. Then we met for dinner and discussed the book. Then I would teach a 1-hour class on leadership. We did this for the 6 months we were in Bosnia." Cooper stated he frequently did not feel safe when he was in downtown areas, and that his briefings on local Islam were well received and distributed via training throughout the task force. In speaking of his 2001 ministry at Camp Dobol in Bosnia, Cooper summarized, "Base camp ministry is an excellent way to know soldiers and do great ministry."[132]

Various US chaplains brought to Bosnia diverse talents and abilities. For Lutheran Chaplain (MAJ) Michael Lembke of the 3d Infantry Division, his talents appeared in his ability to bring together chaplains from various Balkan groups for communication and bridge building. Lembke met regularly with civilian clergy from Croatian, Serbian, and Bosnian Muslim communities. These local clergy were amazed that American military chaplains share chapels that serve all religions. While Lembke performed his routine 0815 Sunday Lutheran service and participated in scheduled bomb threat drills by entering bunkers, he was also able to meet regularly with fellow NATO chaplains from Denmark, Turkey, and the Netherlands. Lembke thrived on building relationships with clergy, whether Jewish, Eastern Orthodox, Muslim, or Roman Catholic. For example, Lembke's visits to nearby Orthodox monasteries allowed him to network with Orthodox priests and learn the Serbian version of the history of tensions in Bosnia. Local civilian clergy from various faith traditions in Bosnia applauded the role of the United States and NATO in attempting to bring peace to their war-torn land. Clearly one of the highlights of Lembke's tour in Bosnia was the large clergy conference he was able to help coordinate. As Lembke explained:

> 24 March 2001—We conducted the first ever Armed Forces in Bosnia-Herzegovina Religious Support Conference. This conference brought together 40 participants from the Bosnian military, civilian clergy to include two bishops (one Orthodox and one Roman Catholic), 4 multinational chaplains (Polish, Danish, Dutch, and Turkish), and 12 American Forces chaplains. It was a great day and capitalized on the desire of the Bosnians to learn more about military chaplaincies. The spirit was positive and the mood upbeat. All present committed to meet again. . . . It was a great day and a wonderful culminating experience.[133]

Army Chaplain Ministries in Bosnia, 2001–2002

By 2001, it became apparent to many observers that the Dayton Peace Accords for Bosnia were not working—at least the agreement was not working very well. Six years had elapsed on a mission that was initially to last only a year; yet at the 6-year mark, Bosnia was completely dependent on outside assistance for its tenuous survival. Ethnic clashes still occurred on a small local scale, and many thought the moment the United States and NATO leave, the killing and ethnic cleansing would resume. Bosnia was slow to rebuild, with the marks of military devastation, namely buildings ridden with bullet holes, bombed out structures, and mass grave sites still noticeable. Factories and ammunition sites bombed by NATO several years earlier still lay in ruins. Unemployment was a plague on the people.

Hopelessness abounded in the lives of the younger generation, many of whom were raised partially in orphanages, their parents the victims of ethnic cleansing and hatred. Crime abounded, prostitution was prevalent, alcohol abuse was rampant, and only a total dependence on outside humanitarian aid and NATO peacekeepers prevented the region from descending into total chaos.

American military leaders in 2001 began to question openly the wisdom of the current policy in Bosnia. US Army Reserve Colonel Alexander A.C. Gerry, fluent in the Serbo-Croatian language, worked in the former Yugoslavia. After touring Bosnia, he made an extensive report to the Reserve Officer's Association. Excerpts from Gerry's report follow:

> Almost 6 years after the beginning of the Dayton Agreement, the Federation of Bosnia and Herzegovina is still on life support, wholly dependent on the international community and foreign aid. . . .

> The country now has two parts, the Muslim-Croat Federation and the Republika Srpska under the administration of the Stabilization Force (SFOR) based on the Dayton Accords. The integration of predominately Croat Bosnia and Muslim Herzegovina with the Serb Republic has proven a massively difficult task that will require an outside military presence for an extended period. . . .

> In the Federation of Bosnia and Herzegovina, nominally multiethnic institutions are in fact split into separate Bosniac (Muslim) and Croat (Roman Catholic) components with little interaction between the two. At the state level, elected officials often work to keep the state from effective political action.

> As long as the basic administrative structures remain weak, elections can do little to foster responsible government. In Serb and Croat dominated areas, the electorate continues to return wartime nationalistic parties to power. For Bosnians, the electoral base is mainly at the municipal and canton level and dependent upon an extremely weak and fractured administrative apparatus.

> The failure of national institutions has forced the international mission, out of necessity, to assume a direct role in the affairs of the Federation of Bosnia. . . . Clearly, this is not a role envisaged in the Dayton Accords nor one

that the international mission ever wanted to play. Bosnia and Herzegovina is not a self-sustaining structure and the consequences of a premature withdrawal could be catastrophic not just for Bosnia but for the entire region.[134]

Army chaplains and chaplain assistants in 2001 continued their diverse ministries in and around Bosnia. Army Reserve Chaplain (LTC) Vernon Chandler and Chaplain Assistant SSG Lucinda Flowers were in Taszar, Hungary, for about 6 months, in direct support of missions in Bosnia. Chandler explained his job: "I was the USASET (US Army Support Element Taszar) chaplain. I supervised the Camp Butmir, Bosnia, BSB [Base Support Battalion] chaplain; I coordinated chaplain support for soldiers at small remote locations in Croatia; I counseled soldiers on 6-month deployments; I conducted reunion briefings and suicide prevention classes; I performed Sunday church services at Taszar; and I coordinated 4-day spiritual retreats in Taszar or Budapest for soldiers coming from Bosnia." In speaking of times he felt in danger, Chandler stated, "One time a vehicle we were in convoy with got in an accident. This was on one of my chaplain visits to Camp Butmir. The area around us had landmines so we had to be very careful where we stood. There were no signs of war that I saw in Hungary or Croatia, but in Bosnia, the ravages of war were quite visible. When we traveled through the Serbian area of Bosnia it was tense, as the harsh stares from the people reminded us that the Christian Orthodox Serbians thought the United States was siding too heavily with the Bosnian Muslims."[135]

Working with Chandler in Hungary was Flowers. As an Active Duty chaplain assistant, Flowers was assigned to the 20th Area Support Group. Located at Taszar from April through October 2001, Flowers stated that she enjoyed setting up the worship services on Sundays, found the Bible Studies and retreats helpful, and ran the daily functions of the chapel. She concluded, "My tour was all in all a great learning experience."[136] Chandler explained the Army mission at Taszar as follows:

> While I was there the base was downsizing. It was still a busy place but not like it had been a few years prior. This was a transition base for the loading and unloading of supplies for other locations in the Balkans. People were always coming or going through our base. C-130 airplanes regularly landed moving troops and equipment in and out of the Balkans. The soldiers who were permanently assigned to Taszar while I was there were mostly from MP units. They did a lot of convoy security missions

as supplies went in and out of our base. They also did our security missions. When I did my chaplain visits, an armed MP would come with us. These soldiers were a mix of AD/RC soldiers and they blended well.[137]

Chandler and Flowers in Taszar had diverse ministry experiences with soldiers coming and going from their location, either going into Bosnia for a tour, departing Bosnia at the end of their tour, or having a time of military leave in the midst of their tour. Some examples of ministry provided to these transient soldiers by Chandler and Flowers are as follows:

a.   Soldiers who got a 4-day pass out of Bosnia would come to our area and either explore the city of Taszar or be bused to Budapest for a religious and cultural tour of that historic city. As the troops came in to Taszar I met them as a chaplain and briefed them and provided chaplain support as needed. In two cases, I had to deliver Red Cross messages of severe problems at home to soldiers that were in my area.

b.   Counseling issues related to the expected marriage and family issues. The longer we were into the 6-month deployment, the more numerous the counseling opportunities. Marriages were strained, and soldiers were disturbed about things changing at home while they were away.

c.   At first, we conducted two Sunday morning services at Camp Butmir, one traditional Protestant service and one more contemporary gospel service. Once a month an Army chaplain Roman Catholic priest would rotate through the camp and conduct a Mass. We adjusted the two Sunday morning worship services into one combined Sunday evening service. This was a good move and attendance increased. We made this adjustment to accommodate the religious and cultural tours that were offered on weekends. Soldiers had to choose between going on a Saturday–Sunday local tour or coming to Sunday morning church. By moving the church services to one combined Sunday evening meeting all were able to attend, since the tours were completed by that time.[138]

The 11 September 2001 terrorist attacks on the United States by Muslim extremists in the al-Qaeda network killed thousands in New York City and hundreds more at the Pentagon and in Pennsylvania. Using hijacked airplanes filled with innocent civilians, these terrorists slammed two airplanes into New York City and one airplane into the Pentagon. A fourth airplane, having failed to reach its intended target, crashed into a field in Pennsylvania, killing all on board. Special Forces soldiers continued their covert operations in Bosnia with renewed intensity, searching for any link between Bosnian Muslims and the al-Qaeda terrorist network. One article stated:

> It was a few hours before dawn when four rented SUVs [suburban utility vehicles] came to a halt outside the three-story gray stucco building in a leafy Sarajevo suburb. Six Green Berets in full battle-rattle jumped from the SUVs and rushed the front door of the Hotel Hollywood, M4s [small rifles] and shotguns at the ready.
>
> They raced up the stairs to the second floor, where they splintered two hotel room doors with sledge hammers. In the rooms, they found their quarry—two Middle Eastern men, bleary eyed but very much aware they were in big trouble.
>
> As some of the Special Forces troops hustled out of the hotel and into their idling vehicles, others swept the rooms scooping up documents.
>
> It was 3:30 am and the counterterrorism campaign in Bosnia had just begun.
>
> Nine hours later, the same 10th Special Forces Group soldiers repeated the operation, this time at the nondescript building that houses a Saudi Arabian relief agency. On this occasion they were joined by a handful of Italian *Carabinieri* from an elite military task force. This raid yielded two more suspects—who were later released—and another gold mine of intelligence.
>
> The raids were the first blows of a counterterrorism campaign in Bosnia that US and NATO officers say has netted more than a dozen Arab terrorist suspects, most with links to Osama bin Laden's al-Qaeda organization. The US government blames al-Qaeda for the September 11th attacks that killed thousands in the United States.[139]

Chaplain (CPT) Sean Wead arrived in Bosnia on 11 September 2001. While he stated, "I participated in combat Operation MARNE DRAGNET against suspected al-Qaeda targets," his primary ministry was to the people stationed at Camp McGovern, Bosnia. Wead was assigned to the 2d

Battalion, 22d Infantry Regiment, a regular Army unit associated with the 10th Mountain Division of Fort Drum, New York. His unit in Bosnia was attached to the 29th Infantry Division, a Texas Army National Guard unit. With responsibilities at Camp McGovern and a few other nearby locations, Wead stated, "I really liked the Army National Guard chaplains of the 29th Infantry Division. They were great chaplains, but a little weak on the Army expectations for procedure. They were easier to work for than many regular Army chaplains."[140] Wead was able to counsel and advise his commander through the unit's reluctance to be subservient to a National Guard unit. Wead described his ministry in Bosnia as follows:

> At night I visited my troops on perimeter guard at Camp McGovern, Eagle Base, and FOB Morgan. I made weekly trips and trained with each company. I did regular services and Bible Studies at Camp McGovern and FOB Morgan. . . . Being present and available worked well. Our UMT road-marched once a month with our soldiers. We made our rounds to the guards during the day and night operations. We were always with soldiers, which paid great dividends.

> Services were attended by only a fraction of the soldiers, only about 30 on a Sunday (there were 500 stationed at McGovern). What really worked were one-on-one visits I made. My ministry was personal and seemed to reach more through the week than corporate Sunday worship.

> I got to design the chapel at Camp McGovern from 'the shoebox' [a small metal container with no windows] into the nice chapel that now exists. Chaplain (COL) Habereck from USAREUR made the discretionary funds available. The chapel was transformed in 2 weeks.[141]

Chaplain Kopec provides a good summary of chaplain activities and life in general in Bosnia at the end of 2001 and the beginning of 2002. In speaking of the improvement of facilities and the decrease in ethnic tensions, Kopec remarked:

> At SFOR-7 [2000] the way our base camps were set out was pretty much close to a separation zone, because Bosnia is divided into Bosnia and Serbia. Basically, when we got into Bosnia we as Americans did not go into Serbia because that's where there was a disagreement. So our base camps were built by the zones that separated Bosnia from Serbia, and our job was to make sure that the zones

are clear and there is no killing going on and nothing nasty going on. Eighteen months later [2002] I go back to Bosnia and we already moved within the territory of Serbia, a couple of forward observation bases were built, FOB Conner and FOB Morgan, which were inside Serbia. The purpose of that was to protect resettlements. Bosnians who decided they wanted to go back to their homes, they got money. I guess the international community was supporting them, pretty much they were going back to where they originally came from, which was within Serbia, rebuilding their houses. And our soldiers were in those areas to protect them from any hostilities from Serbs. So just the simple fact that we moved our bases within the territory of Serbia was a huge improvement.[142]

Throughout 2002 chaplain ministries in Bosnia became predictable and routine. While life in a hostile fire zone was no vacation, the UMTs in Bosnia in 2002 were essentially pastors to congregations confined within the parameters of various base camps. Hazards could be anticipated when chaplains traveled from one base camp to another, but essentially Bosnia in 2002 was in a tenuous peace. Chaplain (MAJ) Al Shrum deployed to Bosnia with the 25th Infantry Division in March 2002. Assigned as the task force chaplain operating out of Eagle Base, Shrum stated that he was "the SFOR-11 chaplain responsible for religious support for the task force and supervision of six chaplains and seven chaplain assistants," and that he "coordinated religious support for the multinational task force and provided direct religious support to the task force staff." In this leadership position, Shrum recalled, "With the five chaplains from the 25th Infantry Division, my relationship was ideal: professional, respectful, supportive, personal, and responsive. However, with the one Indiana Army National Guard chaplain under my supervision, my relationship could not have been any more unprofessional and insubordinate. . . . The Indiana National Guard UMTs were 'lone rangers.'"[143]

Army chaplain ministries in Bosnia in 2002 were fully developed and appreciated. Chaplain Shrum stated, "Worship services went well. Movie nights at the chapel (religious-based movies) were a big hit. Religious retreats to Budapest and Medjugorje went well."[144] Chaplain Assistant David Lee of the 25th Infantry Division was in Bosnia from April through September 2002, assigned primarily to travel and work with Roman Catholic Chaplain Kopec. David Lee remarked, "Chaplain Kopec and I traveled to many locations. We were off base 4 days a week. We had an outstanding working relationship."[145] Working with Shrum and David Lee was Chaplain

(CPT) William Wehlage, also with the 25th Infantry Division. Wehlage was the Plans and Operations Chaplain that coordinated, planned, and helped execute numerous chaplain missions. He recalled, "Trips to Medjugorje were great. We had several prayer breakfasts. We visited an orphanage and distributed humanitarian goods, a great time." As far as being in personal danger, Wehlage said, "No—I was out of the wire several times, and nothing was troubling. Some of the local drivers were reckless. Our division averaged one traffic accident per day while we were deployed." In summary, Wehlage reflected, "I had wonderful and lasting relationships with all chaplains. All chaplains got along extremely well."[146]

Lawson of the 7th Army Reserve Command in Germany, made a 5-day trip to mentor and instruct Reserve component chaplains in Bosnia in May 2002. Brief excerpts from his journal follow:

> Day One (8 May 2002)—Flew on an Air Force C-130 from Ramstein to Tuzla. Met by my host Chaplain (COL) Matthew Horne. Got acclimated to Camp Eagle. More trees and developed than I guessed. . . . A large, active camp. Land mine signs are at the tree lines. . . . Everyone except the chaplains carry weapons at all times.

> Day Two (9 May 2002)—Began mentoring chaplains on Reserve/Active Duty chaplain integration of forces. I handed out lots of religious literature. . . . Sleeping and bathing arrangements humble. Constant traffic from armed vehicles returning from patrols. A tense cease-fire currently exists. Stayed within the fence today.

> Day Three (10 May 2002)—Traveled with Chaplain Horne, a Bosnian translator, and a bodyguard to Camp Connor, then Camp Butmir, Sarajevo. Driving took much of the day. Scenes of warfare, destruction, and evil are in stark contrast to the natural beauty of this war-ravaged country. Bullet holes cover thousands of buildings. Hundreds of homes still stand in ruins. So few men of middle age exist, as many fled or were killed in the genocide a few years ago. Chaplain Horne and I stood at Srebrenica, the killing fields where thousands of Muslim civilians were murdered and buried in shallow graves. . . . The translator said that as soon as the US and NATO leave the killings will again begin. Brought supplies to an orphanage. Too many orphans in this violent place. More religious literature distributed, to both US and allied troops.

Figure 8. CH (MAJ) Al Shrum presides at a memorial service for a soldier who died in Bosnia from a heart attack while exercising.

<u>Day Four</u> (11 May 2002)—More interviews and mentoring with chaplains on Reserve/Active Duty UMT integration of forces issues. A lot of religious literature passed out today. I had a detailed conversation with a French soldier who had many questions about what is true religion. . . . This afternoon we spent at an orphanage in Sarajevo. A nearby gunshot from a suspected sniper had us soldiers looking for cover, while the children ignored the sound. They have all seen so much death and guns that a sniper gunshot did not even make them blink. . . . Sarajevo was a beautiful city now in ruins. Large abandoned skyscrapers stand full of holes from artillery shells, standing like skeletons. Bullet ridden buildings all around. The consequences of human sin are readily apparent. I did not feel safe in Sarajevo but the Lord protected me.

<u>Day Five</u> (12 May 2002)—Slept well. Drove with Chaplain Horne, a bodyguard, and a translator from Sarajevo to Tuzla. Total destruction and despair all along this 2-hour route. Did more Reserve/Active Duty chaplain mentoring on integration of forces. . . . There are too many orphans in Bosnia. It is an unnatural feeling to see so many orphans, their parents dead. A lot of religious pamphlets and tracts

handed out today. . . . Uneventful flight on an Air Force
C-130 from Tuzla to Ramstein AFB, Germany.[147]

While Army UMTs in Bosnia experienced minimal danger in 2002, the region as a whole remained unsafe. An August 2002 civilian travel advisory warned visitors to Bosnia of attacks against returning refugees, unexploded mine-clearing operations, random mob violence, and the occasional closing of the US Embassy in Sarajevo for brief periods.[148] Frequently traveling as an itinerant UMT throughout Bosnia at this time was Kopec and David Lee. Kopec stated, "I was the only Roman Catholic priest and that meant that I had one big parish throughout Bosnia. I had five or six base camps to go to so I was on the road pretty much all week long." Kopec described a typical ministry experience as follows:

> My Sunday would begin on Friday, because I didn't have my own unit, I just served purely as the division Catholic priest. During SFOR-7, I had my squadron and I was a Catholic priest. But during SFOR-11, my Sunday would start on Friday. I would drive with my assistant and another soldier, or a translator, and drive to FOB Morgan, do the Catholic Mass up there for the soldiers, one of the infantry companies in that base camp, then drive to Camp McGovern, I would do an evening Mass and stay over-night, and I would have another Mass on Saturday at noon. Right after that I would leave and go back to Camp Eagle, and have Mass on Sunday at 1030, and then at 1900. On Monday, I would convoy with Chaplain [Anthony] Flores and his assistant, to FOB Conner, and spend the whole day with the soldiers there, just doing counseling and hang-ing around. In the evening, I would do Catholic Mass and he would do Protestant service and then convoy back on the same day to Camp Eagle. Then, Tuesday would be a quiet day, and on Wednesday, again with Chaplain Flores, we would fly by helicopter or convoy to Hill 1326. And the difference was that the ride by helicopter was about 7 or 8 minutes to fly, but convoy was almost 2 hours. So, obviously we always tried to take the helicopter, and the reason is that it was high in the mountains and the roads were treacherous and very slow movement.[149]

Throughout 2002, doubts still lingered about the validity of US troops still in Bosnia. As one author stated, "The Balkans no longer constitute a primary foreign policy challenge. . . . The region itself is in a period of difficult, painful transition, and stands the chance of rapidly succumbing to transnational criminal influences and becoming a 'black hole' of terrorism . . . international corruption, black-market activities, and illegal arms shipments threaten the stability of the region."[150] No reasonable assessment could call for a full withdrawal of international aid and military forces in 2002. The issue for Americans was whether the United States should be involved in an ongoing European squabble. While Horne supervised UMT issues at Eagle Base in Bosnia, and as Chaplain (CPT) Brian Van Dyke completed a 45-day summer tour as chaplain in Taszar, Hungary, the US military continued a huge drawdown of troops in Bosnia.

Chaplain Activities During Military Downsizing in Bosnia, 2003–2005

By 2003 the role of the US military in Bosnia was only a fraction of what it was in 1995–96. This was the case for two main reasons. First, the Balkans as a whole had stabilized: humanitarian missions were being conducted uninterrupted; European nations were aggressively involved in nation building in the Balkans; economic conditions slowly began to improve; and resettlement of refugees was proceeding though not without minor local incidents. The second reason the United States was deemphasizing missions in the Balkans was due to the Global War on Terrorism. This global war resulted from the terrorist attacks on 11 September 2001, after which large numbers of US forces were deployed first to Afghanistan and later to Iraq. While world media attention was riveted on the Middle East, the American military presence in the Balkans became almost an afterthought.

Soldiers sent to Bosnia in 2002–2003 remained focused on humanitarian, peacekeeping, and nation-building missions. Soldiers stated they were surprised that their peacekeeping duties were much calmer than expected, yet they expressed concern that a premature American departure could wreak havoc in the Balkans. The US troop strength in Bosnia originally peaked at 20,000, but by the start of 2003 the total number was around 1,700. As Colonel Mark Milley of the 25th Infantry Division stated, "That's a 10-fold decrease in 6 years, and that speaks for itself. We don't need this overwhelming power anymore." American troops now patrolled among local civilians, something avoided years earlier. US soldiers also stopped wearing their flack vests and Kevlar helmets in public, showing a more relaxed appearance to locals. Hostilities had decreased to the point where US troops were going door-to-door to ask locals to hand over their weapons and were successful in doing so.[151]

Chaplain (LTC) F. Douglas Hudson arrived at Eagle Base, Bosnia, on 2 November 2002, to serve as the Area Support Group (ASG) chaplain. Hudson stated:

> As the ASG chaplain, I was responsible for the base operation needs of the task force UMTs, as well as supervision of the BSB chaplain in Sarajevo, and the ASTs [Area Support Teams] at Taszar and Camp McGovern. I have about $80,000 worth of equipment disbursed throughout the SFOR area for which I am responsible. In addition to what is on hand, if the Task Force UMT has legitimate needs, it is my responsibility to secure those needs. . . . One of the highlights of my rotation has been working with the USAREUR Chaplain's Office to establish a solid library, both Christian books and videos, for the Peacekeeper Chapel located on Eagle Base in Bosnia.[152]

Serving in Bosnia at the same time as Hudson was Chaplain (CPT) Matthew Huisjen. Both Hudson and Huisjen were assigned to the 7th ARCOM in Germany, but were mobilized and deployed to Bosnia as individual soldiers. Huisjen was stationed at NATO HQ in Sarajevo from 1 December 2002 through 1 June 2003. As the BSB chaplain in Sarajevo having additional ministerial duties at Camp Butmir, Huisjen stated, "The two Sunday morning services grew. A new Tuesday evening Bible Study also grew to almost 20 as well, which I co-led with an Air Force chaplain who has become a dear friend. I was thankful to enjoy playing the guitar and singing as this proved to be a valuable asset. I had numerous opportunities to talk through the gospel with people."[153] Huisjen was able to perform a lot of formal and informal marriage counseling. He remarked:

> My personal experience here in Sarajevo has been much richer than I expected. I was confident there would be lots of opportunities for ministry, but I didn't expect the personal growth I've been able to enjoy. I typically strive to help others realize that life is all about relationships— first, our relationship to God through Christ; second, our relationships with those we are closest to; and third, our interaction with the rest of humanity. . . . Personally, I am more thankful for my faith, for my wife, for my friends, for my country, etc., than I have been in a long time. . . .

As I interact more and more with men who've come to discuss struggles in their marriages, I'm reminded again how critical relationships are. At the root of all problems in human relationships is a problem in our relationship with God. As recently as yesterday, I again witnessed the transformation that takes place in a person's heart and marriage as they commit to following God's blueprint for this central area in our lives. It is truly a long, long road to complete healing, but I love the privilege of presenting God's hope to those in pain. I am so thankful to know this hope myself and to model it as a Christian chaplain. [154]

The only Army chaplain or chaplain assistant to write a full-length book on experiences in the Balkans was Chaplain (COL) Ronald Cobb. Serving as the senior chaplain in Bosnia in 2003 allowed Cobb to develop many interesting relationships with both Balkan clergy and NATO chaplains. Assigned to the 35th Infantry Division, Army National Guard, Cobb stated that when he arrived in Bosnia he found the ugly results of religious persecution of the Bosnian Islamic faith, the Croatian Roman Catholic faith, and the Serbian Orthodox faith. Cobb desired to serve US soldiers first, but also to serve the people of Bosnia through interacting with indigenous clergy and humanitarian projects.[155]

The year 2003 was a time of gruesome discoveries of mass grave sites in Bosnia. In the early and mid-1990s, mostly Serbian Orthodox soldiers imposed a genocide-type operation on Muslims. Cobb witnessed the discovery of hidden execution sites and mass graves and made the following comments related to the Potocari Cemetery:

The stench of death will never leave my mind when I think of all the mass graves whose bodies made up this large cemetery. Individual graves scattered throughout the Srebrenica, Bratunac, and Zvornik hills will never all be found. . . . Pictures of hundreds of bodies in the unrefrigerated morgue in Sarajevo waiting to be identified are permanently etched in my soul. I think of the many thousands of friends, children, spouses, parents, and grandparents waiting for someone who will never come home.[156]

Although Bosnia in 2003 was peaceful, the US military still considered the region a hostile fire zone. As with any deployment, soldiers away from loved ones will experience various crises and be in need of chaplain support. Adding to these normal stressors was the discovery of mass graves, creating a gloomy atmosphere for all. Throughout 2003, Cobb spoke about these stressors, taught classes to remedy the situation, and began developing plans for reunion and reintegration of soldiers to families at the end of the deployment. As Cobb said,

> The bottom line for me in Bosnia was focusing on the welfare of every single United States soldier for religious support, emotional support, counseling support, family support, and morale support. In Bosnia I saw significant soldier struggles and problems. There were depression and stress in the lives particularly of those soldiers doing heavy, dangerous tasks. . . . You can imagine the wide variety and many different mental and behavioral areas that young adults, within the confines of concertina wire, in a military cantonment area, can get into which could potentially harm themselves, other soldiers, and the general morale of the entire command.[157]

The focus of chaplains in Bosnia was always religious support. Hudson spoke of his spring 2003 ministry in Bosnia as "providing worship services at a number of locations in Bosnia and Hungary to include Taszar, Hungary, Eagle Base near Tuzla, and FOB Connor." Hudson elaborated, "I was thrust into a more prophetic ministry at Eagle Base and FOB Connor when several task force chaplains were taken ill and had to be returned to the States. . . . With their departure I became the pastor for the General Protestant service at both Eagle Base and FOB Connor." Reciting some of the religious support activities Hudson performed, he remarked, "I also conducted a Wednesday night Bible Study at Eagle Base and a Tuesday night Bible Study at FOB Connor. In addition I have held a weekly Tuesday lunchtime Bible Study at Eagle Base for the ASG and ASG-wide prayer breakfasts."[158]

Benevolent-type humanitarian missions were normal expectations of chaplains in Bosnia. Huisjen at Camp Butmir near Sarajevo said he only occasionally did such missions, while Hudson remarked, "Our ASG adopted several refugee camps nearby. We collected and distributed articles that the people needed. We collected supplies for two schools . . . and some recreational supplies for the students. . . . We have also been involved with two orphanages."[159]

Cobb participated in a memorial service for a US soldier who was killed in Bosnia in a traffic accident. In seeking to avoid a reckless speeding driver on a slick road, SPC Blake C. Kelly was killed and four others were slightly injured. Chaplain (CPT) Douglas Ball was the unit chaplain and quickly responded to the accident scene with medics and others. Kelly was a Roman Catholic lay Eucharistic minister and actively supported the chapel programs. Memorial services were held at Eagle Base and Camp McGovern, with a tearful Cobb stating that "nothing could fill the gap in the hearts of his friends and fellow soldiers from Nebraska."[160]

Figure 9. CH (LTC) F. Douglas Hudson and CA SFC Margarita Brunke at the Grab Potok Refugee Camp, Bosnia.

7th ARCOM Public Affairs Office

In early 2003, the ASG chaplain in Bosnia, Hudson, summarized much of his ministry activities as being available to soldiers in an informal basis, being visible, available, and approachable. This meant he could develop helpful conversations in any number of situations, including before and after patrols. Hudson stated, "Since I spend quite a bit of time traveling around, primarily by NTV [nontactical vehicle], but occasionally by Blackhawk helicopter, I also saw these times as opportunities to bring the presence of Christ to bear in these situations." Hudson was able to develop friendships with his translators and was happy to state that many soldiers who came to him for counseling did improve their situations.[161]

Cobb had an especially favorable experience in Bosnia. The chaplains that worked with him were the recipients of his praise. For example, he spoke of the Gospel Service Chaplain (MAJ) James Messer as an inspiring chaplain; he considered the Protestant service conducted by Ball as outstanding; he appreciated the Latter Day Saint (LDS) (Mormon) lay leader, MAJ Lee Lacy, and supported the LDS activities; and he was especially thankful for his deputy command chaplain, LTC Donald Davidson. In reflecting back on working with these chaplains, it was not surprising for Cobb to state that he was blessed to know these chaplains and to serve with them far away from home. As far as Jewish services, Cobb stated:

> Jewish religious support and worship was led twice on Eagle Base by Chaplain (COL) Ken Leinwand from the USAREUR. First Ken had a delightful Passover Seder Service where he explained in detail how the songs and events of that service were focused on Jewish children so that they would be more emotionally connected to their heritage. Later he returned for a luncheon with Jewish soldiers where his message was how Jews had been refugees for centuries in the context that SFOR-13 soldiers could understand because they were working in a land with many displaced persons.[162]

In 2004, United States involvement in Bosnia continued to downsize. FOBs were closed, task forces were minimized, bases were closed, and troops from all NATO countries were reduced. By late September 2004, there were 1,500 US troops in Bosnia, Croatia, and Hungary, a mere pittance of prior troop strength.[163] The numbers of US troops in Bosnia continued to plummet, and by October 2005, there were only 250 US troops in Bosnia with two chaplains.[164] The UMTs in Bosnia in 2004 and into 2005 were Chaplain (LTC) William Stang, Chaplain (LTC) Eric Ebb, and chaplain assistants SFC James Lee and SSG Jason Brown. All were with the Army National Guard.

Stang, a Roman Catholic chaplain, arrived at Eagle Base, Tuzla, on 15 March 2004 and served there until March 2005. Stang was present when the final SFOR mission was completed. Chaplain strength during 2004–2005 was drastically cut in sequence to the rapidly declining numbers of soldiers stationed in Bosnia. As Stang stated, "I was blessed with a commander and staff that understood the need for religious support to soldiers. The commander's emphasis removed many roadblocks. The commander also regularly attended religious services and promoted chaplain participation at all levels." Ebb served as the deputy to Stang, creating a relationship that worked. Stang remarked, "My deputy chaplain [Ebb] did a fine job. He was put into his job 1 week before deployment. Besides being a very competent minister, he worked hard to learn his job, catch up on training, and respond to the tasks the command assigned. I appreciated his willingness to be part of a team, because that was the only way we could cover all of the tasks with just two chaplains."[165]

Stang and Ebb were responsible for chaplain activities related to the closing of many chapels throughout SFOR and creating the job description for what replaced the SFOR missions, namely the new ENDURING MISSION chaplain position. Stang and Ebb were essentially responsible for working themselves out of their jobs, to facilitate a smooth transition as many US chaplain activities were passed to NATO chaplains or civilian agencies. Stang stated, "Part of our stated mission was to wind down our participation in nation building in order to promote the locals in performing these tasks. Soldiers did support several nongovernment agencies, schools, and orphanages. We also continued to advise local organizations on how they could function without our help."[166]

The rapid downsizing of US involvement in Bosnia did not mean that soldiers still stationed in Bosnia lacked chaplain support. While Stang and Ebb were turning in chapel equipment and supplies and closing chapels, they also maintained an active ministry to the troops. There were religious retreats to Medjugorje, Srebrenica, and Sarajevo; briefings on suicide prevention and family reunions; contracting for Imams and Rabbis to meet specific religious needs; and maintaining the last religious services at the Eagle Base Chapel.

American enthusiasm surrounded the rapid downsizing of US troops in Bosnia.[167] Yet doubts still lingered as to whether or not the Europeans could maintain the peace and rebuild nations in this war-torn region. Muslim extremists had infiltrated Bosnia, especially after the 11 September 2001 attacks on America. Sarajevo had become a gathering place for Saudi Arabian Wahhabi missionaries, promoting an ultraradical Islam and anti-West extremism.[168] Episodes of violence were minor and few. American leaders knew there was still work to do to bring peace to Bosnia, but it was no longer US work—the European Union (EU) was now in control. At the 24 November 2004 disestablishment ceremony for Task Force *Eagle*, General B.B. Bell, Commander of the US Army in Europe, said, "It's appropriate now for the Army. That's why we're here today, as the last vestige of this great joint and combined force under NATO and under EUCOM, to finally disestablish the Army component of this joint, combined, magnificent team."[169]

At one point, there were tens of thousands of US troops in Bosnia. The closing of base camps and consolidation of other facilities meant that by the spring of 2005 the entire former SFOR mission was reduced first to a downsized Eagle Base, two FOBs, and six widely scattered liaison

Eric Ebb

Figure 10. CH (LTC) Eric Ebb greets parishioners after a service at
Eagle Base, Bosnia, 2004.

houses. The SFOR designation was gone, having served as the nomencla-
ture for 15 US troop rotations over a 10-year period. The now designated
ENDURING MISSION was composed of only a few hundred US troops.
The vast majority of chaplains who served in Bosnia from 1995 to 2005
could repeat the summary comments of Stang, the last senior chaplain in
Bosnia. He concluded:

> I deployed to serve the soldiers and there were many
> opportunities to minister. This encouraged me because I
> could see the value of my efforts. I grew spiritually from
> working with such fine soldiers and learning so much
> more about two of the world's major religions [Eastern
> Orthodoxy and Islam]. I became a better chaplain and
> Christian. . . . Several of our staff officers and NCOs
> commented that they didn't realize that the Unit Ministry
> Teams could be so helpful to their missions. I hope to use
> my increased knowledge in training our next generation
> of . . . chaplains.[170]

After the conclusion of the SFOR mission and the subsequent decrease
of US troops in Bosnia, only a minimal chaplain presence remained. Ebb
and Stang had already departed when Chaplain (CPT) Stanley Allen
arrived at Eagle Base, Bosnia. With no overlap with his predecessors,

Allen came to Bosnia on 14 September and was scheduled to leave on 2 December 2005. Assigned to the 101st Military Intelligence Battalion in Germany, Allen was attached to Eagle Base in Bosnia to fill the chaplain vacancy. Allen stated, "The only chapel still open in Bosnia is the one here at Eagle Base near Tuzla." With no US Army chaplains to provide specific denominational religious services to assist Allen, he filled that vacancy with military chaplains from other nations. Allen commented, "I have a general Protestant service Sunday at 1000 hours, the chaplain from Finland has a Lutheran service on Sunday at 1800, and the Polish Catholic priest has Mass on Sunday at 1200 hours." As the year 2005 concluded, Allen was the only US Army chaplain in Bosnia. He had no chaplain assistant support.[171]

Notes

1. Bill Clinton, *My Life* (New York: Alfred A. Knopf Publisher, 2005), 510–512.

2. Madeline Albright, *Madam Secretary: A Memoir* (New York: Miramax Books, 2003), 226.

3. Ibid., 233.

4. Wesley Clark, *Waging Modern War: Bosnia, Kosovo, and the Future of Conflict* (New York: PublicAffairs Books, 2001), 50.

5. For an exhaustive study on Srebrenica, see Jan W. Honig and Norbert Both, *Srebrenica: Record of a War Crime* (New York: Penguin Books, 1997).

6. Clark, *Waging Modern War*, 51.

7. Statement by Secretary of Defense William J. Perry. "On the Deployment of U.S. Troops with the Bosnia Peace Implantation Force." Delivered to the House Committee on International Relations, 30 November 1995.

8. Albright, *Madam Secretary*, 239.

9. Clark, *Waging Modern War*, 33, 35, 37.

10. Albright, *Madam Secretary*, 234–237.

11. Michael A. Warren, *The United States Army Reserve in Operation Joint Endeavor: Mobilization and Deployment* (Atlanta: US Army Reserve Command Historian, June 1996), vol. I, 12.

12. Chaplain (COL) Henry Wake (Retired), interview by Dr. John Brinsfield, 4 March 2004.

13. Questionnaire by SFC Deborah Peek, 20 May 2005.

14. Questionnaire by Chaplain (CPT) Marvin Luckie, 13 April 2005.

15. Chaplain (LTC) Scott McChrystal, interview by Dr. John Brinsfield, 3 March 2004.

16. J.F.O. McAllister, "Uncertain Beacon," *TIME Magazine*, 27 November 1995, 39.

17. George J. Church, "Divided by Hate," *TIME Magazine*, 18 December 1995, 3, 52, 54.

18. Chaplain (CPT) Jeff Giannola, interview by author, 5 August 1997.

19. Questionnaire by SSG Dae Lee, 27 January 2005.

20. Questionnaire by Chaplain (CPT) Brent Causey, 13 April 2005.

21. Warren, *The US Army Reserve in Operation Joint Endeavor*, 20.

22. Paul Glasters, "In the Twilight Zone," *U.S. News & World Report*, 18 December 1995, 44–45.

23. Chaplain (MAJ) Chet Lanious, interview by author, 27 July 2005.

24. William W. Hartzog, *American Military Heritage* (Washington, DC: Center of Military History, 2001), 244–245.

25. Peek questionnaire.

26. McChrystal interview, 2–3.

27. Ibid., 4.

28. Chaplain (CPT) David Brown, interview by author, 27 July 2005.

29. Lanious interview.

30. Dae J. Lee questionnaire.

31. Lanious interview.

32. William Matthews, "Clinton: Bosnia a Defining Moment," *Army Times*, 1 January 1996, 3.

33. William J. Perry, "U.S. in Bosnia," *The Officer*, January 1996, 17.

34. Statistics provided by the US Army Combat Readiness Center, 18 May 2005.

35. "Dead GI was Grad of Lamar High," *Houston Chronicle*, www.chron. com, 23 March 1996.

36. McChrystal interview, 3.

37. Chaplain (MAJ) Jay Hartranft, interview by author, 6 August 1997.

38. Chaplain Jay Hartranft, correspondence with author, 7 June 2004.

39. McChrystal interview, 6.

40. Ibid., 3.

41. Wake interview, 8.

42. McChrystal interview, 7.

43. John M. Shalikashvili, "Initial Posture Statement, 12 February 1997," *Selected Speeches, Testimony, and Interviews by General John M. Shalikashvili, Chairman of the Joint Chiefs of Staff* (Washington, DC: US Government Printing Office, 1998), 188.

44. Stacy Sullivan, "Serb Forces Cut Contacts with NATO," *Washington Post*, 9 February 1996, 1.

45. Kevin Dougherty, "Three Soldiers Injured in Snowy Tuzla Area," *European Stars & Stripes*, 9 February 1996, 1.

46. Bob Djurdjevic, "Bosnia: What's the Full Truth," *Wall Street Journal,* 9 February 1996, 15.

47. Rick Atkinson, "Warriors Without a War: U.S. Peacekeepers in Bosnia Adjusting to New Tasks: Arbitration, Bluff, Restraint," *The Washington Post*, 14 April 1996, A-1.

48. Giannola interview.

49. Ibid.

50. Kenneth Lawson, *AGC Chaplains in Operations Other Than War* (Taylors, SC: Associated Gospel Churches, 1998), 30–31.

51. Luckie questionnaire.

52. Peek questionnaire.

53. Gregory Katz, "Bosnians Say Serbs Must Free Slave Labor Camps," *The Patriot News* [Harrisburg, PA], 18 January 1996, A-9.

54. Harry Summers, "Storm Clouds Over Two Bosnian Fronts," *Washington Times*, 1 February 1996, 17.

55. Jim Hoagland, "On the Wagon in Bosnia," *Washington Post*, 1 February 1996, 18.

56. Scott McChrystal and Marv Wooten, "How a Rock Band Saved Task Force Eagle (Well, Sort Of)," *The Army Chaplaincy*, Spring 1999, 43–44.

57. Dae J. Lee questionnaire.

58. Questionnaire by SFC Wyman Loveless, 13 October 2004.

59. Chaplain David Zalis, interview by author, 4 May 2005.

60. Mike O'Connor, "For U.S. Troops, Bosnia Seems to be a Healthy Place," *The New York Times*, 3 July 1996, 1.

61. Ibid.

62. Causey questionnaire.

63. Ibid.

64. Ibid.

65. Questionnaire by SSG James Nelson, 16 August 2005.

66. Ibid.

67. Dusan Stojanovic, "100,000 Protest Milosevic's Rule," *The Patriot News* [Harrisburg, PA], 26 November 1996, A-7.

68. Clark, *Waging Modern War*, 27, 206, 220, 263, 265, 292.

69. Albright, *Madam Secretary*, 262, 317, 335–338.

70. Wake interview.

71. Chaplain David Hicks and Chaplain Phil Hill, interview by Dr. John Brinsfield, 3 March 2004.

72. Chaplain Charles Howell, correspondence with author, 7 June 2004.

73. Chaplain Charles Howell, interview by Dr. John Brinsfield, 10 December 2003.

74. Ibid.

75. "U.S. Troops in Hungary," *Washington Times*, 30 January 1996, 16.

76. Greg Spencer, "No Reservations," *The Budapest Sun*, 28 November–4 December 1996, 1.

77. Questionnaire by Chaplain (CPT) Scott Sterling, 15 March 2005.

78. Loveless questionnaire.

79. Sean D. Taylor, "Readiness is in the Eye of the Beholder," *Army Times*, 17 February 1997, 18, 30.

80. Shalikashvili, "Initial Posture Statement, 12 February 1997." *Selected Speeches*, 187–188.

81. Chaplain Hank Steinhilber, interview by Dr. John Brinsfield, 9 December 2003.

82. Steve Szasz, "The Chaplain's Chapters: A Monthly Letter Containing Information and Inspiration for Family and Friends," 27 September 1996.

83. Ibid., 16 November 1996.

84. Chaplain Steve Szasz, interview by author, 29 August 2005.

85. Questionnaire by Chaplain (MAJ) Michael Metcalf, 13 April 2005.

86. Questionnaire by Chaplain (CPT) Keith Belz, 6 August 1999.

87. Questionnaire by Chaplain (CPT) Patrick Appleget, 16 August 2005.

88. "Croat Police Blamed in Attack on Muslims," *Washington Post*, 27 February 1997, A-24.

89. "Bosnia Civilians Rain Stones on American Troops," *Rocky Mountain News,* 28 August 1997, 46A.

90. "Rock-Hurling Serbs End Their Anti-NATO Rampage," *The Deseret News* (Utah), 29 August 1997, A-4.

91. "Eighteen U.S. Soldiers Decorated for Restraint Facing Mobs," *The Record* (New Jersey), 30 August 1997, A-12.

92. Questionnaire by SGM Pamela Neal, 15 June 2004.

93. Questionnaire by SSG Yolanda Jackson, 15 June 2004.

94. Chaplain (COL) Janet Horton, interview by Dr. John Brinsfield, 3 March 2004.

95. Szasz, "The Chaplain's Chapters," 28 December 1996.

96. Questionnaire by Chaplain (CPT) Steve Firtko, 15 August 1999.

97. Questionnaire by Chaplain (MAJ) Jay Hartranft, 10 August 2000.

98. "Dear GI: Letters will Brighten Christmas in Bosnia," *St. Louis Post-Dispatch*, 15 December 1997, 2.

99. "On Bosnia: Messages in Clinton Visit Should be Heeded," *Houston Chronicle*, 24 December 1997, 18.

100. "Dealing with Bosnia War Criminals," *Washington Post*, 24 December 1997, A-12.

101. Albright, *Madam Secretary*, 489, 493.

102. "Milosevic May Intervene in Bosnia," *Chicago Tribune*, 28 August 1997, 24.

103. Clark, *Waging Modern War*, 66, 68.

104. Questionnaire by SSG James Johnson, 22 October 2004.

105. Chaplain (MAJ) Jerry Moates, interview by author, 14 June 2004.

106. Robert L. McClure and Morton Orlov II, "Is the UN Peacekeeping Role in Eclipse?" *Parameters*, Autumn 1999, 98, 101.

107. Steinhilber interview.

108. US Army Field Manual (FM) 41-10, *Civil Affairs Operations* (Washington, DC: US Government Printing Office, 1993), 1-1.

109. Jeffery A. Jacobs, "Civil Affairs in Peace Operations," *Military Review*, July–August 1998, 11.

110. Questionnaire by Chaplain (LTC) Frank Wismer, 4 October 2004.

111. Ibid.

112. Questionnaire by Chaplain (CPT) Lonnie L. Locke III, 25 July 2004.

113. Questionnaire by Chaplain (CPT) Philip Smiley, 10 June 2004.

114. Questionnaire by MSG Chris Patterson, 16 August 2004.

115. Ibid.

116. Hartranft questionnaire.

117. Chaplain (CPT) Steven Mark Jones, interview by author, 21 June 2004.

118. Chaplain (MAJ) Erik Erkkinen, "After Action Report for SFOR-4," 15 May 1999.

119. James L. Cairns, "Meanwhile in Bosnia: The Region was Forgotten during the NATO-Yugoslavian Conflict, 1999," *Christian Century*, 14 July 1999, www.findarticles.com.

120. Questionnaire by Chaplain (CPT) Alva R. Bennett, 20 May 2005.

121. Chaplain (CPT) Peter Strong and SPC Phillip Fortner, "After Action Report—Camp Demi," 18 March 1999.

122. Erkkinen, "After Action Report."

123. Questionnaire by Chaplain (CPT) Brad Baumann, 25 July 2005.

124. Ibid.

125. Questionnaire by Chaplain (CPT) Terrance Kesling, 11 February 2005.

126. Chaplain Rajmund Kopec, interview by Dr. John Brinsfield, 9 December 2003.

127. Neal questionnaire.

128. Questionnaire by Chaplain (CPT) Joseph Blay, 5 August 2004.

129. Questionnaire by Chaplain (MAJ) David Crary, 9 June 2004.

130. Ibid.

131. Steven Lee Myers, "Army Will Give National Guard the Entire U.S. Role in Bosnia," *The New York Times*, 5 December, 2000, 1.

132. Questionnaire by Chaplain (CPT) Ronald Cooper, 19 May 2005.

133. Chaplain Michael Lembke, *Greetings from Bosnia, Family and Friends* (self-published, 2001), 65.

134. Alexander A.C. Gerry, "Bosnia and Herzegovina: Questioning the Dayton Agreement," *The Officer*, June 2001, www.findarticles.com.

135. Chaplain (LTC) Vernon Chandler, interview by author, 29 July 2004.

136. Questionnaire by SFC Lucinda Flowers, 29 July 2004.

137. Chandler interview.

138. Ibid.

139. Sean D. Naylor, "Routing out Terrorism in Bosnia," *The Army Times,* 10 December 2001, 12.

140. Questionnaire by Chaplain (CPT) Sean Wead, 20 July 2005.

141. Ibid.

142. Kopec interview.

143. Questionnaire by Chaplain (MAJ) Alvin Shrum, 9 September 2004. The lack of ministry integration by the Indiana Army National Guard UMT was indicative of the tension between this particular National Guard unit and the larger task force. Simply stated, the commander of this Indiana National Guard unit wanted his soldiers under his supervision on his compound, and any outside activities were discouraged. This was the exception, as most National Guard units fully and successfully integrated with their Active Duty partners.

144. Ibid.

145. Questionnaire by SGT David Lee, 5 August 2005.

146. Questionnaire by Chaplain (CPT) William Wehlage, 25 July 2005.

147. Chaplain Kenneth Lawson, unpublished diary, notations from 8–12 May 2002. A copy is available at the US Army Chaplain Center and School Library, Fort Jackson, SC.

148. "Risks Remain in Bosnia-Herzegovina—News Watch," *International Travel News*, August 2002.

149. Kopec interview.

150. P.H. Liotta and Cindy R. Jebb, "Macedonia: End of the Beginning or Beginning of the End?" *Parameters*, Spring 2002, 96.

151. Vince Crawley, "Should we Stay or Should we Go?" *Army Times*, 22 July 2002, 10.

152. Correspondence from Chaplain F. Doug Hudson to Chaplain Gregg Drew, 16 March 2003.

153. Questionnaire by Chaplain (CPT) Matthew Huisjen, 1 November 2003.

154. Ibid.

155. Ronald L. Cobb, *Memories of Bosnia: The 35th Division's SFOR13 NATO Peacekeeping Mission* (Bloomington, IN: AuthorHouse Publishers, 2004), vii–viii.

156. Ibid., 57–58.

157. Ibid., 81–84.

158. Correspondence, Hudson to Drew.

159. Jon Dahms, "7th Army Reserve Command Chaplains Complete Historic Ministry," *US Army Reserve News Service*, 5 May 2003.

160. Cobb, *Memories of Bosnia*, 114.

161. Correspondence, Hudson to Drew.

162. Cobb, *Memories of Bosnia*, 92.

163. *Army Times*, 27 September 2004, 5.

164. Ibid., 17 October 2005, 7.

165. Questionnaire by Chaplain William J. Stang, 2 February 2005.

166. Ibid.

167. "U.S. Troops End Mission in Bosnia," *The State* [Columbia, SC], 25 November 2004, A-20.

168. Stephen Swartz, "The Failure of Europe in Bosnia and the Continuing Infiltration of Islamic Extremists," *The Weekly Standard*, 20 June 2005, 17.

169. Jason Austin, "Task Force Eagle Leaving Bosnia," *Army Public Affairs Press Release*, 23 November 2004, 1.

170. Stang questionnaire.

171. Questionnaire by Chaplain (CPT) Stanley Allen, 1 November 2005.

Chapter 4

The Kosovo Theater of Operations

Background to Contemporary Hostilities in Kosovo

Since the time of the NATO and United States invasion of Bosnia in 1995–96, the nearby region of Kosovo had been a hotspot for rising Balkan tensions. Several hours drive from the closest point in Bosnia, Kosovo has maintained its own ethnic uniqueness and cultural autonomy. Kosovo has for centuries desired to be its own independent nation, free from Yugoslavian or Serbian influence. With an Albanian Muslim heritage, Kosovars see themselves as the historic people of the land of Kosovo.[1] Like Bosnia, Kosovo has a tortured history dating from at least medieval times in the era of Muslim–Byzantine warfare.

Modern Kosovo has only existed as a political or territorial entity since 1945. Before then, Italian-occupied Albania, Serbia, Montenegro, the Ottoman Empire, the Byzantine Empire, Bulgaria, and the Roman Empire partially or entirely ruled Kosovo territory. Some have suggested that Kosovo has been a single distinctive region since ancient times, but this is strongly contradicted by archaeological findings and historic records.[2] Nor has Kosovo's population been ethnically consistent over the years: the province's complex ethnic map has included Latinos, Turks, Roma, Gorani (Slavic Muslims), Circassians, and Jews in addition to Serbs and Albanians.

The Kosovo region lay on the outer fringes of the Byzantine Empire and directly in the path of Slav expansion. From the 850s until about 1014, Bulgaria ruled Kosovo. The forceful emperor Basil, the Bulgar Slayer, subsequently reasserted Byzantine control. Serbia at this time did not exist; a number of small Slav kingdoms lay to the north and west of Kosovo, of which Raška (Rascia, central modern Serbia) and Dioclea (Montenegro and northern Albania) were the strongest. In the 1180s, the Serbian ruler Stefan Nemanja seized control of Dioclea and parts of Kosovo. His successor (also called Stefan) took control of the rest of Kosovo by 1216, creating a state that incorporated most of modern Serbia-Montenegro. This was a period when Greek Orthodox bishops greatly influenced the local populations, with a type of Hellenization occurring throughout the region.[3]

During the rule of the Nemanjić dynasty, many Serbian Orthodox churches and monasteries were built throughout Serbian territory, particularly Kosovo, which became the economic, demographic, religious, and political heartland. The Nemanjić rulers alternatively used both Prizren and Pristina as their capitals. Large estates were given to Serbian monasteries in Metohia (which included parts of Albania and Montenegro), for which the area earned the designation *Metohia* or "monastic land." The most prominent churches in Kosovo—the Patriarchate at Pec, the church at Gračanica, and the monastery at Visoki Dečani near Dečani—were all founded during this period. Kosovo was economically important, as the modern Kosovo capital of Pristina was a major trading center on routes leading to ports on the Adriatic Sea.[4]

Ethnic identity in the Middle Ages was somewhat fluid throughout Europe and people at that time did not appear to have defined themselves rigidly by ethnic group. About all that can be said for sure is that Serbs appear to have been the dominant population culturally, and were probably a demographic majority as well. In 1355, the Serbian state fell apart on the death of Tsar Stefan Dušan and dissolved into squabbling fiefdoms. The Ottoman Empire took the opportunity to exploit Serbian weakness and invaded, meeting the Serbian army on the field of Kosovo Polje on 28 June 1389. The Battle of Kosovo ended in the deaths of both Serbian Prince Lazar and Ottoman Sultan Murad I. Although the battle has been mythologized as a great Serbian defeat, at that time opinion was divided as to whether it was a Serbian defeat, a stalemate, or even a Serbian victory. For centuries, the battle of Kosovo has been a source of patriotic passion for Serbs against Muslims.[5] Serbia maintained its independence and sporadic control of Kosovo until a final defeat in 1455, when it became part of the Ottoman Empire.

The territory of today's Kosovo Province was for centuries ruled by the Ottoman Empire. Despite the imposition of Muslim rule, large numbers of Christians continued to live and sometimes even prosper under the Ottomans. A process of Islamization began shortly after the beginning of Ottoman rule, but it took a considerable amount of time—at least a century—and was concentrated at first on rural towns. It appears that many Christian inhabitants converted directly to Islam rather than being replaced by Muslims from outside Kosovo. A large part of the reason for the conversion was probably economic and social, as Muslims had considerably more rights and privileges than Christians. Christian religious life nonetheless continued with churches largely left alone by the Ottomans, but both the Orthodox and Catholic churches and their congregations suffered from high levels of taxation.

In 1689, the Ottoman-Habsburg war (1683–99)—one of the pivotal events in Serbian national mythology—greatly disrupted Kosovo. In October 1689, a small Austrian force under Margrave Ludwig of Baden breached into Turkish territory and reached as far as Kosovo, following their earlier capture of Belgrade. Many Serbs and Albanians pledged their loyalty to the Austrians, some joining Ludwig's army. This was by no means a universal reaction; many other Serbs and Albanians fought alongside the Ottomans to resist the Austrian advance. A massive Ottoman counterattack the following summer drove the Austrians back to their fortress at Nis, then back to Belgrade, and finally back across the Danube to Austria.[6] This incident produced numerous refugees, brought atrocities against civilians by their neighbors, and caused great disruption with the already fragile Ottoman control of the Balkans.[7] The Ottoman offensive was accompanied by savage reprisals and looting, prompting many Serbs—including Arsenije III, Patriarch of the Serbian Orthodox Church—to flee along with the Austrians. This event has been immortalized in Serbian history as the *Velika Seoba* or "Great Migration." It is traditionally said to have accounted for a huge exodus of hundreds of thousands of Serbian refugees from Kosovo and Serbia proper, which left a vacuum filled by a flood of Albanian immigrants. Arsenije himself wrote of 30,000 souls (i.e., individuals) who fled with him to Austria, a figure confirmed by other sources.[8]

In the late 19th century, with the weakening of the Ottoman Empire independence movements arose within Kosovo. In 1878, one of the four vilayets (provinces) with Albanian inhabitants that formed the League of Prizren was the Vilayet of Kosovo. The League's purpose was to resist both Ottoman rule and incursions by the newly emerging Balkan nations. In 1910, an Albanian organized insurrection broke out in Pristina and soon spread to the entire vilayet of Kosovo, lasting for 3 months. The Ottoman Sultan visited Kosovo in June 1911 during peace settlement talks covering all Albanian-inhabited areas. Following the First Balkan War of 1912, the Treaty of London in May 1913 internationally recognized Kosovo as part of Serbia and Metohia. In 1918, Serbia became part of the newly formed Kingdom of Yugoslavia. The influence of the Ottoman Turks was gone, allowing lands lost to Serbs since medieval times to be regained.[9]

Between the two world wars, the Yugoslavian government tried to evacuate the Albanian population from Kosovo and Macedonia. Albanian Kosovars were sent to Turkey and Albania with Serbs transplanted to colonize Kosovo with a Serbian population. On 7 March 1937, a memorandum titled "Expulsion of the Albanians" was presented to the Yugoslavian government from the Serbian Academy. The 1941 and 1945 partitions of Yugoslavia by the Axis Powers awarded most of Kosovo to the Italian-occupied Greater Albania, and smaller parts of it to German-occupied Serbia and Bulgaria. During the occupation, armed Albanian groups, notably the Vulnetari militia, expelled thousands of Kosovo

Serbs. It is still not known exactly how many fell victim to this forced displacement, but Serbian estimates put the figures at 10,000 to 40,000 killed with 70,000 to 100,000 expelled.[10]

Following the end of World War II and the establishment of Tito's communist regime, in 1946 Kosovo was granted the status of an autonomous region of Serbia and in 1963 became an autonomous province. The communist government did not permit the return of many of the Serb refugees. With the passing of the 1974 Yugoslavia constitution, Kosovo gained virtual self-government. The province's government then applied Albanian curriculum to Kosovo's schools; they obtained and used surplus and obsolete non-communist textbooks. Life in Kosovo under communism had an emphasis on brotherhood and unity, with the objections by Serbs to gaining Kosovar influence being suppressed by Tito's demand for unity within Yugoslavia.[11]

Throughout the 1980s, tensions between the Albanian and Serb communities in the Kosovo province escalated. The Muslim Albanian community favored greater autonomy for Kosovo, while Eastern Orthodox Serbs favored closer ties with the rest of Serbia. There was little appetite for unification with Albania itself, which was still ruled by a Stalinist government and had considerably worse living standards than Kosovo. Serbs living in Kosovo complained of being discriminated against by the provincial government, notably by the local law enforcement authorities failing to punish reported crimes against Serbs. The increasingly bitter atmosphere in Kosovo meant that even minor frictions could become major incidents. Perhaps the most politically explosive complaint leveled by the Kosovo Serbs was that the communist authorities in Belgrade were neglecting them. Adding fuel to the fire of tensions at this time was the so-called Paracin Massacre where an apparently deranged soldier from their unit killed several Serb soldiers, an incident that Belgrade widely misreported as a large-scale attack by Albanians against Serbs.[12]

In August 1987, during the dying days of Yugoslavia's communist regime, Milosevic visited Kosovo.[13] He appealed to Serb nationalism to further his career. Having drawn huge crowds to a rally commemorating the Battle of Kosovo, he pledged to Kosovo Serbs, "No one should dare to beat you." He became an instant hero. By the end of the year, Milosevic was in legitimate control of the expanding Serbian government.

In 1989, a Serbia-wide referendum drastically reduced the autonomy of Kosovo and the northern province of Vojvodina. The referendum implemented a new constitution that allowed a multiparty system, introduced freedom of speech, and supposedly promoted human rights. In practice, it was subverted by Milosevic's government, which resorted to rigging elections, controlling much of the news media, and was accused of abusing the human rights of its opponents and national minorities. Civilian protests against government corruption led to dozens of deaths. The referendum significantly reduced the provinces' rights, permitting the government of Serbia to exert direct control over many previously autonomous areas of governance, including Kosovo. In particular, the constitutional changes handed control of the police, the court system, the economy, the education system, and the language policies to the Serbian government.[14]

Map 5. A 2000 map of Kosovo.

Many of Serbia's national minorities, who saw it as a means of imposing ethnically based centralized rule on the provinces, strongly opposed the new constitution. Kosovo's Albanians refused to participate in the referendum, portraying it as illegitimate. As it was a Serbia-wide referendum and Albanians were a minority in Serbia, their participation would not have changed the outcome of the referendum. The provincial governments also opposed the new constitution. It had to be ratified by their assemblies, which effectively meant voting for their dissolution. Kosovo's assembly initially opposed the constitution but in March 1989, when the assembly met to discuss the proposals, Yugoslavian tanks and armored cars surrounded the meeting place, forcing the delegates to accept the amendments. By the end of the month, over 20 people were killed and a curfew was imposed.

The constitutional changes dissolved the parliaments of all Yugoslavian republics and provinces, which until then had leaders only from the Communist Party of Yugoslavia, and held multiparty elections. Kosovo Albanians refused to participate in the elections and instead held their own unsanctioned elections. Because election laws required turnout higher than 50 percent, the parliament of Kosovo was not established. The new Serbian constitution abolished the individual provinces' official media, integrating them with the official media of Serbia while retaining some programs in the Albanian language; suppressed the Albanian-language media in Kosovo; withdrew funding from state-owned media, including that in the Albanian language in Kosovo; and banned state-owned Albanian language television or radio from broadcasting from Kosovo. Serbian secret police intimidated the people. Kosovar Albanian police were ineffective as Yugoslavian-Serbian security forces imposed conformity amidst various incidents of abuse and harassment.[15]

The new Serbian constitution also transferred control of state-owned Kosovar companies to the Serbian government. In September 1990, up to 123,000 Albanian workers were fired from their positions in government and the media, as were teachers, doctors, and workers in government-controlled industries. This provoked a general strike and mass unrest. Some of those not fired quit in sympathy, refusing to work for the Serbian government. Although the government claimed it was simply getting rid of old communist directors, the firings were widely seen as a purge of ethnic Albanians. The old Albanian educational curriculum and textbooks were revoked and new ones were created. The curriculum was (and still is, as that is the curriculum used for Albanians in Serbia outside Kosovo) the same as the Serbian curriculum and that of all other nationalities in Serbia except that it contained education on and in the Albanian language.

Education in Albanian was withdrawn in 1992 and reestablished in 1994. Pristina University, the center of Kosovo Albanian cultural identity, abolished education in the Albanian language and fired Albanian teachers en masse. Albanians responded by boycotting state schools and setting up an unofficial parallel system of Albanian-language education.[16]

What they saw as an attack on their rights outraged Kosovar Albanians. There was mass rioting and unrest from Albanians as well as outbreaks of intercommunal violence. In February 1990, a state of emergency was declared, and the presence of the Yugoslav army and police was significantly increased to quell the unrest. Unsanctioned elections were held in 1992, which overwhelmingly elected Ibrahim Rugova as president of a self-declared Republic of Kosovo. However, these elections were not recognized by the Serbian government or by any foreign government. In 1995, thousands of Serb refugees from Croatia settled in Kosovo, which further worsened relations between the two communities.

Historic Albanian opposition to the sovereignty of Yugoslavia and especially Serbia had previously surfaced in rioting (1968 and March 1981) in the capital Pristina. In 1995, Ibrahim Rugova advocated non-violent resistance. Later when it became apparent that this was not working, opposition took the form of separatist agitation by political opposition groups and after 1996 armed action by the clandestine Kosovo liberation army. By this time, the former nation of Yugoslavia was in chaos. Years of ethnic tensions and religious antagonism had degenerated into local acts of intimidation, violence, and even genocide, forcing the United States and NATO into military action.

From 1996 through 1999 the United States, the United Nations, NATO, and the European community were unable to create an acceptable intervention plan for Kosovo. Meanwhile, thousands of ethnic Albanian Muslims were victims of widespread and increasing atrocities.

Preparations for the First US Army Chaplains to Arrive in Kosovo

The United States' commitment to military intervention in Kosovo was slow to develop. By 1998, the momentum to send US troops to the region became virtually irresistible. Nevertheless, recent lessons learned in Somalia, Haiti, and Bosnia created a passive resistance to deploying more US troops into another internal Balkans dispute. The mission in nearby Bosnia, stated in 1995 to last only 1 year, was nowhere near completion. In 1998, US Secretary of State Albright attributed the eventual US military intervention in Kosovo to one source—the familiar adversary Slobodan Milosevic. Having previously considered Milosevic a brute, a ruthless opportunist, and a man of great cruelty, his agenda of terror in Kosovo infuriated Albright.[17] In her memoirs, Albright states that the primary mistake made by Milosevic that prompted the United States toward military intervention in Kosovo was the massacre in and around the small town of Prekaz. Albright stated:

> Kosovo was extremely tense but not at war. After the 1995 Dayton Accords were signed, however, the situation began to heat up further. Kosovo's Albanians looked around and saw that the Bosnians, Croats, Slovenes, and Macedonians had all left Yugoslavia to form independent states. The Albanians shared the same ambitions, but the Dayton Accords did nothing for them. Many grew inpatient with the denial of their rights and appeals for patience from civilian leaders. . . . From sources in the region, we received word in January 1998 that Milosevic was preparing to respond with a crackdown. . . .

> In late February and early March [1998] around the small town of Prekaz, in the Yugoslavian province of Kosovo, Serb paramilitary units stormed through ethnic Albanian villages, killing scores of people. Whole families were burned alive in their homes. Women, children, and the elderly were among the victims; thousands of people fled. It was the worst violence in the province since World War II. . . .

> Prior to the Prekaz massacre, Yugoslav authorities had assured our chief Balkans negotiator, Ambassador Robert Gelbard that they would respond with restraint to any attacks. Obviously they had lied. . . .[18]

As far back as Christmas 1992, President George H.W. Bush informed Milosevic that the United States would be prepared militarily if the Serbs initiated an armed conflict in Kosovo. Three weeks after Clinton took office in 1993, he reaffirmed that warning. As US attention in the Balkans in the 1990s focused on Bosnia, Albright warned that rising tensions in Kosovo had implications for all of Europe. She stated, "We had to approve concrete measures that would expand our leverage over Belgrade. That was how Milosevic had been brought to the table at Dayton, and that was the only language he would respond to now."[19] In contrast, the Defense Department was initially resisting another Balkans mission. In late spring

1998, when Milosevic stepped up helicopter strikes and ordered the burning of villages in Kosovo, the United States went to NATO looking for military support. Meanwhile, the United States and NATO sent troops to Macedonia and Albania to discourage the spread of violence. Aggressive military planning began with the threefold intention of keeping the conflict from spreading, planning air strikes in case Serb atrocities would not cease, and coordinating a potential peace implementation force to enter Kosovo after a political settlement was reached.[20]

The senior US military officer with knowledge of Kosovo was Clark. As the NATO Supreme Allied Commander, Clark was the top military officer over NATO and US forces in Europe. All plans of potential military intervention in Kosovo went through Clark for refinement or approval. In 1998, as war in Kosovo seemed likely, Clark outlined his goals as follows: "Get Milosevic to agree to a cease-fire; to halt the fighting; and to comply with the terms of the Security Council Resolution 1199. In this resolution was the requirement that the Serbs withdraw the additional forces that had moved into Kosovo after February 1998."[21]

Clark had the difficult job of balancing all the unique concerns of individual NATO countries with a vacillating US policy in the Balkans. In addition, he had to manage the legitimate concerns of Kosovo's neighbors who feared an escalation of hostilities could overflow into their countries, namely Macedonia and Albania. Through late 1998, Serbian troops under Milosevic infiltrated Kosovo and continued a campaign of terror, ethnic cleansing, and stabilization of military fortifications with Serbian soldiers and paramilitary forces committing violent deprecations on Kosovar civilians.

A deadly chess game ensued between Serbian forces and the small number of NATO peacekeeping troops and civilian UN observers sent to Kosovo. Peace negotiators met in Rambouillet, France, on 23 February 1999. At the end of more than 2 weeks of intense efforts, they attempted to reach an agreement on substantial autonomy for Kosovo while respecting the national sovereignty and territorial integrity of the Federal Republic of Yugoslavia. As peace negotiations proceeded, Serbian troops repositioned themselves to deceive NATO representatives, only to continue their campaign of terror in other locations. Deceit and manipulation by Milosevic's forces dragged negotiations into early 1999. By 20 March 1999, international television networks were reporting live media coverage of Albanian refugees streaming barefoot in the mud and snow from the recently looted village of Srbica. On 24 March 1999, NATO forces under the command of Clark began an extensive bombing campaign against Serbian forces in and around Kosovo.

Much of the world watched in amazement and trepidation as the first-ever use of a combative military force by NATO was unleashed on Kosovo. Designated as Operation ALLIED FORCE, the NATO goals of the air strikes were explicit. Air strikes would be pursued until President Milosevic:

- Ensures a verifiable stop to all military action and the immediate ending of violence and oppression.
- Ensures the withdrawal from Kosovo of the military, police, and paramilitary forces.
- Agrees to the stationing in Kosovo of an international military presence.
- Agrees to the unconditional and safe return of all refugees and displaced persons and unhindered access to them by humanitarian aid organizations.
- Provides credible assurance of his willingness to work on the basis of the Rambouillet Accords in the establishment of a political framework agreement for Kosovo in conformity with international law and the Charter of the United Nations.[22]

The bombing campaign against Serb forces lasted from 24 March through 20 June 1999. A few temporary lulls in the bombing were achieved during that time based on the work of negotiators, none of which produced lasting peace. On 15 April 1999, US Secretary of Defense William Cohen stated the objectives of Operation ALLIED FORCE as follows: "Our military objective is to degrade and damage the military and security structure that President Milosevic (Yugoslav President) has used to depopulate and destroy the Albanian majority in Kosovo."[23] As far as the actual military tactics employed by NATO and US forces involved in the bombing, Clark stated:

In the first place, we were going to execute two operations plans simultaneously, the first of which was the Phased Air Operation and the second of which was the Limited Air Operation. Both plans had been approved through the NATO approval process. While the Phased Air Operation called for a first phase limited to the enemy's air defense system and any deployed forces in Kosovo, it also provided authority to strike the air defense system throughout Yugoslavia. There were no off-limits areas. The Limited Air Operation, on the other hand, gave us the authority to strike headquarters, forces, and facilities in and around

Kosovo that were connected to the forces that had perpetrated the ethnic cleansing or some other incident.[24]

As the 24 March 1999 air strikes were about to begin, Clark developed some "measures of merit" to help him and his staff evaluate the success of the bombing campaign. "The first measure of merit," Clark stated, "is not to lose aircraft, minimize the loss of aircraft. . . . The second measure of merit is to impact the Yugoslavian military and police activities on the ground as rapidly and as effectively as possible. We had to attack and disrupt—destroy if possible—the actual elements doing the ethnic cleansing. . . . The third measure of merit is to protect our ground forces. . . ."[25] Adding to these three measures of merit were the larger strategic international issues that Clark addressed, namely, enforcing the ongoing peacekeeping mission in Bosnia, maintaining the support of front-line states Macedonia and Albania, and providing humanitarian assistance to the Kosovar people.[26] Later a fourth measure of merit was added, maintaining the NATO military alliance. All this was to be accomplished while maintaining the sometimes strained and fickle political alliances within the NATO cooperative structure.

The NATO bombing campaign against Serbs in Kosovo lasted just under 90 days. Serb facilities, troops, equipment, and supply depots were quickly destroyed all over Yugoslavia. Using NATO and US fighter jets, a variety of bombers including the B-52s, A-10 Warthog antiarmor aircraft, and US Navy cruise missiles and Tomahawk missiles, Serbian positions were plummeted. The command bunker of Milosevic was destroyed, the command and control communication assets of the Serbians were decimated, and the Serbian troops not hiding below ground were destroyed. During the air strikes, some air-to-air combat between Americans and Serbian pilots flying Russian-made jets did occur to the demise of the Serbians. Throughout the air campaign, one American pilot was shot down and rescued the next day; three American soldiers on the Macedonian-Serbian border were captured and later released; and on 26 April, two US pilots were killed in an Apache helicopter accident in a support mission in Albania.[27]

NATO contributions to the air campaign were substantial. France provided almost 100 aircraft, second only to the United States. Germany, France, Greece, the United Kingdom, Italy, Belgium, the Netherlands, and later Hungary, the Czech Republic, and Turkey provided air bases. While the United States provided all of the stealth aircraft and most of the refueling and electronic warfare assets, the Allies flew some 40 percent of the air strikes.[28] All 19 NATO countries contributed in some way to Operation ALLIED FORCE, including countries with minimal military assets such as Iceland, Portugal, and Luxembourg.[29] The rising refugee population on roadways throughout the region was an unforeseen factor that greatly complicated the NATO air campaign against Serbs in Kosovo. In a frantic last-minute attempt to impose as much ethnic relocation in Kosovo as possible, Serbs herded thousands of Albanian Muslims out of Kosovo so that at the end of hostilities Serbians could easily relocate into this area. Other Kosovars fled their ravaged province for Albania, further adding congestion to an already complicated war zone. Early in the air campaign, intentionally displaced refugees were estimated at 540,000, with 100,000 more in Albania and 50,000 relocated in Macedonia. Toward the end of the air campaign, the displaced Kosovars ethnically cleansed from their homes and scattered throughout was estimated at 800,000.[30]

The bombing campaign ended on 20 June 1999. Milosevic agreed to the cease-fire principles: the expulsion of remaining Serb military and paramilitary forces from Kosovo, the acceptance of an international NATO-led military ground force in Kosovo, the full return and resettlement of all refugees, and participation in a later political agreement to determine the final political status of Kosovo.[31] The Allied ground forces to enter Kosovo would be called the Kosovo Force (KFOR). Clark created four new "measures of merit" to guide the KFOR ground forces entering Kosovo: deploy troops smoothly and quickly; avoid anarchy—get all Serb forces out, stop crimes of revenge with full support of the International Criminal Tribunal; provide humanitarian assistance as much as possible; and protect the KFOR personnel, especially from minefields.[32]

During the preparation and execution of the air campaign, Army chaplains were training with their units for potential deployment to Kosovo. Some of the senior chaplains in Europe at that time were Hicks at USAREUR and Janet Horton at V Corps. Hicks was at USAREUR from June 1997 through July 1999 and was a senior chaplain in Europe during the air campaign and the initial deployment of KFOR into Kosovo. Hicks supervised, supplied, and coordinated chaplains for the KFOR mission, administering UMT assets throughout Europe. Janet Horton of V Corps in Heidelberg served in that capacity from June 1997 through June 2000. She stated that Milosevic was more sophisticated in his ethnic cleansing in Kosovo than he had been a few years earlier in Bosnia. US Army preparations for the Kosovo mission were conducted simultaneously with other missions, so between 1800 and into the morning of the next day detailed Kosovo and Albania planning was conducted. In comparing preparations for the Kosovo mission to the ongoing mission in Bosnia, Janet Horton stated:

I think what we learned was that we had to be more flexible. We had to understand each sector, because there was such a difference. People wanted immediately to compare Bosnia to Albania, and the Kosovo mission, and each one of them was quite different. Even though they were in the same region, and some of the same factions, there was still a difference between where we set up, what the infrastructures were, what the needs were, how long the mission was going to be. You had to get to the point where you realized that a specific religious support analysis was necessary. You can't necessarily take what works even a year ago and say that it is going to work the same.[33]

Chaplains training for deployment to Kosovo during the bombing campaign understood that they and their soldiers could soon be placed in danger. Chaplain Howell of the 21st Theater Support Command (TSC) was extensively involved in supporting his soldiers who were preparing supplies and logistics for the invasion force into Kosovo. As the bombing campaign in Kosovo was proceeding, Howell's unit was bringing huge amounts of supplies to Croatia and Greece. From February through April 1999, his unit unloaded supplies destined for Kosovo in the port of Rijeka, Croatia. Their headquarters in Rijeka was never really completed, as the short duration of the air campaign meant supplies needed to be pushed forward quickly to units entering Kosovo. As the bombing campaign ended and troops poured into Kosovo, Howell's unit developed a supporting operation in Greece. He stated:

At the last minute, our President announced that now ground troops would fight. As soon as he announced that, within 72 hours Slobodan Milosevic and his forces we were fighting decided to withdraw. . . . So with that announcement we opened up a port in Greece, and the USS *Bob Hope* was the ship that we used to bring in the equipment from Fort Hood. We brought the troops and equipment in as a safeguard, loaded them up in June, July, and August, and moved them into Kosovo as a ground force.[34]

Chaplains preparing to enter Kosovo in 1999 had various experiences during their preparation period. Chaplain (CPT) Scott Jones of the 67th Combat Support Hospital stated that his unit had good briefings for the soldiers about to deploy,[35] while Chaplain (CPT) Darin Powers of the 2d Battalion, 18th Field Artillery remarked that he had positive ministry opportunities working with spouses and children of soldiers who were about to deploy, and that unit morale was high.[36] Chaplain Causey of the 3d Brigade, 1st Infantry Division listed his preparation activities for Kosovo as follows: "Deployment briefings for both families and soldiers, marriage retreats, deployment briefings for children, local cultural and religious assessment and training, personal force protection training for the chaplain assistants, and worship rites and religious assessment training for UMTs."[37]

Chaplain Assistant SSG Craig Gardner was assigned to the 3d Brigade Combat Team (BCT) under the 1st Infantry Division. The extensive training his unit completed in Germany while the air bombing campaign was expanding in Kosovo is an interesting glimpse from a sergeant in this stressful time of predeployment preparations.

> I got a call from the Division Chaplain, Chaplain (LTC) Jack Pendergrass. He explained to me that 3d Brigade was in the chute to deploy to Kosovo and their 56M30 [senior chaplain assistant] was not deployable due to a profile from a motorcycle accident. They needed me to cross-level over to 3d BCT to deploy. I did one MRE (Mission Readiness Exercise) with Chaplain (MAJ) Brent Causey at Hoenfels, Germany. I also prior to that did a CPX (Command Post Exercise) with him at Grafenwehr, Germany. . . . The US was in talks with Serbs about the deployment so the deployment date kept changing. The 3d BCT did three different MREs getting ready. We were wrapping up the last one when word came to deploy as soon as possible.[38]

Initial Chaplain Activities and Ministries in Kosovo, 1999

Basic chaplain organization and activities in Kosovo had similarities to those in Bosnia. The USAREUR chaplain in early 1999 was Hicks, replaced later that year by Haberek. The largest combatant command in Europe, V Corps, in 1999 had Janet Horton as their senior chaplain. Since many of the deployed units in Kosovo came under the V Corps command structure, Janet Horton and her USARUER counterparts were intimately involved in higher-level planning for all chaplain operations in the Balkans. The senior chaplain on the ground in Kosovo was designated as the KFOR chaplain, the first one being Zalis. Under Zalis in Kosovo was a task force chaplain. With the designation of Task Force *Falcon*, the first chaplain to serve in this capacity was Chaplain (MAJ) Allen Kovach.

After coordination with the USAREUR and V Corps chaplain offices, Zalis, a Rabbi, arrived in Kosovo in the spring of 1999. Much of the on-the-ground chaplain coordination with diverse US forces and with NATO chaplains would come through Zalis. Several years after his Kosovo adventures, Zalis reflected on his experiences:

> I was in Kosovo for several months in 1999. I was the first KFOR chaplain. I supervised directly or indirectly about 60 chaplains from various countries. I visited these chaplains at their units all over Kosovo. I really got to know the geography of the region from all these trips. I had a German deputy KFOR chaplain that worked for me. I think I might have been the only Army chaplain in history who worked directly for a foreign general officer. The commander was a four-star general at the NATO headquarters in Pristina. There was always a sense of danger in Kosovo in 1999. We had good military intelligence that told us when civilian riots were happening and we avoided those areas at those times. There was a lot of hate in the people's faces, toward each other and toward the NATO troops in their country. The US and NATO troops did a remarkable job of peacekeeping and were very restrained in dealing with the ethnic and religious hatred in the region.[39]

Zalis mentioned, "I frequently conducted Jewish religious services, several at Camp Bondsteel and many more at other remote locations. We lived humbly in NATO tents; it was very cold and the bases were underdeveloped. Rosh Hashana services were a special blessing to perform." In elaborating on his experiences in traveling throughout Kosovo on supervisory chaplain visits, Zalis stated, "Personally, I felt in danger every time I went out on civilian roads, which was all the time. Traffic in the small villages slowed down to a crawl and the driver and guards were very vigilant to ensure nothing happened to us." In his capacity as the senior chaplain in Kosovo, Zalis organized some nation-building chaplain events. He commented, "While in Kosovo I organized two special chaplain meetings, where all the NATO and other chaplains in Kosovo came together for conferences." When a US soldier died in an accident in Kosovo, Zalis recalled, "I spent time with the corpse and the unit chaplain and the unit. I then accompanied the body to the mortuary affairs unit at Landsthul Hospital in Germany where the remains were prepared for shipment to the United States."[40]

Janet Horton, of V Corps, used her skills as a religious adviser to assist her commander, Lieutenant General (LTG) Jay Hendricks, in understanding the manipulative use of religion by Serbians and others in Kosovo. Realizing that Milosevic and his followers had never been religious people, Janet Horton provided research that showed religious issues were becoming a propaganda tool to incite nationalistic and pietistic fervor among a people who had mostly been irreligious for almost 70 years of communist rule. Calling Milosevic and his cabinet "the people of the propaganda," Janet Horton warned that religious manipulation was being used to persuade people to achieve secular goals and militancy against the US and NATO peacekeeping forces.[41]

In her capacity at V Corps HQ in Germany, Janet Horton helped to coordinate the response to tons of donated items sent from the United States to the people of Kosovo. Commanders of units in Kosovo naturally looked to their chaplains to distribute these humanitarian supplies. The chaplains in units were so busy distributing donated items to Kosovars that they could potentially neglect the primary religious support mission to US soldiers. In coordination with Chaplain (LTC) James Goodwill in Kosovo, Janet Horton recommended a policy where chaplains would keep track of how many hours they spent on humanitarian missions, with primary emphasis being on the religious support mission. When 8,000 pounds of school supplies were donated to Kosovar children, Goodwill and Janet Horton ensured that benevolent missions to the civilian community, though important to win the hearts and minds of the local population, were secondary to meeting the religious needs of US troops in a hostile fire zone in Kosovo.[42]

The role of the task force chaplain in Kosovo was essentially like a typical brigade chaplain position in the US Army. While most of the chaplains in Kosovo fell under the task force structure, many did not. Kovach supervised those who were under the task force hierarchy, while KFOR Chaplain Zalis supervised those chaplains in Kosovo not under the task force. Serving with the 2d Brigade under the 1st Infantry Division, Kovach arrived at Camp Bondsteel, Kosovo, as the task force chaplain in July 1999. He was assigned to the 2d Brigade only a few weeks before deploying to Kosovo. Arriving first at Camp Able Sentry in Macedonia, Kovach spent the majority of his Balkans tour working out of Camp Bondsteel, Kosovo. In speaking of his role as task force chaplain, Kovach stated, "My main job was to ensure quality religious support throughout the task force. Initially this meant I had to do a lot of traveling in convoys of three armed vehicles in order to visit my Unit Ministry Teams (UMTs). As the Task Force *Falcon* chaplain, I directly supervised seven UMTs."[43]

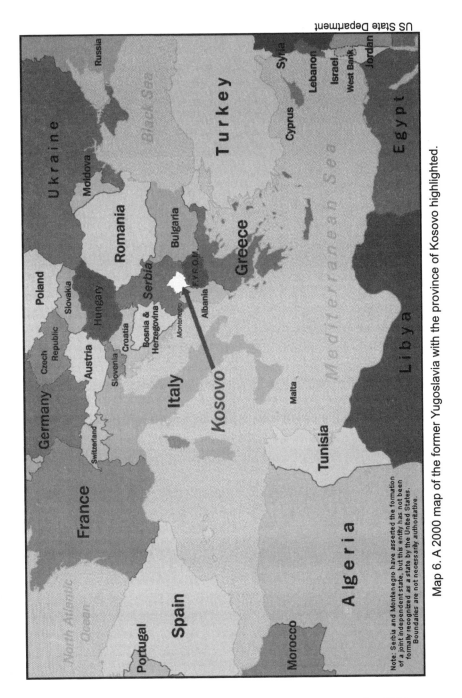

Map 6. A 2000 map of the former Yugoslavia with the province of Kosovo highlighted.

Note: Serbia and Montenegro have asserted the formation of a joint independent state, but this entity has not been formally recognized as a state by the United States. Boundaries are not necessarily authoritative.

Kovach remarked that living conditions in Kosovo in 1999 were humble. He commented, "The camp was very austere. We lived in tents and worshiped any place we could get out of the weather. First, we held religious services in tents but later on we had a chapel constructed. The region outside the camp was sparsely populated, as this area suffered ethnic cleansing and the local people were reluctant at first to move back into their homes." As far as types of ministries Kovach performed or coordinated, they consisted of religious services of numerous denominations, counseling, ministering to the injured at the hospital, coordinating subordinate chaplain activities, and interacting with local indigenous clergy. Kovach praised Chaplain Assistant SSG Edwardo Apodaca, who kept the office running smoothly and supervised force protection. When asked if there were times in Kosovo that he did not feel safe, Kovach stated, "Yes. Initially when we first arrived, we were part of the teams that went to mosques and churches to look for stashed weapons. We knew from place to place that angry locals had rifles, mortars, hand grenades, and placed land mines in many areas. But the longer we were there the less intimidated we were about these things." He somewhat jokingly remembered an eccentric Serbian who randomly harassed Camp Bondsteel, calling him "the mad mortar man" who occasionally lobbed mortars toward the camp.[44]

In October 1999, Causey replaced Kovach in Kosovo as the Task Force *Eagle* chaplain. Assigned to the 3d Brigade under the 1st Infantry Division, Causey stated, "I worked for two commanders, the task force commander and the brigade commander. I was very close to both of them as a pastor, adviser, and special staff member." The expanding mission throughout 1999 and into 2000 meant that Causey supervised 15 UMTs assigned to base camps scattered throughout Kosovo. Causey commented that some of the things that worked well during his tour in Kosovo were the moving of chaplains to various areas to provide comprehensive religious support, the worship services, the force protection provided by chaplain assistants for chaplains, and the bringing together of local religious leaders to promote peace. As far as being in personal danger, Causey stated, "We took direct fire only one time on a convoy. No one was injured."[45]

One of the chaplain assistants that worked in Kosovo in the fall of 1999 was SSG Elbert Jackson of the 3d Brigade, 1st Infantry Division. As the senior Task Force *Eagle* chaplain assistant, Elbert Jackson was responsible for chaplain assistant issues at Camp Bondsteel and Camp Montief, Kosovo, and Camp Able Sentry, Macedonia. He also managed supplies and chaplain assistant personnel issues for the 12 chaplain assistants in the task force. Elbert Jackson stated that he enjoyed administrating "prayer night, choir, holiday services, prayer breakfasts, and movie nights" and that he enjoyed the working harmony between chaplains of different faiths. He also remarked that he found it interesting to meet religious leaders from the local communities as well as chaplains from other NATO nations. When asked if he ever felt like he was in danger, he responded "Once or twice. These were times we were asked to join elements looking for mass grave sites as well as weapons stored in religious structures in the area."[46]

Chaplains experienced diverse ministries, challenges, and opportunities in Kosovo. Traditionally the chaplain assigned to a unit deploys with that unit. Some chaplains serve in field units, others in administrative headquarters, and others in hospitals, at airfields, or have itinerant ministries. For example, Chaplain Powers of the 2-18th Field Artillery was assigned to an airfield in Albania from June through July 1999 in support of operations in Kosovo. He remarked that he had a good relationship with the commander, made many friends, and enjoyed being a chaplain to his soldiers.[47] Chaplain Scott Jones was assigned to the 67th Combat Support Hospital, a unit that took over and ran the hospital at Camp Bondsteel. Arriving in July 1999, Scott Jones recalled that he "provided religious services and Bible Studies for staff and patients" and had a challenging ministry working with the 120 trauma victims that came through the hospital while he was there.[48]

Special Forces Chaplain (CPT) Steven Mark Jones performed a unique and challenging ministry in Kosovo at this time. Serving with the 10th Special Forces (SF), Mark Jones was in Kosovo in April–May and again in December 1999. In the events leading up to deployment, Mark Jones stated, "1999 was a volatile time in Kosovo. When we got our orders, the stress level raised. FRG [Family Readiness Group] meetings were all well attended. My unit had the best FRG I ever saw in the Army, as the SF community sticks together." In speaking of his relationship with other chaplains during his deployments, he recalled, "I always knew a chaplain I could refer people to. The SF chaplains had a good relationship with the troops. If I was in a remote location and a chaplain was needed in another area, I knew who to contact." Mark Jones related an interesting ministry experience as follows:

> I participated in a worship service with a Polish Army chaplain who was an Orthodox priest. The service was conducted on the Polish compound. Some of my soldiers and I attended. I participated by singing a solo, doing a Bible reading, and leading in public prayer. The local Serbian Orthodox choir sang. The service was in three languages, Polish, English, and Serbian. It was a unique experience for me and I thoroughly enjoyed it.[49]

Kosovo in 1999 was not a safe place. The NATO bombing campaign forced the warring Serbian factions to come to peace. Tensions were seething between Christian Orthodox Serbians and Muslims of mostly Albanian descent in Kosovo. Serbian military and paramilitary forces still roamed the countryside, first seeking to evade NATO air strikes then attempting to evade NATO troops on the ground in Kosovo. Then, with NATO peacekeepers separating rival factions, some deprecation by Muslims toward Serbians reciprocated in kind. As Mark Jones recalled:

> During my April–May 1999 trip to Kosovo there were frequent small arms fire fights between US troops and Kosovar bandits. On one patrol my men found a cave with lots of ammunition inside. Within the cave were side chambers, one of which was piled high with decomposed human corpses. The dead were mostly men with some women and children. This was the results of an ethnic cleansing event. I was there to reinforce a reverence for the dead and to minister to soldiers. This was nasty duty, as the bodies were in a horrible state of decay and had a horrid stench. Our unit respectfully loaded the corpses onto trucks and transported them to civilian Serbian officials so they could be identified and properly buried. I spent a lot of time talking and in prayer with individual soldiers to help them get through this gruesome experience.[50]

Chaplain Assistant SFC Craig Gardner was assigned to Camp Bondsteel, Kosovo, in 1999 to work primarily with Chaplain (MAJ) Robert Loring. He experienced the danger still prevalent in Kosovo during his first night:

> The first night at Bondsteel [August 1999] I was in the Engineer Brigade TOC [Tactical Operations Center] walking with other soldiers and sergeants. Someone yelled for everyone to be quiet and everyone gathered around the radio. The task force was operating off one radio frequency. The Serbs would try to creep through the wire at night. The OP/LP [Observation Post/Listening Post] would see them and report it. Then the commander would send out a tank and a Bradley squad to intercept them and the soldiers in the TOC would listen to the whole exchange. It reminded me that there were people outside the wire that wanted to hurt us.[51]

Mark Jones remembered the following dangerous incident from his December 1999 ministry in Kosovo.

In December 1999 my SF unit had a memorable experience. We were planning a convoy operation, so the day before one vehicle with a few well armed soldiers did a recon of the proposed route. There was a Russian convoy about to use this route, and the route was mined and ready for an ambush. Our one vehicle inadvertently drove into this ambush before the Russian convoy arrived. The vehicle hit a mine and flipped over. When the enemy forces saw that it was a US vehicle that was hit they disbursed. The Russian convoy then arrived and rescued the men, even though the area was loaded with antipersonnel mines. One soldier died and another had a broken arm. Four of the Russian soldiers who rescued our men were awarded medals by our two-star commander, certainly a unique thing to observe. I spent most of December with this US Army SF unit.[52]

Gardner related the following harrowing experience while he was on a routine patrol mission. After leaving Loring at a secure location,

I met up with the Engineer platoon leader and an Infantry platoon leader. They asked if I wanted to go on a walking patrol with them. We had just left the camp and were walking through the barricades when somebody threw a grenade and popped off three rounds about 80 meters in front of us. I wasn't scared then. I got down behind a basket full of rock and started looking for targets. It was later on as we continued to patrol through the dark alleys that I began to become fearful, crossing lit areas and main roads. I started to come to grips with what had happened.[53]

At the close of 1999, chaplain ministries in Kosovo were developing from initial and temporary attempts at providing religious support to soldiers in a hostile fire zone to more established routines and better facilities. At first, chaplains and chaplain assistants conducted religious services on the hoods of vehicles or in a clearing in the woods or in tents within the wire. Logistically, UMTs in Kosovo had fantastic support from Germany. Janet Horton helped commanders realize that for a temporary mission an itinerant chaplain ministry is fine. However, for a sustained mission in a developing theater of operations, more structure and stability were needed to maximize chaplain support to soldiers. In speaking to her commanders, Janet Horton remarked, "We needed a planned, cleared, designated worship space by asking, how long do you want our chaplains to do gypsy ministry?" The commanders got the point and chaplains began to get designated chapel and office tents. Then a containerized chapel was sent to Kosovo, and plans were developed to build wood chapels throughout Kosovo for US troops. Although chaplains still enjoyed performing religious services on the hoods of vehicles when necessary, much had changed in Kosovo throughout 1999 for Army chaplain ministries.

A unique ministry related to Kosovo in 1999 actually occurred in Germany. In the late summer, enemy prisoners of war (EPW) from Serbia were transferred to Manheim, Germany, for holding and interrogation. Chaplain Baktis, already stationed in that area with an aviation battalion, was put on special orders for 6 weeks to serve as a chaplain to the detainees. Baktis was selected for this mission because he was an Eastern Orthodox priest and able to relate to the culture of the Balkans people. There were only two prisoners at this incarceration center, one Eastern Orthodox and one Muslim in name but not in practice. Because of media, military, and Red Cross interest, Baktis commented, "I frequently had to brief the V Corps [Chaplain Janet] Horton and USAREUR Chaplain David Hicks. This was a highly visible and scrutinized ministry, the most ever in my career." Baktis stated it was hard to get religious supplies in the Serbian language on short notice for these detainees, and he provided pastoral counseling through a translator for both prisoners and shared the sacrament with the Eastern Orthodox prisoner. "I visited them weekly," Baktis recalled, "and I got the Muslim prisoner a Koran and a prayer rug and I shared the sacrament weekly with the other prisoner."[54] Not to be overlooked was the ministry to the prison guards on this special high-visibility assignment in Manheim. Baktis stated, "There was a lot of pressure on these special project soldiers assigned to a separate building that few knew existed. I counseled with the guards." Baktis elaborated, "I did some debriefing mostly having to do with stress caused by phone calls from the Defense Department in Washington. The commander and soldiers guarding the EPWs were held to confidentiality, so they could not even speak to their family or friends. I became their only vent."[55]

Ministry to Displaced Kosovar Refugees

Aggressive Serbian military and paramilitary activities in Kosovo in 1999 created a catastrophic refugee crisis. As negotiations for peace dragged from 1998 to 1999, Serbians who stalled and delayed at the negotiating table made allowances for their Serbian brethren in Kosovo to conduct extensive and vicious ethnic cleansing. After the NATO bombing campaign began, Serbs were very active in vindictive and brutal offenses against Albanians or those of Muslim descent in Kosovo. US Secretary of State Albright narrated this scenario as follows:

> Before NATO bombing began, the Serb offensive had already driven a hundred thousand Kosovars from their homes. This figure grew rapidly in subsequent days. . . . Homes in hundreds of villages were burned. Scholars, journalists, and political leaders who had advocated independence were tracked down and killed. Tens of thousands of people were made to board trains, which were then sealed from the outside and sent to the Albanian border. Thousands of others were herded along the same route by car or on foot. Serb security forces stripped the departing Kosovars of birth certificates, driver's licenses, car registrations, and other proof of identification. Their message to the Albanians was clear: 'You must leave and we will not let you back.'[56]

On 21 April 1999, Vice President Al Gore announced US plans to relocate up to 20,000 Kosovar refugees. He said those with family ties in America and those in vulnerable circumstances, such as single mothers or people with medical conditions, would be given priority. The first Kosovar refugees reached America in early May. Those with relatives in the United States arrived on commercial flights to meet family members at New York's John F. Kennedy Airport. Those to be linked with sponsors arrived at McGuire Air Force Base in New Jersey on charter flights. From there, they boarded buses bound for Fort Dix's Doughboy Gymnasium where an interagency task force welcomed them. The Department of Health and Human Services headed the effort, supported by the Defense Department, Immigration and Naturalization Service, State Department, American Red Cross, New Jersey National Guard, and nongovernmental resettlement agencies. When each refugee family finished processing, soldiers and Immigration and Naturalization Service interpreters escorted them to assigned dormitories. Army chaplains made up a valuable part of this team.[57]

The Kosovars entered the United States with the legal status of refugees according to immigration officials. As such, they could work in the United States and could decide to stay. They could apply for permanent residency after 1 year and for citizenship after 5 years. US officials, however, said they expected most of the refugees will want to return to Kosovo, and the US government is committed to helping them return once it is safe to do so. The flow of refugees to Fort Dix stopped at the end of May 1999. US officials said future refugees bound for the United States would complete processing overseas and go directly to relatives or sponsors.[58]

Figure 11. Ethnic Albanians wave to military and civilian officials on arrival at New Jersey's McGuire Air Force Base. The refugees traveled from Macedonia to reach temporary safe haven in America.

Throughout the spring and early summer of 1999, Fort Dix, New Jersey, was the site for a huge refugee relocation program entitled Operation PROVIDE REFUGE. This joint task force (JTF) was responsible for the safe and professional inprocessing of Kosovar Albanians into the United States. Over 4,000 ethnic Albanian refugees processed through Fort Dix, arriving there after a 13-hour flight from Macedonia. Men and women of all ages arrived exhausted and frightened, but were quickly greeted at Fort Dix by reception teams of military and civilian professionals.

Army Chaplain (LTC) Eric Wester was the JTF chaplain for Operation PROVIDE REFUGE. From the very beginning of this mission, it was imperative that the religious needs of the refugees be respected while not overlooking the religious needs of the task force workers. Wester outlined the responsibilities of chaplains involved in Operation PROVIDE REFUGE as follows:

a. Provide for religious services and related chaplain activities for the JTF.

b. Advise the command on matters of morals, religion, and morale.

c. Prepare a daily SITREP [Situational Report].

d. Maintain Chapel 5, Bldg 5959 (Hope Chapel).

e. Track religious census of refugees arriving at the Welcome Center.

f. Provide information about religion, customs and courtesies to the JTF.

g. Respond to critical incidents involving JTF personnel.

h. Maintain records related to chaplaincy activities.

i. Establish a baseline of religious supplies and equipment for the JTF.

j. Coordinate with interagency personnel and nongovernment agencies.

k. Operate safely and integrate risk management to the daily operations.[59]

Chaplains with the JTF Operation PROVIDE REFUGE mission coordinated all activities with Wester. The refugees stayed in an area of Fort Dix called The Village, with Chaplain (MAJ) John Stepp and Chaplain (CPT) Mohammad Khan assigned directly to provide religious support to

The Village military personnel. Religious support to the Albanian Muslims was contracted out to Albanian speaking Muslims or other Muslim Imams who used Albanian translators to communicate. Organizationally, the Joint Task Force Unit Ministry Team (JTFUMT) was responsible for supervision of all UMT activities; supervising religious volunteers; contracting with civilian clergy; consulting with commanders on religious, moral, and morale issues; and serving as an initial point of contact for all chaplain or religious issues. The Village UMTs had the mission of direct religious support to the soldiers who worked in The Village and advised the JTF chaplain on any major issues. The Village UMTs also conducted a religious census of each arriving refugee as part of their inprocessing. With all of these activities related to the refugee mission, the religious support mission of the entire Fort Dix community was not to be neglected. The installation UMTs provided administrative, budget planning, and funds distribution to the JTFUMTs through the JTF chaplain; served as a central location for all outside religious visitors; and provided for the religious needs of the larger Fort Dix community.

During the short duration of this mission, among the Kosovar refugees' there was one wedding, five or six births, and two deaths. Wester, Stepp, and Donald Holdridge coauthored an article describing their experiences with Operation PROVIDE REFUGE. They stated:

> We had the privilege of working with the ethnic Albanian Kosovar refugees as part of Joint Task Force Operation PROVIDE REFUGE at Fort Dix, New Jersey, in the spring and summer of 1999. Refugees were inprocessed and medically cleared before joining sponsoring congregations or communities throughout the United States.

> All but 6 of the 4,200 refugees who came through Fort Dix were Muslim. These six were Roman Catholics. Our advice to the commander and our recommendation to the Department of Health and Human Services was to use Albanian-speaking Imams and Roman Catholic clergy to enable the refugees to practice their faith.

> In the weeks prior to arriving at Fort Dix, many of the refugees we met had their land stripped away, their homes torched, their legal documents destroyed, and family members raped and killed. All they brought with them were a few hand-carried items and their faith. Respecting their faith and encouraging hope were two cornerstones of our religious support planning.

As Army chaplains, our primary missions were to minister to soldiers working as part of the task force and to advise the command about the importance of religion in this humanitarian mission. But we also spent many evening hours trying to get to know the refugee families. They loved being around American soldiers, and we loved them. This mission gave us the chance to practice our constitutional duty of protecting and respecting everyone's right to freedom of religion, whether they were a US soldier or an ethnic Albanian refugee.[60]

At the time of the Kosovar refugee mission, Holdridge was in the Army Reserve, assigned to the 365th Engineer Battalion, Pennsylvania. Assigned to Task Force Operation PROVIDE REFUGE, Holdridge recalled:

I was excited to be able to interact with another culture and try to help these displaced people through a difficult time in their lives. . . . Chaplain Stepp and I spend every evening talking with the refugees, kicking the soccer ball around with the kids, pushing them on the swings, and trying to learn their language (The children were picking up English much faster than we were picking up Albanian!). . . . I remember hearing their ethnic music being played out of the chapel steeple loudspeakers in the evenings. Yet, at 2155 every night, Kate Smith's "God Bless America" was played.

As chaplains, we wanted to show these predominately-Muslim people that there are Christians who cared for them. Some refugees did say that some Eastern Orthodox neighbors warned them of Milosevic's troops coming, or helped hide them. America can't help everyone, but we can do something where we are at. The charity of the American public ought to be commended by the media more than it is.[61]

Stepp stated: "My ministry was the same as all chaplains—perform or provide for the free exercise of religion of each soldier in the task force and to advise the commander on how to meet the religious needs of the refugees." He elaborated, "To begin, we always put the spiritual needs of the soldiers first. Worship for soldiers was conducted at the Fort Dix post chapel. The ministry to the refugees was to show by actions to these Kosovar Muslims that true Christians can be trusted. We demonstrated that through providing for their spiritual needs."[62] Six years after his ministry as The Village chaplain for Operation PROVIDE REFUGE, Stepp had the following reflections:

> I believe that the soldiers and refugees went away knowing that spiritual freedom is alive in America, and the refugees left knowing that true Christians know the meaning of love and can be trusted. We deliberately chose not to shoot them with the gospel, but instead to plant seeds of Christ's love through our relationships with them. Then, we trust God to send someone to water that seed and help it to grow. I believe it is Christian to remove barriers from other's lives that prevent them from having a personal relationship with Jesus Christ. Each person we meet should be closer to God from knowing us. We, UMTs, helped remove the barrier of hate and prejudice toward the Christians (hate and prejudice created by the war) that permeated the refugees lives. I believe we successfully accomplished that mission.[63]

The only Muslim US Army chaplain assigned to JTF Operation PROVIDE REFUGE was Khan of the 519th Military Intelligence Battalion, Fort Bragg, North Carolina. Khan served at the refugee camp in May and June 1999, after being ordered to report immediately to Fort Dix from Fort Bragg. Because of the immediate need to have a Muslim chaplain at the refugee center, Khan received no preliminary briefings or training. Khan stated, "Being the only Imam and Islamic faith chaplain, I was very welcomed by the commander and I had a very cordial relationship with the staff and all NCOs." On meeting the mostly Muslim refugees, Kahn recalled the human tragedy of Kosovo in the faces of the very young and the very old, as well as those pregnant or injured in various ways. Khan stated: "This was a very draining human drama," and "the other chaplains in this task force were friendly and cooperative."[64]

MAJ Ronald Kopp, USAR

Figure 12. CH (CPT) Mohammed Khan ministers to the religious needs of Muslim ethnic Albanians at Fort Dix, NJ.

As a Muslim chaplain, Khan served as a religious adviser to the commander and to JTF Chaplain Wester. Khan stated, "I was advising the commander and the UMTs regarding dietary needs of Kosovar Muslim refugees and helped establish worship places for them and arranged Albanian speaking Imams for their Jumma [Friday evening] services." Being unable to speak Albanian, Khan used Albanian-speaking civilian volunteers from New York City, Department of the Army linguists, and Albanian speakers from the US Department of Immigration. One of the many duties of Khan and the other chaplains on this mission was to screen civilian religious groups who wanted to influence, proselytize, or in some way influence the refugees. Khan remarked it was an emotional and disturbing event to listen to the refugees' stories of their persecution in Kosovo. While referring the refugees to the appropriate aid agencies, Khan stated that most refugees were more concerned about the welfare of their loved ones left behind than their own well being. Khan stated, "The Kosovar refugee resettlement mission at Fort Dix, New Jersey, was overwhelming as well as challenging to all chaplains who worked with them. . . . We had only one chaplain assistant [SPC James T. Mack]. He helped all us chaplains all the time. This 30-day experience with the refugees I will remember for a very long time."[65]

Developing Chaplain Issues in Kosovo, 2000–2001

Kosovo in 2000 was a region in chaos. The rebuilding necessary after the NATO bombing campaign, which ended 9 June 1999, was only beginning. Approximately 45,000 NATO troops, including a large US force, entered a seething Kosovo. United Nations Security Council Resolution 1244 established the UN mission in Kosovo (UNMIK) to administer and help rebuild the shattered region with the cooperation of the European Union. Both would share responsibility for humanitarian affairs, institution building, and reconstruction.[66] Militarily the mission in Kosovo was maintained with a combination of NATO, European Union, and United Nations support. For civilians, sanitation in Kosovo was deplorable. An outbreak of tularemia became a scourge to the Kosovars. Tularemia is a bacterial disease found in humans and animals that develops from water contaminated by decaying carcasses. Often spread by rats, the disease affects humans in their eyes and throats and may produce ulcers. As one news report stated:

> A large outbreak of tularemia occurred in Kosovo in the early postwar period, 1999–2000. Epidemiologic and

environmental investigations were conducted to identify sources of infection, modes of transmission, and household risk factors. Case and control status was verified by enzyme-linked immunosorbent assay, Western blot, and microagglutination assay. A total of 327 serologically confirmed cases of tularemia pharyngitis and cervical lymphadenitis were identified in 21 of 29 Kosovo municipalities. Matched analysis of 46 case households and 76 control households suggested that infection was transmitted through contaminated food or water and that the source of infection was rodents. Environmental circumstances in war-torn Kosovo led to epizootic rodent tularemia and its spread to resettled rural populations living under circumstances of substandard housing, hygiene, and sanitation.[67]

US troops deploying to Kosovo in 2000 lived at a higher quality of life than the majority of the Kosovo people. Although the initial US and NATO base camps constructed in 1999 were quite humble, they quickly became safe and sanitary locations for soldiers to live and for chaplains to minister. As a Roman Catholic priest with the 82d Airborne Division, Chaplain (CPT) John McLain arrived in April 2002 on a specific tasker and not with his unit. First stationed at Camp Able Sentry in Macedonia, he thereafter moved north into Kosovo and rotated his ministry with Camp Montieth, Camp Bondsteel, and various checkpoints. The Task Force *Falcon* chaplain at that time was Causey; McLain served as the deputy task force chaplain. While describing his relationship with Causey as tense, McLain stated that he spent a lot of time visiting troops, including the Special Forces soldiers at various A-Team locations. McLain recalled that there was a slight anti-American sentiment, but he experienced no violence while traveling around Kosovo with a Special Forces soldier for protection.[68]

US Army chaplains served in Kosovo for various lengths of time. Chaplain Firtko of the 1st Battalion, 36th Infantry Regiment was in Kosovo from 15 May through 15 July 2000. Stationed at Camp Montieth, Firtko served as the installation chaplain and chapel manager at Montieth. Soldiers at that time at Camp Montieth lived in dome-shaped metal sea huts with plywood floors and electricity, with separate common use male and female bathrooms. Firtko stated there was an ongoing dangerous situation because his battalion was stationed along the Serbian border at a time when Serbs were forming for an attack into Kosovo—an attack that never materialized. Firtko stated that providing field services at the Serbian border for his soldiers was a memorable event, and that he did "much counseling to homesick soldiers and those with marital problems." Firtko recalled the time when Wiccan soldiers asked him to designate for them a place of worship, with the commander allowing them a location outdoors under the moonlight. Firtko stated, "Morale was generally good," and that he had little contact with family support groups back home.[69]

Eastern Orthodox Chaplain Baktis had a longstanding ministry in Kosovo. Baktis thoroughly enjoyed being in this land steeped with Eastern Orthodox history, and he frequently networked with indigenous Orthodox clergy in a variety of capacities. Baktis stated, "I was in Kosovo from May through July 2000. Then I went on a monthly basis to hold Eastern Orthodox church services and to help the IO [Information Operations] cell with religious and cultural issues, to try and help the Serbian population in Kosovo." As far as his best memories of ministry in Kosovo, Baktis recalled that he enjoyed fellowship with another Eastern Orthodox American priest, he happily visited numerous Eastern Orthodox religious sites, he was thrilled to concelebrate at the ordination of a local priest at a nearby monastery, and he was delighted to concelebrate an Eastern Orthodox church service with a Russian Army chaplain.[70] Baktis remarked, "Destruction was horrible. Churches were destroyed for no military reason. . . . This was a bittersweet experience. As a US Army chaplain, ministry was good. Relationships to local clergy and NATO allies were satisfying. It was sad to see the suffering of innocent children. Seeing tanks parked next to churches was a weird experience." Assigned to an Engineer unit, Baktis stated:

> Our unit had a mission of uncovering mass graves. Our Engineers took booby traps from graves, whether it was one grave or a mass grave site. Then an international team did the recovery of corpses. A lot of Finnish civilians did the forensic work. My troops also secured the area so shallow grave sites could be identified. I saw the corpses and it reminded me that war is an ugly business.[71]

Chaplain (CPT) Steven Simpson and Chaplain Kenneth Hubbs had occasions for complaint in their summer and fall 2000 tours in Kosovo. Simpson, assigned to the 2d Battalion, 37th Armored Regiment, claimed that an "inexperienced brigade chaplain caused much turmoil among the UMTs," further stating that there was "no UMT cohesion, only conflict."[72] Hubbs of the 141st Signal Battalion lamented the fact that even though his widely dispersed soldiers were often in the area of other chaplains, those chaplains did not visit his soldiers. The Army chaplaincy calls this area coverage, meaning chaplains in a geographic area minister to soldiers in that area even though the soldiers are from other units. Hubbs stated, "For the vast majority of my soldiers, I was the only chaplain who saw them . . . even though there were chaplains in their immediate area."[73]

The experiences of Chaplain (CPT) William Horton in Kosovo show how aggressive planning and training can make for a successful deployment. William Horton was assigned to the 2-327th Infantry Battalion, stationed in Kosovo from August 2000 through February 2001. William Horton stated that "morale was very high" for the Kosovo mission, and that his chaplain-to-commander relationship was "very strong." As a battalion chaplain located near Vitina, Kosovo, William Horton found that "weekly training and fellowship with the other task force chaplains kept communication lines open and allowed time to reflect spiritually."[74]

With soldiers spread in three main locations in Kosovo, including along the tense Albanian border, William Horton was able to encourage soldier participation in religious services by arriving at each forward observation base (FOB) at least 1 hour before the scheduled religious service. By designating unit religious coordinators at each FOB, William Horton was able to publicize and encourage soldiers to attend chapel services. In a unique ministry experience, William Horton was able to minister to a grieving Kosovar family. He recalled, "The US paid to relocate a family, which had their daughter killed by a US trooper. I made monthly chaplain visits to this grieving family with a translator and others. The family was very forgiving and received us well. We played with the other kids in the family and brought gifts. They were very accepting."[75]

Two chaplains who found themselves in dangerous situations around this time were William Horton and Steven Mark Jones. For William Horton an incident occurred in February 2001 as his unit was transitioning with their replacement unit. In the village of Vitina there was a house blown up next to the FOB where some of his soldiers were stationed. The explosion shook the building where William Horton and the troops were located, but none of the shocked, dust-covered soldiers were injured.[76] Mark Jones of the 10th Special Forces Group related his dangerous experience as follows:

> I had an interesting experience in October 2000 in Kosovo. The battalion commander, sergeant major, and I joined an A-Team for a routine SF mission. The patrol came upon a typical humble shepherd's dwelling in a field, but our troops discovered booby traps around it. The men did a probe of the area and assaulted this 20'x 40' building, which contained three rooms and a separate shed. The US troops were so professional that they captured the

two Kosovar Muslims inside without firing a shot, and discovered six to seven rifles and thousands of rounds of ammunition. On this same mission later on we took fire from some smugglers near the northern border of Kosovo, mortar and rifle fire. My SF troops dismounted, assaulted the enemy positions, killed two enemy thugs, suffering no injuries to my men.[77]

As the Kosovo mission transitioned from 2000 to 2001, concerns were raised about the trauma of combat or semicombat experiences on the soldiers rotating home. Chaplains and mental health workers briefed soldiers returning from a 6-month rotation in the hostile fire zone of Kosovo on how to smoothly transition back to family life. Soldiers received mandatory briefings in Kosovo as part of their outprocessing, while family members back home were invited to voluntary reintegration and reunion meetings in their local areas. As one news report stated:

CAMP BONDSTEEL, Kosovo (December 15, 2000)— As more than 3,000 soldiers prepare to leave Kosovo this week, officials want to make sure the transition back home is as stress-free as possible. The vast majority of troops have no problems returning home, but a few can run into difficulties, including alcohol-related incidents and domestic violence.

Commanders, chaplains, and doctors have worked since September to give reunion briefs to homeward bound troops, talking to spouses in Germany and handing out mental health surveys to combat some problems. . . .

Officials are fanning across the US sector of Kosovo, giving the reunion briefs unit by unit. First, soldiers are given the mental health survey, and then chaplains tell them what to expect. . . . Besides the survey, religious leaders are meeting with soldiers, said Chaplain (MAJ) Tim Bledsole.[78]

Kosovo in 2001 was a potentially volatile place struggling with rebuilding and autonomy. The US and NATO forces had been in the country since 1999. The intention was to terminate military and paramilitary aggression in Kosovo by signing a peace treaty and temporarily inserting NATO-led peacekeepers. Difficulties developed in determining when to turn over NATO and US operations to legitimate Kosovar civilians or government entities. Questions arose as to what the desired end state in Kosovo really was, and how to achieve it. As one article mentioned, "It is critical to articulate the desired end state for an ethnic conflict before establishing conditions for successfully transferring control from military to civilian agencies. . . . The greatest concern continues to be restoring some form of normalcy with limited resources and dealing with competing demands that are usually associated with functions outside of military jurisdiction."[79] Complicating the NATO military handover of responsibilities to qualified Kosovars was the friction between the military and nongovernmental organizations (NGOs). Although there were over 300 civilian aid agencies from throughout the world operating in Kosovo in 2001, the relationship of these NGOs to the military and to military chaplains was poorly structured.[80]

Chaplain (MAJ) Robert Land arrived in Kosovo in December 2000 as the Task Force *Falcon* chaplain, serving at Camp Bondsteel through June 2001. Assigned with the 2d Brigade Combat Team under the 1st Armored Division, Land supervised 12 chaplains who were scattered throughout Kosovo and Macedonia. In reflecting on his time in Kosovo, Land remarked:

> When we arrived Camp Bondsteel was pretty well developed. There were two new beautiful chapels, so we had the temporary containerized chapels redeployed to Germany. I had a good team of 12 chaplains. There were only a few times that I had to get firm with them. We laid out the ground rules early and there were no major issues. We had good support reacting to crisis situations. My team was mostly Active Duty with some Reserve component UMTs.[81]

As the Task Force *Falcon* chaplain, there were many unique duties placed on Land. For example, at times there was a need for specific religious faith group coverage, these being occasions for Roman Catholic Chaplain Habereck or Jewish Chaplain Leinwand to come from Germany to Kosovo to minister. When the need for a Muslim chaplain arose, Land arranged for Chaplain (CPT) Muhammad Shabazz to come and help. The Army Chief of Chaplains, Chaplain (MG) Gaylord Gunhus, came to Kosovo at Christmas 2000 to celebrate and worship. Problems arose when chaplains came temporarily to visit troops in Kosovo without coordinating with Land's office. Land stated, "There were visiting chaplains from USAREUR that did not coordinate well. Some came to visit small numbers of soldiers and did not coordinate with me. This was awkward and took a lot of my time to coordinate with these visiting chaplains."[82] While in Kosovo, Land mentioned, "There were a few flare-ups of hostilities. One event was when tensions arose with the border conflict with Macedonia, when a civilian bus blew up nearby with casualties. At another time, we were traveling on narrow dirt roads to attend a funeral for a local girl and we heard artillery rounds going off nearby, but we were unhurt. Further, when we first arrived a lieutenant stepped on a mine and was seriously injured." In summarizing his tour in Kosovo, Land commented, "It was very rewarding to meet chaplains from other nations. I was thankful we had no fatalities in our unit. This tour was a highlight of my ministry. It was a real world experience. Overall, the mission was very successful. We worked as a team. I held them to a high standard and they did great, with God's providence over all."[83]

The relationship between the commander and the chaplain is a crucial relationship that must be enhanced for the chaplain to succeed. Chaplain (CPT) Martin Kendrick of the 2-502d Infantry Regiment said that, "I had a very close relationship with my commander. He relied on me heavily to provide necessary spiritual guidance. I also did research on the religious nature of Kosovo and then briefed the commander."[84] Chaplain (CPT) Steven Cantrell of the 716th Military Police Battalion said of his relationship with his commander, "We met a week before we flew into Sophia, Bulgaria. We traveled by bus convoy to Camp Able Sentry, Macedonia. Once we had inprocessed, we convoyed to Camp Bondsteel. LTC Gyrisko was ecstatic to receive a chaplain. He and I were as close as brothers."[85] Having the full support of their commanders allowed Kendrick and Cantrell to have full freedom of ministry, to have access to supplies and transportation, to have cooperation on local benevolent projects, and to network with indigenous clergy to encourage peacekeeping.

An example of a chaplain making the transition in Kosovo from 2001 to 2002 is Chandler. Serving at Camp Bondsteel from December 2001 through November 2002, Chandler was the first ASG chaplain for Task Force *Falcon*. During this tour, he was promoted to colonel. Chandler stated:

> As the ASG chaplain, I was the senior chaplain in theater. I worked with but did not supervise or rate the task force chaplain or his staff. In my ASG, there were usually about 12 chaplains and 12 chaplain assistants. I would help them with their training and occasionally teach them classes. But my main ministry was to the ASG HQ staff. I also supervised the Camp Able Sentry [CAS] Chaplain in Macedonia. At first it was Chaplain David White. Then there was a gap for a few months where I preached in the CAS chapel until Chaplain (MAJ) Steve Jerles arrived.

I had an excellent chaplain assistant named SFC Tracy Williams. She was proactive, professional, and fun to be with. She did her job very well and was quite capable and competent. She supported and complemented my ministry, a real ministry multiplier.

I conducted a Bible Study once a week in Pristina. A small group would meet with me for prayer, Bible Study, fellowship, singing, and sometimes refreshments. We met in a small metal trailer-type building which was redesigned as a nice air conditioned chapel that could hold about 20 people comfortably.

I made frequent chaplain visits to small numbers of US troops stationed in Albania. There must have been a US Army chaplain there previously, as there were at one time a large number of US troops there. There was a former US Army chapel, a small humble building made out of a concrete bunker. There was an Italian RC priest there who said the Mass regularly for the international military population. When I visited, I would conduct Protestant services. I would go there either by helicopter, which I preferred, or by a long vehicle ride in convoy.

Albania was not safe after dark. Trucks were often ambushed along the road by criminals or paramilitary groups. We were told never to stop any place in Albania except at a US facility. Drug smuggling, prostitution, and crime were epidemic in Albania. Although I met a few very nice Albanian people, the country was poor, filthy, and unsafe. . . . The Muslims in mostly Eastern Orthodox Kosovo want to be aligned with the mostly Muslim nation of Albania. But the Albanians look to Italy for much of their culture, as they share ancient roots that go back to the old Roman Empire. Albanians like Italian food, music, language, and culture.[86]

Chaplain Duties in Maintaining the Peace in Kosovo, 2002–2004

By 2002, there were serious doubts as to the wisdom of the US policy in the Balkans. Bosnia was at a tense peace with thousands of US peacekeepers still deployed to that area. In Kosovo, tensions were still apparent as refugees resettled into homes, war criminals were pursued, and ethnic tensions seethed beneath the NATO attempt at rebuilding the region. In 2002, the United States considered Kosovo a trouble spot that could produce future threats to US security. Peacekeepers in Kosovo attempted to break the cycle of impunity for criminals while training local Kosovars to provide their own security, stability, and safety.[87] By 2002, advances in these areas were minimal. Because the fighting had ceased in Kosovo, there were many cries to bring the US troops home. With a tense peace prevailing in Kosovo, the number of US troops began to decrease. As one news source reported:

> The United States and its allies continue to gradually reduce the number of peacekeepers in the Balkans, but US commanders in the region say their work is far from done.
>
> 'It's still quite early, at the 3-year mark . . . to figure out the endgame,' Army Brig. Gen. Douglas Lute said at his headquarters at Kosovo's Camp Bondsteel. 'And that's the fundamental question: What's the future of Kosovo look like?'
>
> The US-led air war in Kosovo ended in 1999. . . . Three years later, US troops . . . still provide 24-hour security at Serb Orthodox churches. They still wear helmets and don't mix as closely with the locals as their counterparts in Bosnia. . . .
>
> More than 5,000 US peacekeepers remain in Kosovo. In June, NATO agreed to a 25-percent reduction by June 2003, with the US force to shrink by 1,300 troops.
>
> But it is still unclear how long US troops will stay. . . .[88]

Chaplain (CPT) Brian Chepey and Chaplain Assistant SPC De-Angelo Coatie deployed together to Kosovo as a UMT with the 2d Aviation Battalion under the 1st Infantry Division. Serving in Kosovo at Camp Bondsteel from April through November 2002, Coatie said, "My chaplain and I were in synch. We shared the same vision and were able to implement some good ministry." Coatie also stated that he enjoyed helping provide wholesome entertainment for the troops, he liked the Bible Studies, he was happy to visit local religious sites, and he enjoyed coordinating the two to four baptisms held per week for the soldiers. Coatie successfully did all that was expected of a chaplain assistant and more. He administered the chapel, arranged local religious tours, coordinated helicopter transportation for himself and Chepey, helped rebuild and paint local schools, protected the chaplain while on convoys, and worked as a liaison for US Army chaplains to meet indigenous clergy in Kosovo. Coatie was promoted to sergeant E5 while in Kosovo. Coatie had a very positive experience in Kosovo, and while admitting there were stressors, he stated, "Kosovo was a really good deployment."[89]

Camp Bondsteel in 2002 was a bustling community supported by several chaplains. Both Chaplain Chepey and Chaplain Yoon of the 1-7th Battalion Field Artillery were at Bondsteel throughout the summer of 2002. Chepey was the worship leader for the South Chapel on Sunday mornings and the pastor for the evening service at the South Chapel. Yoon led a Bible Study on Tuesday evenings at the South Chapel and provided weekly church services for the US and NATO forces at Pristina. Chepey saw as a highlight of his deployment the fact that he was able to baptize dozens of soldiers and Marines at a natural lake some 7,000 feet high on the nearby mountain affectionately called "Big Duke" by the Americans.

Figure 13. US Army Chief of Chaplains (MG) David Hicks (center) and CA CSM Robert Bush (second from left) meet with US and NATO chaplains in Kosovo, February 2002.

Yoon rejoiced in that he had "freedom of ministry," and stated, "The task force chaplain gave each UMT full support—minimum micromanagement. Because of him, there was a spiritual revival in Kosovo and record high chapel attendance."[90]

Army chaplain ministries in Kosovo were an example of the integration of Reserve component chaplains and chaplain assistants with their Active Duty peers. At any location or time in Kosovo there could be any combination of Reserve and Active Duty chaplains and chaplain assistants working together as UMTs. Senior chaplains in the United States and in Europe were concerned that this integration went smoothly. Chaplain (MAJ) Kenneth Lawson of the 7th ARCOM in Germany made a 15 to 19 July 2002 trip to Kosovo to check on the integration issues, provide training, and assess the Reserve component to Active Duty UMT status and report back to the USAREUR chaplain, the National Guard Bureau chaplain, and the USARC chaplain. Excerpts from his unpublished journal follow:

> 15 July 02—I am now on the bus from Pristina to Camp Bondsteel, Kosovo. Terrible road. Pockets of destruction are all around, ruined buildings and twisted steel everywhere. . . . Culture appears poor and agricultural, some new buildings and industry. . . . On the bus we have to wear body armor and our Kevlar helmets. There is an armed guard on board. . . . Arid rolling hills and a huge valley ideal for the airport, about a ¾-hour ride to Bondsteel.

> 16 July 02—A good night sleep in humble housing conditions. Hundreds of churches in this area have been blown up by Muslims, mostly of Albanian descent. . . . The senior chaplain at Bondsteel wondered why the US was here to protect the Muslims from the Serbs when the Muslims abuse the Serb Christians at every opportunity. . . . Bondsteel has a small prison in which five or six Serbian suspected killers are held awaiting trials. . . . Participated in a Bible Study at Pristina at 1900. There were riots in Pristina but not near us. . . . Had a small class on Reserve to Active Duty chaplain integration issues.

> 17 July 02—UN police are removing gruesome posters made from a real photograph of a Serbian soldier cutting the throat of a teenage Muslim. The caption of the poster read in Albanian and English, 'Do not let criminals come back to Kosova.' The posters were placed in locations to

incite riots. . . . Spent the afternoon in UMT training at the North Chapel, Bondsteel. Taught a large class on UMT issues with Reserve and Active Duty integration. . . . This evening had an especially beautiful sunset, as the clouds reflected a golden color upon the mountains. Truly God the creator of the universe is awesome. Yet how tragic are the sinful acts of humanity in contrast. I had to view the beauty of God's creation through a barbed wire fence.

18 July 02—This morning I had a small class with two chaplains on chaplain integration issues. . . . The rest of the day I was on my own, exploring Camp Bondsteel. . . . I was late to bed this evening. On the way to my room I could hear civilian small mortars being fired. The ethnic hatred still goes on in isolated areas. One village will fire a mortar into another village at night, and then hide in the hills while the US or an allied force seeks them out. Small scale killings still go on. . . . Sometimes these events make the newspapers but mostly they do not.

19 July 02—Went for an early morning jog within the fence around Camp Bondsteel. The fog was very thick, poor visibility. The sounds of small arms fire was easy to hear, a few miles west of camp. The Serbians (Muslims) use every advantage (the fog) to commit atrocities then flee into hiding. As soon as the gunshots began, a US helicopter took off after the assailants, but they will never find the shooters because of the fog. . . . Flight delays and an exhausting day before I arrived back in Germany.[91]

Army Reserve Chaplain Assistant SPC Kelli Overturf served with the KFOR first at Camp Able Sentry, Macedonia, and then at Camp Bondsteel, Kosovo. Camp Able Sentry was a small NATO compound with one chapel and one American UMT, namely Chaplain (MAJ) Steven Jerles and Overturf. Overturf maintained the chapel, did administrative and office automation work, coordinated all religious activities, and was responsible for the security of all chapel equipment. Overturf and Jerles provided religious services for US and NATO troops as well as civilians from various countries who worked at Camp Able Sentry. A highlight of Overturf's time at Camp Able Sentry was the spiritual retreats to Greece visiting the Bible sites associated with the Apostle Paul that she and Jerles coordinated and conducted. In December 2002, Camp Able Sentry began to downsize drastically and the chapel closed. Overturf then went to Camp Bondsteel,

Kosovo, where she worked with Chaplain Assistant SGT Darnell Rambert and Chaplain (LTC) Gregg Drew. The newly married Overturf stated that the only downside to this deployment was being away from her husband.[92]

In August 2002, Lawson of the 7th ARCOM made a quick 5-day trip to Kosovo and Macedonia to visit soldiers from his unit. In his journal, Lawson recorded:

> 19 Aug 02—Uneventful flight from Germany to Kosovo. . . . The bus ride from Pristina to Camp Bondsteel showed continued rebuilding after their civil war. A new huge mosque was under construction in a new town which just appeared in a field recently cleared of land mines. The distinct Muslim attire is evident among the people. One young Muslim man pointed his finger like a gun and pretended to shoot us on the bus. Slept at Bondsteel tonight. . . .

> 20 Aug 02—Departed Bondsteel after breakfast for Camp Able Sentry (CAS), Macedonia. The border between Kosovo and Macedonia was heavily guarded by UN soldiers. Both countries require that all vehicles entering their countries drive through a manmade shallow river, a symbol of spite in washing the dirt off of one country before entering the other. . . . Driving through Skopje was dangerous, as cows, people, bicycles, and vendors all clog the roadways, and anti-American sentiments run strong among the Serbians. . . . Minarets from mosques are a common sight. No Eastern Orthodox Church buildings anywhere, they were all destroyed. CAS is located next to the Skopje airport, which is not very busy. . . .

> 21 Aug 02—Today was relaxing. . . . I saw the soldiers I needed to see from my home unit, they are all doing fine. . . . One was on guard duty in a tower. . . . we talked and he gladly took Christian literature. . . . The chapel here at CAS is brand new, in pristine condition, seating about 90 people comfortably.

> 22 Aug 02—I went with Chaplain (MAJ) Steve Jerles and soldiers from my unit and others to visit the mental hospital at Demijkapj, about 90 minutes on the bus. This mental hospital/orphanage was very sad. Terrible living conditions, horrid smell, lots of flies in the eyes, noses, and

mouths of the mentally ill patients. These are the forgotten victims of war in the Balkans. Most are mentally disturbed from seeing their parents raped and murdered. It was built by the British and Macedonian governments. . . .

23 Aug 02—Spent all day waiting to travel or traveling. . . . I continued a long conversation with a sergeant from Florida that I had [started] with him on my way here 5 days ago. He was all mixed up theologically and had a lot of questions. . . . While waiting at the Tuzla airport an E4 who had a death in the family asked me to pray for him as he was going home on emergency leave. I was glad to do so. . . . An exhausting day but arrived safely home late at night Germany time.[93]

Drew, an Army Reserve chaplain of the 7th ARCOM, replaced Chandler as the ASG chaplain for Kosovo. Simultaneous to this, the senior ASG chaplain in Bosnia was Chaplain F. Douglas Hudson, also of the 7th ARCOM. That meant that both senior chaplains in theaters of operations Bosnia and Kosovo were from the same unit at the same time. This was the first and only time this has happened. As one news report stated:

This marked the first time in the history of the US Army in the Balkans that the senior SFOR and KFOR chaplain positions were held by chaplains from the same unit at the same time. . . . The fact that the unit is an Army Reserve unit stationed in Europe makes this distinction even more significant. . . . 'Folks here are hungry to hear the word of God,' said Chaplain Drew, who took part in more than 50 worship services and about 100 small group Bible Studies at Camp Bondsteel, Kosovo. . . . Chaplain Hudson also provided worship services for troops in Hungary, in Bosnia at Eagle Base near Tuzla, and Forward Observation Base (FOB) Connor, near Srebrenica. 'I spent a lot of time there [Taszar, Hungary] during the first couple of months,' Hudson said. 'I especially enjoyed the Christmas season with the soldiers.'[94]

As 2002 came to a close, Drew and the other UMT members had time to reflect on the holiday season and what the new year might bring. Clearly, ministries throughout Kosovo were going well. Chaplains throughout the region were having active and engaging ministries not only with US troops, but also with international peacekeepers and with civilians assigned to work on the installations. The downsizing of facilities and reductions in troop strength were an optimistic sign. In a somewhat reflective mood as

Christmas 2002 approached, Drew wrote the following summary of his prior months in Kosovo:

> The blessings for a chaplain serving soldiers in the Balkans are endless. Working with exceptional chaplain colleagues, gifted chaplain assistants, having fellowship with multinational soldiers and chaplains, and of course humanitarian activities in orphanages and schools. Yet there are two additional blessings for this chaplain that would cause any military leader a measure of pride. First, I've lost count now of the times civilians, contractors, soldiers from other nations, and those in the Active component have said, 'We can't tell the difference anymore between Active Duty, Reserve, or National Guard.' The fact that we are now viewed as equal in ability, even though we have much less training time, is a testament to the commitment and excellence of today's Reserve and National Guard. Second, when you hear the Active Component USAREUR and Regular Army UMT SGMs [Sergeant Majors] tell your very own chaplain assistants, that they have heard time and again, how well they are doing, while rewarding them with coins and praises; you stand 10 inches taller, and in the evening times of prayer, you thank God, for allowing you the privilege to work with such gifted young soldiers.[95]

Chaplain (CPT) Richard Brown of the 2d Battalion, 2d Infantry Regiment served through July of 2003 at Camp Montieth, Kosovo. Richard Brown commented, "I was the only chaplain on the camp. Nearest camp was 45 minutes to 1 hour away. Due to vehicle movement rules, I was unable to get there often. I did have the priest visit for Roman Catholic services once a week." Richard Brown summed up his job description succinctly, saying, "I was responsible for the spiritual care of all soldiers and civilians on camp." He believed that at this time in Kosovo there were only slight differences in ministry compared to a typical garrison ministry on any Army facility. Never sensing that he was in any personal danger, Richard Brown stated that he enjoyed distributing clothing, candy, and school supplies to local orphanages and schools, and that he tried to bring some understanding related to local Orthodox and Muslim traditions.[96]

Chaplain assistants in Kosovo in 2003 were enablers and coordinators for chaplains. They needed abilities in resource management, administration, military customs and courtesies, computer technology, vehicle maintenance, force protection, hospitality, and initial counseling. The ASG chaplain assistant in Kosovo in early 2003 was SGT Darnell Rambert. As the ASG chaplain assistant, Rambert essentially was an enabler, a facilitator for other UMTs in Kosovo. As Rambert stated, "The easiest word to explain what we do is 'support.' We support the task force in all ways possible." Rambert elaborated, "The Field Fund is probably the most visible thing we manage. This fund is currently in excess of $8,000, and all of the monies collected go back to the soldiers. . . . We also order ecclesiastical supplies for the task force UMTs, and manage the facilities, to ensure that all is working and any problems are taken care of."[97]

Lawson made two short-term trips to Kosovo in 2003, the first from 6 to 10 January and the second from 3 to 11 June. As with his previous short visits in Kosovo, the purpose of these visits was to resolve any Reserve to Active Duty integration issues and to minister to soldiers from his unit, the 7th ARCOM. The January visit to Camp Bondsteel consisted of several meetings with chaplains to discuss integration issues. Another briefing was with Drew, Rambert, and Overturf of the 7th ARCOM. This briefing consisted of informing Drew, Rambert, and Overturf about the 7th ARCOM's operations related to sending troops to Afghanistan in retaliation to the 11 September 2001 terrorist attacks on America. Essentially, Drew, Rambert, and Overturf were told that when they returned from their deployment to Kosovo, the 7th ARCOM will be operating at an aggressive pace and will need their services right away. The weather on this January 2003 visit to Kosovo was cold but not very snowy. Lawson's June visit to Kosovo was to see 7th ARCOM troops at Camp Bondsteel, Pristina, and Camp Montieth. There were many opportunities on this June visit to minister in a hospital, to counsel those with marital problems, to distribute religious literature, to discuss theological issues with interested soldiers, and to dialogue with various UMTs on Reserve to Active Duty integration issues.[98]

On completion of his tour in Kosovo, Drew commented that he had many unique and rewarding ministry experiences from the Balkans. He stated, "We participated in the KFOR chaplain's meetings and hosted one meeting here at Camp Bondsteel with 40 chaplains representing 16 countries. We provided countless suicide prevention briefs and reunion briefs, not to mention the many, many counseling sessions. Perhaps our greatest form of ministry though has been that of presence, and relationships." Drew continued, "In Kosovo we delivered close to 300 boxes of donated items to schools, a hospital for the handicapped, an orphanage, and other charity organizations."[99] In conclusion, Drew reflected, "This level of ministry (working with an Active Duty task force), has caused all of us to grow and mature incredibly in our profession, and in our dependence on God to carry us through. We have learned to lean on one another, and take care of each other, and to keep each other accountable. All in all, this has been a truly remarkable experience."[100]

Figure 14. CH (LTC) Gregg Drew with residents of a mental health hospital in Kosovo.

The US Army Chaplaincy and Downsizing in Kosovo, 2004–2005

In 2004, Kosovo suffered from the pains of achieving more autonomy while the United States and NATO lowered their troop strength. Meanwhile, the United Nations had no clear plan for the future peaceful administration of Kosovo, whether the region would become an independent nation, an autonomous state within Serbia, or somehow joined to Albania. Disgruntled Kosovars of both Muslim and Eastern Orthodox beliefs took advantage of this transition period to settle old grudges or inflict anguish on their enemies. In the spring of 2004, sections of Kosovo were at peace while other sections were rife with tension and disturbances. Riots by both Muslims and Orthodox protestors forced NATO and US peacekeepers to use armed force when necessary to squelch the uprisings. For example, as one news report stated:

153

PRISTINA, Serbia-Montenegro—Ethnic Albanians torched Serb homes and churches Thursday as Kosovo convulsed in a second day of rioting. The worst violence since the province's war ended in 1999 has killed at least 31 people and injured hundreds.

Serbian nationalists set mosques elsewhere on fire and threatened to retaliate with 'slaughter and death.' NATO sent reinforcements to quell tensions in the UN run province and ease the threat of renewed conflict in the volatile Balkans. . . .

Some peacekeepers were already carrying out the orders, shooting and wounding protesters who used violence in clashes Thursday, said Col. Horst Pieper, the chief NATO spokesman in Kosovo. The number of injured peacekeepers rose to 51 since clashes began Wednesday. . . .

The bloodshed underscored the bitter divisions that have polarized Kosovo's mostly Muslim ethnic Albanians, who want independence from Serbia, and Orthodox Christian Serbs, a minority in Kosovo who consider the province their ancient homeland.

The violence . . . dealt the Bush administration a potential setback in efforts to reduce the number of peacekeepers in the Balkans and redeploy them to Iraq, Afghanistan, and other hotspots. About 2,000 Americans now serve with the force, down from 5,000 after the war, and the entire force has shrunk from 50,000 to 18,500. . . .

Serbia–Montenegro's military raised the combat readiness of some units to their highest level, and Kosovo's ethnic Albanian Prime Minister, Bajram Rexhepi, warned that the situation was not under control. The US Embassy in Belgrade closed to the public temporarily as a precaution. . . .[101]

Balkan tensions and hostilities in the spring of 2004 were not confined to the province of Kosovo. Within Serbia itself, riots by Orthodox Serbs against Muslim Albanians grew in prominence. One report stated, "Angered by ethnic clashes in Kosovo that targeted their kin, Serb nationalists rampaged Thursday in Serbia, torching mosques and threatening Kosovo's ethnic Albanians with 'slaughter and death.'" This article lamented the fact that "The protests in Belgrade and other Serbian towns

154

were reminiscent of similar nationalistic outbursts at the start of the Balkan wars in the early 1990s, when former President Slobodan Milosevic's propaganda deliberately incited hatred toward other ethnic groups then living in the former Yugoslavia." In mentioning a specific example of ethnic hatred and violence, the report stated, "In Nis, Serbia's second largest city, 5,000 extremists gathered midmorning on the square, chanting 'Slaughter, death to all' Kosovar Albanians, and 'Let's all go to Kosovo.'"[102]

The US Army troop levels in Kosovo were around 2,000 in the spring of 2004, elevating quickly to 2,500 and remaining at that level throughout the year.[103] From February through August, Army National Guard Chaplain (LTC) Timothy Peterson of the 34th Infantry Division of Minnesota was the senior Army chaplain in Kosovo. While soldiers on patrol in Kosovo experienced a temporary elevation of tension and danger from sporadic civilian riots, life in base camps for US troops remained stable and safe. Peterson commented:

> I was the senior chaplain in the deployment KFOR 5B. The other chaplains were Bill Klavetter, Joel Steverson, Tom Jensen, and Eric Feig. All were from the Minnesota National Guard. . . . I was the staff chaplain, serving on the general's personal staff and supervising the religious program for the whole task force. I was also the senior US chaplain in Kosovo and provided religious support to other US personnel and US civilians working for the United Nations.[104]

Peterson said of his relationship to his commander, "We had a ½-hour weekly scheduled meeting and talked many other times each week. He fully supported our ministry and urged us to be creative in finding ways to minister to soldiers and families." Peterson elaborated on his relationship with his commander: "I accompanied the commanding general in his visits with religious leaders. I had input into the plans regarding the religious impact upon operations." In speaking of his interaction with other chaplains in Kosovo, Peterson stated, "The US chaplains and chaplain assistants meet weekly for encouragement, coordination, and training. We also met once a month for training with the other chaplains involved in KFOR. All the US chaplains worked together to provide a comprehensive plan of worship and religious education."[105]

In 2004, the future of Kosovo was uncertain. Before considering an independent Kosovo, UN officials insisted the province have a firmly established democracy, a respect for human rights and the rule of law, and a viable reconstruction program in place. The US and other world leaders took a cautious approach on Kosovo independence, fearing that any redrawing of borders in the Balkans could lead to new conflicts. Specifically of concern was Macedonia, where ethnic Albanians want statehood, and Bosnia, whose Serbs have also pressed for statehood.

Flare-ups of violence in Kosovo in 2004 were common. Homesteaders who refused to leave confronted resettling refugees returning to their homes. Threats, random violence, and ethnic tensions were evident. Skeptics could state that this was normal for Kosovo and, in fact, a sense of prewar normalcy had returned to the region. What was not normal was the 18 April prison shootout in the city of Kosovska Mitrovica. A press report stated:

> KOSOVSKA MITROVICA, Serbia-Montenegro—A Jordanian policeman fired on a group of fellow UN police officers in a prison compound in Kosovo, killing two Americans before being shot and killed in the ensuing gunbattle. Eleven others, including ten Americans, were wounded.
>
> A group of 21 American correctional officers, along with two Turks and an Austrian officer, were leaving the detention center after a day of training in northern Kosovo on Saturday when they came under fire from at least one member of a group of Jordanians on guard at the prison, said Neeraj Singh, a UN spokesman.
>
> The officers shot back. In the 10-minute gunbattle, the attacker and two American officers were killed, while 10 more Americans and one Austrian were wounded.
>
> It was not clear what touched off the violence. Four Jordanian police officers were arrested, a NATO source told the Associated Press on condition of anonymity. . . .
>
> The shooting took place in Kosovska Mitrovica, a city that has long been the scene of ethnic violence between Serbs and ethnic Albanians, including riots that broke out a month ago, killing 19 and injuring 900.[106]

By the end of 2004, Kosovo appeared to be on the mend. One report stated Kosovo "has the international community tied in knots," and that Kosovo "has become a showplace for the difficulties and dangers of trying to heal a fractured society through a lumbering international bureaucracy," there were signs that Kosovo was beginning to heal.[107] Seeking to remedy the short supply of fresh water and inconsistent electricity along with addressing the huge unemployment rate in Kosovo, the UN created two agencies that made an immediate difference. One agency, the UN Interim Administration Mission in Kosovo, addressed police, utilities, and economic issues. The other new agency was the Kosovo Trust Agency, a group of economists and bankers who administrated real estate, privatization of businesses, and financially sponsored redevelopment projects. Progress was noticeable throughout Kosovo.[108]

As 2004 transitioned into 2005, US Army chaplains continued to minister to about 2,500 US troops in Kosovo, NATO soldiers, and authorized civilians. Serving these US soldiers were five chaplains and four chaplain assistants. Chaplain (LTC) Lawrence Hendel was the Task Force *Eagle* chaplain and Chaplain (LTC) Daniel Viveros was the deputy staff chaplain. Working with Hendel and Viveros in the task force were Chaplain Assistants SSG Frank Tsai, SGT Oscar Guerrero, and SGT Jasmine Yates. UMT members not in the Task Force *Eagle* structure but also in Kosovo were Chaplain (MAJ) Oran Roberts, Chaplain (MAJ) Douglas Compton, and Chaplain (CPT) Chris Guadiz, along with Chaplain Assistant SSG Richard Johnson. Hendel, a Roman Catholic priest with the California Army National Guard, described his position in Kosovo:

> I am the brigade chaplain, or staff chaplain for Multinational Brigade East in Kosovo. I am responsible for supervising, mentoring, and guiding the four other UMTs within the task force. I am responsible to brief the commander weekly, attend weekly staff calls, attend the update brief and commanding general's calendar scrub along with the weekly commander's brief. We conduct weekly UMT meetings and bi-monthly training sessions. As the sole US Roman Catholic priest, I am responsible for the welfare of all the Catholics in the task force at both Camp Bondsteel and Camp Montieth. Per guidance from the USAREUR chaplain, I support Task Force *Orion* in Bosnia with Catholic support once a month. I oversee the bi-monthly 4-day spiritual retreat trips to Greece but the chaplain OIC [officer in charge] and his chaplain assistant do all of the work. Like any other chaplain, there are pastoral counseling sessions, many reports, and coordination that must go on. I also coordinate with the international theater chaplain as the need arises.
>
> Principally I work with my deputy chaplain, Chaplain Daniel Viveros, who is the OIC of one of two chapels on

Bondsteel and collaborate with the other chaplains serving on this mission and in particular as we prepare and plan for redeployment. I believe we have a reasonably cohesive team as we share responsibilities for the Greece retreats, participate in the international activities and task force religious and pastoral support.[109]

Chaplain Roberts and Chaplain Assistant Yates made up the UMT at Camp Montieth, Kosovo. Roberts, affectionately called the "Bishop of Montieth" since he was the only chaplain at that installation, worked with Yates to provide religious support, suicide prevention classes, reunion briefings, and other lectures to improve the morale and welfare of the troops. When asked if he ever felt in personal danger in Kosovo, Roberts responded:

> Even though we are receiving hostile fire pay, I have never felt in danger due to threat of arms. The majority of the population, Kosovo-Albanians, seems to love us and refer to us as their liberators and allies. The Imams that I have met refer to us as their 'miku im,' beloved friends. The children are constantly waiving at us and saying hello. The reception has not been quite so warm by Kosovo-Serbians, but they have been friendly as well. The Serbian Orthodox priests have been quick to point out the injustices that have occurred during the NATO occupation; nevertheless, they have remained civil. Driving on the narrow Kosovo roads is probably the most dangerous thing we do, especially during the wintertime. The roads are traveled by livestock, pedestrians, horse-drawn wagons, tractors, and suicidal drivers in automobiles that attempt to pass on blind hills and curves. We have seen plenty of accidents and have had multiple near misses. Mirror strikes are common. There are no sidewalks in the country, so pedestrians tend to walk in the car lanes when snow is covering the shoulders of the road.[110]

One of the issues that chaplains and chaplain assistants had to deal with in Kosovo in 2005 was boredom. Soldiers were performing routine missions, Kosovo was no longer very dangerous, soldiers had idle time, and morale could potentially plummet. Yates recalled:

> This is a very long deployment in which basically nothing happens the entire time you are here. It is very important (especially on an infantry post) to keep the morale of the soldiers up by keeping them busy. This is not Iraq or

Afghanistan, and things get boring and morale gets low. It is, however, very safe and I feel very content here.

I work with Chaplain Roberts as the only UMT on Camp Montieth, an infantry post with over 400 male soldiers. We balance our time between missions with spiritual leaders outside of the camp, NGO leaders, and most importantly soldier care. On a good day I work 0900–1700 and have time to work out, eat dinner with friends and watch a movie. On a normal day my hours vary greatly and we spend many of those hours outside the wire visiting the leaders in our community. I provide security for the chaplain outside the wire and make sure all maintenance is taken care of. Although he has an open door policy, when possible, I make appointments for soldiers to meet with Chaplain Roberts.[111]

The US and NATO presence in Kosovo was contributing to peace and the rebuilding of the nation. When various incidents of local violence erupted in Kosovo in 2005, no escalation of hostilities occurred and Kosovars resolved the conflicts with little NATO assistance. The province was starting to stand on its own. For example, on 15 March 2005 a bomb blew up near the convoy of Kosovo President Ibrahim Rugova in Pristina, injuring a bystander and some property. Kosovar police, with Italian peacekeepers in support handled the situation with no escalation.[112] On 2 July 2005, three almost simultaneous explosions in Pristina produced no casualties and no escalation of hostilities.[113] The discontented were still randomly violent, but Kosovo was well on its way to recovery.

An integral part of the ongoing healing of ethnic tensions within Kosovo can be credited to US and NATO chaplains working in local communities on humanitarian, benevolence, and religious dialogue activities. From the moment NATO and US chaplains arrived in Kosovo, they began to build bridges of communication, understanding, tolerance, and respect between local antagonistic religious and civil leaders. By 2005, the results of these efforts were obvious. Chaplain Assistant Tsai succinctly stated, "The UMTs in Kosovo continually interact with nongovernmental organizations and a few individual families to provide spiritual and financial support."[114] Hendel elaborated on the American UMTs working outside the wire to locals in need:

We provide monies through designated offerings to a few NGOs that function here in Kosovo. The Mother Teresa Society has an office in every major municipality, but we focus on the one in Vitina within our AOR. The director serves 216 households, the poorest of the poor. The soldier's offerings are the primary source of funding for their carefully documented work. Chaplain Guadiz and his assistant, SPC Aaron Stevens, see the director regularly and we were taken on a tour once to see some of the households the Mother Teresa Society helps. It was a profound experience, seeing the poorest of the poor in person. We provide assistance to a women's shelter in Gjilane, named Liria, and Chaplain Oran Roberts in that area visits the center regularly with his chaplain assistant, SGT Jasmine Yates. The Aviation chaplain, Chaplain Doug Compton, visits an orphanage in Pristina with his chaplain assistant, SSG Richard Johnson, and we have provided some funding for that NGO. Other than that we don't directly minister to the local population. Our responsibility is to minister to the soldiers and provide for the spiritual needs of the contractors who work at the installations. We have to be careful to be consistent and impartial in our efforts when and if we reach out to the local communities. I recently had the experience of meeting with a local Catholic priest and learned about the challenges he faces as priest and pastor.[115]

Roberts and Yates found working with local Kosovars to be a rewarding experience. Such ministries were refreshing to the UMT members as well as to the soldiers who accompanied them on these local humanitarian assistance visits. Such benevolent activities let soldiers see the people of Kosovo and the ravages of civil war, and allowed the troops to feel like they were contributing to the welfare of others. Roberts stated:

My UMT has continued the work started by the previous UMT. We provide humanitarian assistance with the approval of our S5 [Civil Affairs] to the Liria Center for the Protection of Women and Children in Gjilan and to the Kamenica Red Cross. We take designated chapel offerings for these NGOs and provide donated clothing, food, and other supplies. The Liria Center is a women's shelter that shelters and educates women and children who have been traumatized by the war, domestic violence, and human trafficking. I have done radio and TV interviews with them to advertise their services that are available to all ethnic groups in Kosovo. The Kamenica Red Cross is a local NGO that provides basic necessities and emergency aid to the poorest families in the Kamenica area. Recently, Chaplain (LTC) Daniel Viveros and I have taken on the Soup Kitchen in Novo Brdo. As the deputy staff chaplain, Dan performs a Protestant worship service at the chapel in Film City that takes a designated offering for the soup kitchen. Novo Brdo is primarily a Serbian area, but the kitchen serves all ethnic groups in their area. We have tried to limit our efforts to the most worthy NGOs, but we have also helped individuals, such as baby Albert, who needed surgery for a cleft palate.[116]

Figure 15. SGT Jasmine Yates (rear) with children from the Kamenica area.

The people of Kosovo have a deep respect for their religious leaders. Whether Muslim, Eastern Orthodox, or Roman Catholic, these religious leaders are often the most important people in the community. Kosovar civil leaders look for religious endorsement of their plans and policies. Average residents in rural Kosovo venerate clerics, even if they personally are mostly secular in disposition. Simply stated, to achieve emotional and spiritual healing in Kosovo after centuries of tension and hatred, the diverse clergy of Kosovo must support peace. US and NATO chaplains since entering Kosovo in 1999 have always sought and usually succeeded in bringing rival indigenous clergy together for conferences to promote peace and unity. Roberts continued the routine of his predecessors by consistently networking with local clergy. Roberts recalled:

> I have met with and formed friendships with the key Muslim, Orthodox, Catholic, and Protestant religious leaders in my sector. I have been their escort to various KFOR events, and I have served as a liaison between my task force and them. I do not participate in IO targeting, but my relationship with these religious leaders has given me a better understanding of how to advise my commander on the influence of religion on our peace-enforcement mission and as to the religious perspective on the current situation.[117]

No emotional or civil reconstruction was possible in Kosovo without imposing justice on those who committed heinous war crimes against civilians. In early March 2005, Kosovo's former Prime Minister Ramush Haradinaj surrendered to the UN War Crimes Tribunal following a special flight from Pristina to The Hague, Netherlands.[118] Haradinaj pleaded not guilty to 37 charges of war crimes including murder, rape, and deportation of Serbs during the 1998–99 war between ethnic Albanians and Serb forces and was in confinement.[119] In 2005, the war crimes trial of former Serbian President Slobodan Milosevic was in session at The Hague. Milosevic was charged with a multitude of war crimes including genocide.

Meanwhile, US military operations in the region were ongoing, with one tragedy. On 1 April 2005 a C-130 aircraft took off from an airport in Tirana, Albania, on a routine training mission in conjunction with Albanian forces. A news report stated:

> TIRANA, Albania—Search teams recovered all nine bodies Friday from the wreckage of a US military aircraft that crashed in mountainous southern Albania during a joint exercise, authorities said.
>
> A US military C-130 airplane crashed in bad weather late Thursday near the remote village of Rovie, in the Drizez Mountains, about 100 kilometers (60 miles) southeast of the capital, Tirana, officials said. The exact cause was unclear. . . . The military transport was assigned to the 352d Special Operations Group based in Mildenhall, England. . . .[120]

As this tragedy was on an Air Force mission, an Air Force chaplain was the lead in providing memorial services and counseling. However, Army Chaplain Hendel stated he did speak to two liaison officers who went to Albania from Kosovo and remarked that they were doing fine.[121] Army Chaplain Compton remarked that his aviation unit helped support the Air Force with Black Hawk helicopter operations, but the Air Force chaplain ministered to those involved and did memorial services.[122]

While US and NATO forces still maintained their potentially dangerous peacekeeping missions, in 2005 Kosovo politically experienced the growth pains of a fledgling democracy. The Christian Serb minority in Kosovo resisted the efforts of the majority Muslim Albanians in developing a power-sharing plan. Serbs wanted more self-government in their enclaves throughout Kosovo. The Albanian majority, desiring complete independence from Serbia, was under international pressure to accommodate these desires of the Serbs. Quibbling continued over the details of this power-sharing plan throughout 2005.[123]

In the fall of 2005, Hendel was the senior chaplain in Kosovo. There were three US Army chapels still operating in Kosovo, two chapels at Camp Bondsteel, and one chapel at Camp Montieth. Hendel's reflections on his prior 12 months of service in Kosovo bear repeating:

> Serving in Kosovo is not glamorous or headline news, but I believe the efforts of all Kosovo Forces, being part of this multinational effort is the opportunity to make a difference to implement the spirit of UN Resolution 1244. We are a small part of an international effort to afford a region the opportunity to maintain peace, have a safe and secure environment, and restore confidence in the population's efforts to engage in the self-governing process. There are many more issues for the people of Kosovo to resolve and work through, but they are on the way. I have been proud to serve with all the soldiers in this peacekeeping mission, US and multinational. . . .[124]

Notes

1. Frank Columbus, ed., *Kosovo-Serbia: A Just War?* (Commack, NY: Nova Science Publishers, 1999), 5.

2. Wikipedia contributors, "History of Kosovo," *Wikipedia: The Free Encyclopedia,* www.en.wikipedia.org/wiki/history_of_kosovo. Much of the following narrative is based on this insightful article.

3. Noel Malcolm, *Kosovo: A Short History* (New York: New York University Press, 1998), 41–44.

4. "History of Kosovo," *Wikipedia.*

5. Tim Judah, *Kosovo: War and Revenge* (New Haven: Yale University Press, 2000), 4–7.

6. "History of Kosovo," *Wikipedia.*

7. Malcolm, *Kosovo: A Short History,* 139–141.

8. "History of Kosovo," *Wikipedia.*

9. Glen E. Curtis, ed., *Yugoslavia: A Country Study* (Washington, DC: GPO for the Library of Congress, 1992), 26.

10. "History of Kosovo," *Wikipedia.*

11. Josef Korbel, *Tito's Communism* (Denver: University of Denver Press, 1951), 53.

12. Julie A. Mertus, *Kosovo: How Myths and Truths Started a War* (Berkeley: University of California Press, 1999), 141–143.

13. Ibid., 145.

14. "History of Kosovo," *Wikipedia.*

15. Mertus, *Kosovo: How Myths and Truths Started a War,* 182–187.

16. "History of Kosovo," *Wikipedia.*

17. Madeline Albright, *Madame Secretary: A Memoir* (New York: Miramax Books, 2003), 225, 481.

18. Ibid., 483–484, 481.

19. Ibid., 485.

20. Ibid., 488–489.

21. Wesley Clark, *Waging Modern War: Bosnia, Kosovo, and the Future of Conflict* (New York: PublicAffairs Books, 2001), 137.

22. "Operation Allied Force," www.defenselink.mil/specials/kosovo.

23. Ibid.

24. Clark, *Waging Modern War,* 176.

25. Ibid., 183.

26. Ibid., 187–189.

27. Ibid., 214, 219, 281, 286.

28. Ibid., 426–427.

29. "Operation Allied Force," www.defenselink.mil/specials/Kosovo.

30. Clark, *Waging Modern War,* 234, 267.

31. Ibid., 326.

32. Ibid., 371.

33. Chaplain (COL) Janet Horton, interview by Dr. John Brinsfield, 3 March 2004.

34. Chaplain Charles Howell, interview by Dr. John Brinsfield, 10 December 2003.

35. Questionnaire by Chaplain (CPT) Scott Jones, 9 August 2005.

36. Questionnaire by Chaplain (CPT) Darin Powers, 11 August 2005.

37. Questionnaire by Chaplain (CPT) Brent Causey, 13 April 2005.

38. Questionnaire by SFC Craig Gardner, 25 March 2005.

39. Chaplain (BG) David Zalis, interview by author, 4 May 2005.

40. Ibid.

41. Janet Horton interview.

42. Ibid.

43. Chaplain (MAJ) Allen Kovach, interview by author, 17 August 2005.

44. Ibid.

45. Causey questionnaire.

46. Questionnaire by SFC Elbert Jackson, 20 September 2004.

47. Powers questionnaire.

48. Scott Jones questionnaire.

49. Chaplain (CPT) Steven Mark Jones, interview by author, 21 June 2004.

50. Ibid.

51. Gardner questionnaire.

52. Steven Mark Jones interview.

53. Gardner questionnaire.

54. Chaplain Peter Baktis, interview by author, 13 August 2004.

55. Chaplain Peter Baktis, correspondence with author, 4 October 2005.

56. Albright, *Madame Secretary*, 520.

57. Linda D. Kozaryn, "U.S. Offers Kosovar Albanians Safe Haven," *Armed Forces Press Service*, n.d. Accessed on 3 October 2005 at www.defenselink.mil/specials/provide_refuge/2background.html.

58. Ibid.

59. "Standing Operating Procedures/Chaplain," Joint Task Force Operation PROVIDE REFUGE, 10 May 1999.

60. Eric Wester, John Stepp, Donald Holdridge, "Initial Ministry to Persecuted People," *The Army Chaplaincy*, Winter–Spring 2000, 36–37.

61. Chaplain Donald Holdridge, correspondence with author, 4 October 2005.

62. Chaplain John Stepp, correspondence with author, 4 October 2005.

63. Ibid.

64. Questionnaire by Chaplain (CPT) Mohammad Khan, 25 July 2005.

65. Ibid.

66. "Disaster Response: Efforts of Interaction Agencies in Kosovo," *InterAction*, May 2001, located at www.interaction.org/kosovo.

67. Ralph Reinties, ed., "Tularemia Outbreak Investigation in Kosovo: Case Control and Environmental Studies Research, *Emerging Infectious Diseases*, January 2002. Accessed at www.findarticles.com.

68. Questionnaire by Chaplain (CPT) John McLain, 10 July 2004.

69. Questionnaire by Chaplain (CPT) Steve Firtko, 6 August 2000.

70. Baktis interview.

71. Ibid.

72. Questionnaire by Chaplain (CPT) Steven Simpson, 4 November 2004.

73. Questionnaire by Chaplain Kenneth Hubbs, 10 July 2004.

74. Questionnaire by Chaplain (CPT) William Horton, 5 August 2004.

75. Ibid.

76. Ibid.

77. Steven Mark Jones interview.

78. Gary J. Kunich, "Soldiers Prepare to Leave Kosovo by Preparing for Transition Back into Home Life," *European Stars & Stripes*, 15 December 2000, 3.

79. Joseph Anderson, "Military Operational Measures of Effectiveness for Peacekeeping Operations," *Military Review*, September/October 2001, 36.

80. Ibid., 37.

81. Chaplain (MAJ) Robert Land, interview by author, 9 July 2004.

82. Ibid.

83. Ibid.

84. Questionnaire from Chaplain (CPT) Martin Kendrick, 31 January 2005.

85. Questionnaire from Chaplain (CPT) Steven E. Cantrell, 31 January 2005.

86. Chaplain (LTC) Vernon Chandler, interview by author, 29 July 2004.

87. Kimberly C. Field and Robert M. Perito, "Creating a Force for Peace Operations: Ensuring Stability with Justice," *Parameters*, Winter 2002–2003, 77–78.

88. Vince Crawley, "Despite Drawdown, Endgame's Unclear," *Army Times*, 22 July 2002, 10–11.

89. Questionnaire by SGT De-Angelo Coatie, 8 August 2005.

90. Questionnaire by Chaplain Paul Yoon, 19 July 2004.

91. Unpublished diary of Chaplain Kenneth Lawson, 15–19 July 2002. A copy is on file at the US Army Chaplain Center and School Library, Fort Jackson, SC.

92. SPC Kelli Overturf, correspondence with author, 6 December 2002.

93. Lawson unpublished diary, 19–23 August 2002.

94. Jon Dahms, "7th Army Reserve Command Chaplains Complete Historic Ministry," *US Army Reserve News Service*, 5 May 2003.

95. Chaplain Gregg Drew, correspondence with author, 19 December 2002.

96. Questionnaire from Chaplain (CPT) Richard E. Brown, 24 July 2004.

97. SGT Darnell Rambert, correspondence with author, 2 February 2003.

98. Lawson unpublished diary, 6–10 January, 3–11 June 2002, and August 2002.

99. Dahms, "7th Army Reserve Command Chaplains Complete Historic Mission," 1–2.

100. Chaplain Gregg Drew, correspondence with author, 16 March 2003.

101. "NATO Sends Troops Into Strife-Torn Kosovo," *Associated Press*, 18 March 2004.

102. "Serb Mobs Target Muslims, Albanians," *Associated Press*, 18 March 2004.

103. The *Army Times* placed the troop levels on 16 September 2004 at 2,500 in Kosovo and repeated that figure on 6 December 2004.

104. Questionnaire by Chaplain Timothy Peterson, 13 April 2005.

105. Ibid.

106. "Three U.N. Officers Die in Kosovo Prison Shootout," *Associated Press*, 18 April 2004.

107. Andrew Higgins, "Could U.N. Fix Iraq? Word from Kosovo Isn't Encouraging," *Wall Street Journal*, 2 August 2004, 1.

108. Ibid., 2.

109. Questionnaire by Chaplain (LTC) Lawrence Hendel, 25 October 2005.

110. Questionnaire by Chaplain (CPT) Oran Roberts, 26 October 2004.

111. Questionnaire by SGT Jasmine Yates, 27 October 2005.

112. "Bomb Near Kosovo Presidential Convoy," *Associated Press*, 15 March 2005.

113. "Blast Hits U.N. HQ in Kosovo," *Associated Press*, 2 July 2005.

114. Questionnaire by SSG Frank Tsai, 29 October 2005.

115. Hendel questionnaire.

116. Roberts questionnaire.

117. Ibid.

118. Anthony Deutsch, "Kosovo's Ex-Premier Surrenders to UN," *WORLD Magazine*, 9 March 2005, 6.

119. "Kosovo ex-PM Denies 37 War Charges," *CNN.com*, 14 March 2005.

120. "Bodies found after C-130 Crash," *CNN.com*, 1 April 2005.

121. Chaplain Lawrence Hendel, correspondence with author, 3 November 2005.

122. Chaplain Douglas Compton, correspondence with author, 3 November 2005.

123. "Serbs Reject Kosovo Power-Sharing Plan," *USA Today*, 11 August 2005, 5A.

124. Hendel questionnaire.

Chapter 5

Conclusion

After 10 years of military involvement in the Balkans, the US military can rightly be satisfied that they have saved lives and maintained peace. Considering the volatile and tortured history of this region, the calm presently experienced throughout the Balkans is remarkable. In the early 1990s, Bosnia was a killing zone—a place of genocide and vile atrocities. After the intervention of the United States and NATO in 1995, the killings stopped and a tentative but growing peace surrounded the region. Having failed in his political and military objectives in Bosnia, the Serbian tyrant Slobodan Milosevic turned his frightful ambitions toward Kosovo. Serbians in Kosovo resisted more firmly than they did in Bosnia. An air bombing campaign followed by an invasion of NATO and US troops quickly squashed Serbian resistance, and the occupation of Kosovo began.

In the Balkans, the United States and NATO have been active and successful in peacekeeping and nation-building activities. At the same time, war criminals from throughout the Balkans have been arrested and placed on trial. At the time of this writing, Slobodan Milosevic was on trial in an international court at The Hague in the Netherlands, accused of crimes against humanity. Others accused of crimes in the Balkans are also awaiting trial. For example, as one news report stated, "Nebojsa Pavkovik, Yugoslavia's former Army chief, surrendered to a United Nations tribunal in The Hague, Netherlands, to face charges of war crimes during the 1998–99 civil war in the southern Serbian province of Kosovo. The former general was indicted in 2003 on five charges related to the forced deportation of 800,000 Kosovo Albanian civilians and the murder of hundreds of them."[1] Near the end of 2005, many suspected war crime trials at The Hague were concluding, notably the sentencing of Haradin Bala to 13 years in prison for executing 9 unarmed civilian prisoners in July 1999.[2]

While international courts of law sorted out the innocence or guilt of numerous Serbians, Bosnians, or Kosovars, the common people of the Balkans attempted to locate missing relatives or identify the remains of the dead. The following news report states progress in this area:

> SARAJEVO, Bosnia-Herzegovina—A Bosnian based international agency for missing persons said Friday it had identified 2,000 victims of the Srebrenica massacre whose bodies were found in mass graves in Bosnia.
>
> The International Commission on Missing Persons has a list of 7,800 persons who disappeared in the worst massacre

of civilians in Europe since World War II. Bosnian Serb forces overran the Muslim enclave of Srebrenica in July 1995 and executed thousands of men and boys.

Rifat Kesetovic, chief pathologist of the organization, signed the 2,000th Srebrenican-related death certificate at a morgue in the northern city of Tuzla.

'We are proud to have passed this landmark, but there are still around 6,000 missing victims from Srebrenica and we are working hard to find them, to identify them and return them to their families,' Kesetovic said. . . .

Also Friday, Serbian police arrested a fifth suspect incriminated in the Srebrenica killings in a 1995 execution video of Muslim prisoners, Belgrade media reported.[3]

Public memorial services to honor the dead throughout Bosnia were an indication that peace was prevailing and emotional scars were beginning to heal. The memorial service at Vuk Karadzic in May 2002 allowed family members to return to the site where they were separated from their loved ones, never to be reunited. Other smaller ceremonies, such as the one in the spring of 2002 at the Drina River, allowed loved ones to morn, pray, and grieve at the location where the corpses of their loved ones were thrown in the river. An eyewitness stated, "This is the first time people were able to gather together in the city of Bratunac for the observance without violence. This was a major step toward reconciliation in BiH [Bosnia-Herzegovina]."[4]

Nevertheless, factions within Bosnia were resistant to change. Just before the 10th anniversary memorial service at Srebrenica in 2005, explosives were found and disarmed at the memorial service location. No injuries occurred and the 50,000 people expected to attend the event were able to eulogize and grieve in peace.[5] Others resistant to change were the Bosnian Serbian Parliament that, after years of haggling over details, accepted the European Union's (EU) demand for reform of Bosnia's ethnically divided police force, fulfilling the last condition for an agreement to bring the country closer to membership. The Bosnian Serb Parliament adopted by an overwhelming majority the EU guidelines for the police reform a day before the deadline was to expire. Bosnian Serbs had initially rejected the EU guidelines for reform, while the Muslim-Croat federation accepted the reforms months before. By October 2005, all major factions within Bosnia had agreed to the reforms that would diminish corruption, provide more accountability, and ethnically diversify regional police forces.[6]

While Bosnia restructured and instituted reforms with the goal of recognition in the EU, Kosovo remained farther behind in its reforms. At the end of 2005, Kosovo languished in a 6-year governmental limbo as a UN administered province of Serbia. As UN Envoy Martti Ahtisarri lamented, "Everybody's fed up with these transitional periods. Nobody wants to see Kosovo as a failed state."[7] Determining the final status of Kosovo is seen as the key to wider stability throughout the Balkans. While the fighting stopped in 1999, fears of extremists set to disrupt the peace process have forced NATO to maintain an 18,000-strong military presence in Kosovo, of which about 2,000 are from the United States. Ethnic tensions remain in Kosovo, as those of Albanian Muslim descent look to Pristina for leadership while Serbian Christians see their leadership in Belgrade. Civilians who travel from Serbia in and out of Kosovo frequently stop on the side of the road and change license plates to avoid any regional animosities. Kosovo is also troubled by constant power outages, an unemployment rate of up to 60 percent, and estimated monthly wages of about 150 to 200 euros, that being equivalent to 100 to 150 US dollars. The main hindrance to stability in Kosovo remains the Bosnian Serbs in Belgrade, who are reluctant to concede that their dream of a Serbian Christian Kosovo at the expense of Muslim Kosovars will not be a reality.

US Army chaplains serving throughout the Balkans from 1995 to 2005 were essential in the reconciliation process for the diverse religious populations. Clearly, the role of the chaplain as a religious adviser to commanders, long an expectation in the military, was solidified and enhanced by Army chaplains serving in the Balkans. Army commanders in the Balkans did not face a forceful and well-armed professional Army, but rather regional militias and paramilitary forces that thrived off ethnic racism and religious hatred. Army chaplains networked with local clergy and political leaders, brought rival religious factions to clergy events, promoted harmony among rival groups, and encouraged forgiveness and acceptance by long-standing belligerents. Chaplain Chandler stated:

> I attended a meeting at Eagle Base in Bosnia [2001] to help the Bosnian military develop a chaplaincy. Both Bosnian Muslims and Bosnian Eastern Orthodox Christians attended. Through translators we showed how an interdenominational and pluralistic chaplaincy can function. The whole concept of a military chaplaincy was foreign to them, even more so when they learned about how chaplains of all faiths [serve] in the US military chaplaincy.[8]

While in Bosnia in 1996, Chaplain (CPT) David Brown made numerous visits to local clergy to get a better understanding of the religious and ethnic tensions in Bosnia. His frequent visits to Eastern Orthodox churches and his discussions with Orthodox priests allowed him to make friends and to help build a level of credibility among local clergy for the US presence in Bosnia. The following article mentions the role of chaplains as spiritual diplomats and promoters of reconciliation:

> Efforts to regain peace in war-torn Bosnia and Herzegovina continue, and the United States Army chaplains in the region are assuming the role of spiritual diplomats. The Army chaplains are teaching local military leaders the benefits of creating a chaplaincy within the Bosnian military to teach harmony and tolerance. Military clergy from Britain, Denmark, Poland and Turkey are joining the US Army chaplains in this spiritual diplomatic initiative. . . .

> 'Who better than a chaplain to talk about healing and reconciliation in a peacekeeping environment,' said Chaplain (MAJ) Mike Lembke, who helped organize the discussions.

> Chaplain Lembke served as the Plans and Operations Chaplain during Operation JOINT FORGE, Stabilization Force 8, in Bosnia-Herzegovina for Task Force *Eagle*. He coordinated with the Joint Military Commission and the Civil Military Cooperation Cell, a series of meetings with local military advisers and Muslim, Orthodox, and Catholic clergy from Bosnia. These meetings resulted in convening the first Armed Forces in Bosnia-Herzegovina Religious Support Conference.

> 'It has been very meaningful to me to be able to employ chaplain doctrine in providing advice to our commander and to participate in ongoing discussions with local Orthodox, Muslim, and Roman Catholic clergy as part of my work and ministry in Bosnia,' said Lembke.[9]

Chaplain Wead provides an example of a chaplain having direct positive input into a tactical situation. The chaplain's voice of compassion and reason helped to avoid a potential disaster in Bosnia in the fall of 2001.

> Our unit was going to raid a suspected al-Qaeda terrorist hideout. Our commander suggested using CS gas [tear gas]. He asked for input. I pointed out that our mission stated we were to gather papers, and if we used CS gas it could ignite the building and destroy intelligence materials. I also suggested that our own intelligence had

been very inaccurate before. It was possible that they were wrong about this being a terrorist cell location. We did not use the CS gas. It turned out the house we took down contained an 80 year old woman, her daughter of 35, and grandchild of 11. I believe my role as chaplain gave me a different way of looking at these operations than the other officers. This assisted the Commander in making a prudent decision that showed compassion and restraint.[10]

The role of the US Army chaplain in the Balkans peace process varied based on time and personalities. The initial US presence in the Balkans was reluctant to engage with local clergy, there being no standing operating procedures for such activities. As US troops rotated in and out of Bosnia and later Kosovo, there was more willingness for chaplains to engage with local clergy to facilitate peacekeeping and reconciliation. As Chaplain Steinhilber recalled:

We're a stabilization force; it's been stabilized. We're religious leaders. Why can't we go out and meet with the local clergy and help out and meet with our neighbors? For instance, Chaplain Michael Hoyt had very much of an 'Oh, no, we don't go out of our compound; we take care of our own,' attitude. Chaplain Jim Goodwill had more of an openness but was hampered on that. Later chaplains were more open to moving about the countryside and working with orphanages, etc.[11]

By 1998 Army Chaplain Baktis was able to travel throughout Bosnia in an itinerant ministry capacity, he being in high demand as an Eastern Orthodox priest. One way Baktis was able to facilitate harmony and reconciliation in Bosnia was with his frequent meetings with indigenous Eastern Orthodox clergy. In this capacity, Baktis was able to present the US and NATO peacekeepers as those who respected the religious traditions of Bosniacs and friends who desired to enhance and encourage wholesome religious expressions among the people. Baktis was also able to be a peacemaker with the US allies in the Balkans. For example, the Russian army had a heavy presence in Bosnia. As an Eastern Orthodox priest, Baktis had immediate legitimacy with Russian Orthodox soldiers and chaplains. Baktis was able to communicate, coordinate, and fellowship with his fellow Eastern Orthodox clergy within the Russian army chaplaincy, helping to establish trust and appreciation for Russians toward Americans as allies in the Balkans.[12]

Balkans ministries enhanced the role of the chaplain as a religious adviser for the commander. Another consequence of the US Army in the Balkans from 1995 to 2005 was the full integration and coordination of chaplains from the Regular Army, the Army Reserve, and the Army National Guard. Not since World War II had the Army been so fully integrated with its Active Duty and Reserve components. Chaplains and chaplain assistants could be from either one of the three Army components with any variation of supervisory responsibilities. Culturally, the Active Army, the Army National Guard, and the Army Reserve have unique traditions, experiences, and ways of doing business. Initially some of these distinct cultural traits caused some examples of UMT uncooperativeness, but this was the exception and quickly faded away through subsequent Balkans troop rotations. The popular expression at the time of "One Army—One Fight" was a reality among chaplains and chaplain assistants in the Balkans. Distinctions quickly faded away amidst the pressures of ministry in a hostile fire zone far away from home.

The civil unrest and destruction throughout the Balkans forced UMT members to re-identify their ministry related to humanitarian operations. Orphanages abounded, mental health facilities were overcrowded, and schoolchildren were educated in ramshackle buildings with few if any school supplies. Some chaplains, deeply moved by the despair of local civilians, poured themselves into the local civilian population. Other chaplains adopted a nearby school, orphanage, or hospital and kept their benevolent ministry to only one facility. Some chaplains saw themselves as ministers to the US military only and did little if any ministry toward the local population. Ultimately the decision whether or not a chaplain would be involved in a benevolent ministry to the local population depended on the approval of the commander. Chaplains sold the idea of humanitarian missions to their commanders and got approval, then developed a relationship with an indigenous facility based on the guidance of the commander and the personal goals of the chaplain.

Army chaplain ministries in the Balkans were for most chaplains the first time they had ministered in a JTF NATO-sponsored organization. This was an enriching educational and practical experience for US Army chaplains. Being collocated on isolated military facilities with troops from various countries meant the US chaplain had many opportunities to minister and fellowship with chaplains and soldiers from other nations. This allowed for a greater respect for the religious and cultural norms from various countries and created friendships across denominational lines between chaplains. Chaplains from various countries exchanged ideas for ministry, and religious events were often co-celebrated. This interaction between chaplains from allied nations built unity and camaraderie between clergy and soldiers and helped solidify the resolve of allied troops toward the ultimate goal of peace in the Balkans.

Unknown to US Army chaplains who served in the Balkans before 11 September 2001, their experiences in Bosnia and Kosovo were a preamble to a much larger American military operation throughout the world, the Global War on Terrorism. It is a fact that a large number of chaplains who served in the Balkans were soon after asked or ordered to join the US Global War on Terrorism effort in such remote places as Iraq, Afghanistan, eastern Africa, Cuba, and other places. This is a reoccurring pattern in American history. As the Mexican War prepared soldiers for the Civil War, as the Mexican Border Conflict prepared the military for World War I, and as the Korean War prepared a whole generation of soldiers for fighting in Vietnam, so the peacekeeping operations in the Balkans prepared the US Army for similar humanitarian and nation-building missions in Iraq and other parts of the world. These experiences were invaluable for both Active Duty and Reserve component units. Lessons learned in the Balkans would be implemented throughout the world in the Global War on Terrorism.

In the fall and early winter of 2005, Chaplain (1LT) Chris Guadiz was assigned to Camp Bondsteel, Kosovo. Working under the supervision of Chaplain (LTC) Doug Compton, Guadiz regularly preached on Saturday and Sunday evenings. The everyday ministry experiences of Guadiz were typical of numerous Army chaplains throughout the Balkans. He listed his most significant events as counseling soldiers, performing chapel and field services, hospital visitation, Red Cross responses, suicide interventions, and advising the commander on ethical, religious, and moral issues within the command. Specifically, Guadiz enjoyed dialogue with local civilian religious leaders in the Vitina area on issues of ethnic, religious, and cultural significance. He further remarked that he was happy to network with NATO chaplains and learn about the chaplaincies from allied countries. Guadiz stated, "I would just like to say that this has been an incredible opportunity to hone my skills as a chaplain. I see God working miracles in the lives of soldiers everyday and I am amazed at how he has sustained us."[13]

Notes

1.   "Ex-Yugoslav Army Chief Surrenders to U.N. Court," *USA Today*, 26 April 2005, 11A.

2.   "Kosovo Separatist Acquitted of War Crimes," *USA Today*, 1 December 2005, 5A.

3.   "Two Thousand Bosnian Massacre Victims Identified," *Associated Press*, 10 June 2005.

4.   "Vuk Karadzic Memorial Ceremony," *TALON*, 17 May 2002, 12.

5.   "Explosives Found at Srebrenica Memorial," *Associated Press*, 5 July 2005.

6.   "Bosnian Serbs Give in on Police," *CBS News*, 5 October 2005.

7.   Beth Kampschror, "Six Years in Transition, Kosovo Eyes Final Status Talks," *The Christian Science Monitor*, 23 November 2005, 4.

8.   Questionnaire by Chaplain (CPT) Vernon Chandler, 29 July 2004.

9.   "U.S. Army Chaplains Assume the Role of Spiritual Diplomats," *The Military Chaplain,* September/October 2001, 4.

10.   Questionnaire by Chaplain (CPT) Sean Wead, 20 July 2005.

11.   Chaplain Hank Steinhilber, interview by Dr. John Brinsfield, 9 December 2003.

12.   Chaplain Peter Baktis, interview by Dr. John Brinsfield, 11 December 2003.

13.   Questionnaire by Chaplain Christopher Guadiz, 5 November 2005.

About the Author

Chaplain (LTC) Kenneth E. Lawson served as an enlisted soldier from 1979–85. He entered the chaplain candidate program through the Ohio Army National Guard in 1989, and served as a National Guard chaplain and a civilian pastor for 10 years. In 1999, Ken went on Active Duty in the Active Guard and Reserve (AGR) program. His Active Duty assignments include Fort Devens, Massachusetts (1999–2001); Heidelberg, Germany (2001–2004); and the US Army Chaplain School (2004–present). Ken also has 8 years teaching experience as an adjunct Bible College instructor. While assigned in Germany, Ken spent extensive time in Bosnia, Kosovo, and Macedonia as part of the NATO peacekeeping mission.

Ken was born in Lawrence, Massachusetts, in 1961. He received a Bachelor of Science from Salem State College, a Master of Arts from Bob Jones University, a Master of Divinity from Cincinnati Bible Seminary, a Doctorate of Sacred Theology from Bethany Theological Seminary, and a Doctor of Philosophy from Preston University. His military education includes Basic Training and Advanced Individual Training at Fort Gordon, Georgia (1979–80); Chaplain Officer Basic Course (1990); Chaplain Officer Advanced Course (1996); US Army Command and General Staff College (2000); and the Installation Chaplain (O5) Course (2002). Ken is endorsed by the Associated Gospel Churches and serves on their Cooperating Board. He is the author of five books, the most recent being *Religion and the U.S. Army Chaplaincy in the Florida Seminole Wars, 1817–1858.*

Ken and Vera Lawson were married in 1986. They are the parents of four children, and reside in Columbia, SC.

Glossary

1LT	first lieutenant
AAR	after action review
ACR	armored cavalry regiment
AD	armored division; Active Duty
AFB	Air Force Base
AOR	area of responsibility
ARCOM	Army Reserve Command
ARPERCEN	Army Personnel Center
ASG	area support group
AST	area support team
BCT	brigade combat team
bde	brigade
BG	brigadier general
bldg	building
bn	battalion
BSB	base support battalion
CA	chaplain assistant; Civil Affairs
CAS	Camp Able Sentry
CH	chaplain
CIMIC	Civil Military Cooperation
CMRP	Command Master Religious Program
COL	colonel
COMSFOR	Commander, Stabilization Force
CPT	captain
CPX	command post exercise
CSM	command sergeant major
CST	chaplain support team
DISCOM	division support command
DMZ	demilitarized zone
DOD	Department of Defense
EPW	enemy prisoner of war
etc.	and so forth
EU	European Union
EUCOM	European Command
FIST	fire support team
FM	field manual
FOB	forward observation base
FRG	family readiness group
FSB	forward support battalion
GA	Georgia
GI	Government Issue
HQ	headquarters
ID	infantry division

IFOR	Implementation Force
IN	Indiana
IO	information operations
JSOTF	Joint Special Operations Task Force
JTF	joint task force
JTFUMT	joint task force unit ministry team
KFOR	Kosovo Force
LDS	Latter Day Saint
LP	listening post
LSA	Life Support Area
LTC	lieutenant colonel
LTG	lieutenant general
MAJ	major
MASCAL	mass casualties
MASH	Mobile Army Surgical Hospital
MD	multinational divisions
MG	major general
MOPP	mission oriented protective posture
MP	military police
MRE	meals, ready to eat; mission readiness exercise
MSG	master sergeant
MWR	Morale, Welfare, Recreation
NATO	North Atlantic Treaty Organization
NCO	noncommissioned officer
NCOIC	noncommissioned officer in charge
NGO	nongovernmental organization
NSE	National Support Element
NTV	nontactical vehicle
OIC	officer in charge
OJF	Operation JOINT FORGE
OP	observation post
OSCE	Organization for Security and Cooperation in Europe
PA	Pennsylvania
PDP	Party for Democratic Prosperity
PFC	private first class
POC	point of contact
PSYOP	psychological operations
RC	Reserve component
RPG	rocket propelled grenade
RV	recreational vehicle
SACEUR	Supreme Allied Commander, Europe
SC	South Carolina
SDSM	Social Democratic Union of Macedonia
SF	Special Forces
SFC	sergeant first class

SFOR	Stabilization Force
SGM	sergeant major
SGT	sergeant
SITREP	situation report
SPC	specialist
SPOE	sea port of embarkation
SSG	staff sergeant
SUV	suburban utility vehicle
TAACOM	Theater Army Area Command
TAB	target acquisition battery
TDY	temporary duty
TF	task force
TOC	tactical operations center
TSC	theater support command
TV	television
UMT	Unit Ministry Team
UN	United Nations
UNMIK	UN mission in Kosovo
UNPROFOR	UN Protection Force
US	United States
USACRC	United States Army Combat Readiness Center
USARC	US Army Reserve Command
USAREUR	United States Army, Europe
USASET	US Army Support Element Taszar
ZOS	zone of separation

Bibliography

Articles and Reports

Army Times. Various articles from 1995 through 2005.

Anderson, Joseph. "Military Operational Measures of Effectiveness for Peacekeeping Operations." *Military Review*, September/October 2001.

Atkinson, Rick. "Warriors Without a War: U.S. Peacekeepers in Bosnia Adjusting to New Tasks: Arbitration, Bluff, Restraint." *The Washington Post*, 14 April 1996, A-1.

Austin, Jason. "Task Force Eagle Leaving Bosnia." *Army Public Affairs Press Release*, 23 November 2004, 1.

"Blast Hits U.N. HQ in Kosovo." *Associated Press*, 2 July 2005.

"Bodies Found After C-130 Crash." *CNN.com*, 1 April 2005.

"Bomb Near Kosovo Presidential Convoy." *Associated Press*, 15 March 2005.

"Bosnia Civilians Rain Stones on American Troops." *Rocky Mountain News,* 28 August 1997, 46A.

"Bosnian Serbs Give in on Police." *CBS News*, 5 October 2005.

Cairns, James L. "Meanwhile in Bosnia: The Region was Forgotten During the NATO-Yugoslavian Conflict, 1999." *Christian Century*, 14 July 1999, 12.

Church, George J. "Divided by Hate." *TIME Magazine*, 18 December 1995, 3, 52, 54.

Crawley, Vince. "Despite Drawdown, Endgame's Unclear." *Army Times*, 22 July 2002, 10–11.

_____. "Should We Stay or Should We Go?" *Army Times*, 22 July 2002, 10.

"Croat Police Blamed in Attack on Muslims." *Washington Post*, 27 February 1997, A-24.

Dahms, Jon. "7th Army Reserve Command Chaplains Complete Historic Ministry." *US Army Reserve News Service*, 5 May 2003.

"Dead GI was Grad of Lamar High." *Houston Chronicle*, 23 March 1996, available from www.chron.com.

"Dealing with Bosnia War Criminals." *Washington Post*, 24 December 1997, A-12.

"Dear GI: Letters will Brighten Christmas in Bosnia." *St. Louis Post-Dispatch*, 15 December 1997, 2.

Deutsch, Anthony. "Kosovo's Ex-Premier Surrenders to UN." *WORLD Magazine*, 9 March 2005, 6.

"Disaster Response: Efforts of Interaction Agencies in Kosovo." *InterAction*, May 2001, available from www.interaction.org/kosovo.

Djurdjevic, Bob. "Bosnia: What's the Full Truth." *Wall Street Journal,* 9 February 1996, 15.

Dougherty, Kevin. "Three Soldiers Injured in Snowy Tuzla Area." *European Stars & Stripes*, 9 February 1996, 1.

"Eighteen U.S. Soldiers Decorated for Restraint Facing Mobs." *The Record* (New Jersey), 30 August 1997, A-12.

Erkkinen, Erik. "After Action Report for SFOR-4." 15 May 1999.

"Explosives Found at Srebrenica Memorial." *Associated Press*, 5 July 2005.

"Ex-Yugoslav Army Chief Surrenders to U.N. Court." *USA Today*, 26 April 2005, 11A.

Field, Kimberly C. and Robert M. Perito, "Creating a Force for Peace Operations: Ensuring Stability with Justice." *Parameters*, Winter 2002–2003, 77–78.

Gerry, Alexander A.C. "Bosnia and Herzegovina: Questioning the Dayton Agreement." *The Officer*, June 2001, 23.

Glasters, Paul. "In the Twilight Zone." *U.S. News & World Report*, 18 December 1995, 44–45.

Higgins, Andrew. "Could U.N. Fix Iraq? Word from Kosovo Isn't Encouraging." *Wall Street Journal*, 2 August 2004, 1.

Hoagland, Jim. "On the Wagon in Bosnia." *Washington Post*, 1 February 1996, 18.

Jacobs, Jeffery A. "Civil Affairs in Peace Operations." *Military Review*, July–August 1998, 11.

Kampschror, Beth. "Six Years in Transition, Kosovo Eyes Final Status Talks." *The Christian Science Monitor*, 23 November 2005, 4.

Katz, Gregory. "Bosnians Say Serbs Must Free Slave Labor Camps." *The Patriot News* [Harrisburg, PA], 18 January 1996, A-9.

"Kosovo ex-PM Denies 37 War Charges." *CNN.com*, 14 March 2005.

"Kosovo Separatist Acquitted of War Crimes," *USA Today*, 1 December 2005, 5A.

Kozaryn, Linda D. "U.S. Offers Kosovar Albanians Safe Haven." *Armed Forces Press Service*, n.d. Available from www.defenselink.mil/specials/provide_refuge/2background.html; accessed on 3 October 2005.

Kunich, Gary J. "Soldiers Prepare to Leave Kosovo by Preparing for Transition Back Into Home Life." *European Stars & Stripes*, 15 December 2000, 3.

Liotta, P.H. and Cindy R. Jebb, "Macedonia: End of the Beginning or Beginning of the End?" *Parameters*, Spring 2002, 96.

Matthews, William. "Clinton: Bosnia a Defining Moment." *Army Times*, 1 January 1996, 3.

McAllister J.F.O. "Uncertain Beacon." *TIME Magazine*, 27 November 1995, 39.

McChrystal, Scott and Marv Wooten. "How a Rock Band Saved Task Force Eagle (Well, Sort Of)." *The Army Chaplaincy*, Spring 1999, 43–44.

McClure, Robert L. and Morton Orlov II. "Is the UN Peacekeeping Role in Eclipse?" *Parameters*, Autumn 1999, 98.

"Milosevic May Intervene in Bosnia." *Chicago Tribune*, 28 August 1997, 24.

Myers, Steven Lee. "Army Will Give National Guard the Entire U.S. Role in Bosnia." *The New York Times*, 5 December, 2000, 1.

"NATO Sends Troops Into Strife-Torn Kosovo." *Associated Press*, 18 March 2004.

Naylor, Sean D. "Routing out Terrorism in Bosnia." *The Army Times,* 10 December 2001, 12.

O'Connor, Mike. "For U.S. Troops, Bosnia Seems to be a Healthy Place." *The New York Times*, 3 July 1996, 1.

"On Bosnia: Messages in Clinton Visit Should be Heeded." *Houston Chronicle*, 24 December 1997, 18.

"Operation Allied Force," www.defenselink.mil/specials/Kosovo.

Perry, William J. "On the Deployment of U.S. Troops with the Bosnia Peace Implantation Force." Delivered to the House Committee on International Relations, 30 November 1995.

_____. "U.S. in Bosnia." *The Officer*, January 1996, 17.

Peterson, David. "Memorandum on Religious Conflict in Yugoslavia," 30 December 1994.

Reinties, Ralph, ed. "Tularemia Outbreak Investigation in Kosovo: Case Control and Environmental Studies Research." *Emerging Infectious Diseases*, January 2002.

"Risks Remain in Bosnia-Herzegovina—News Watch." *International Travel News*, August 2002.

"Rock-Hurling Serbs End Their Anti-NATO Rampage." *The Deseret News* (Utah), 29 August 1997, A-4.

"Serb Mobs Target Muslims, Albanians." *Associated Press*, 18 March 2004.

"Serbs Reject Kosovo Power-Sharing Plan." *USA Today*, 11 August 2005, 5A.

Shalikashvili, John M. "Initial Posture Statement, 12 February 1997." *Selected Speeches, Testimony, and Interviews by General John M. Shalikashvili, Chairman of the Joint Chiefs of Staff*. Washington, DC: US Government Printing Office, 1998.

Spencer, Greg. "No Reservations." *The Budapest Sun*, 28 November–4 December 1996, 1.

"Standing Operating Procedures/Chaplain," Joint Task Force Operation PROVIDE REFUGE, 10 May 1999.

Stojanovic, Dusan. "100,000 Protest Milosevic's Rule." *The Patriot News* [Harrisburg, PA], 26 November 1996, A-7.

Strong, Chaplain (CPT) Peter, and SPC Phillip Fortner. "After Action Report—Camp Demi." 18 March 1999.

Sullivan, Stacy. "Serb Forces Cut Contacts with NATO." *Washington Post*, 9 February 1996, 1.

Summers, Harry. "Storm Clouds Over Two Bosnian Fronts." *Washington Times*, 1 February 1996, 17.

Swartz, Stephen. "The Failure of Europe in Bosnia and the Continuing Infiltration of Islamic Extremists." *The Weekly Standard*, 20 June 2005, 17.

Szasz, Steve. "The Chaplain's Chapters: A Monthly Letter Containing Information and Inspiration for Family and Friends." 27 September 1996.

Taylor, Sean D. "Readiness is in the Eye of the Beholder." *Army Times*, 17 February 1997, 18, 30.

"Three U.N. Officers Die in Kosovo Prison Shootout." *Associated Press*, 18 April 2004.

"Two Thousand Bosnian Massacre Victims Identified." *Associated Press*, 10 June 2005.

Unpublished Diary of Chaplain Kenneth Lawson. A copy is on file at the US
Army Chaplain Center and School Library, Fort Jackson, SC.
"U.S. Troops End Mission in Bosnia." *The State* [Columbia, SC], 25 November
2004, A-20.
"U.S. Army Chaplains Assume the Role of Spiritual Diplomats." *The Military
Chaplain,* September/October 2001, 4.
"U.S. Troops in Hungary." *Washington Times*, 30 January 1996, 16.
"Vuk Karadzic Memorial Ceremony." *TALON*, 17 May 2002, 12.
Wester, Eric, John Stepp, and Donald Holdridge. "Initial Ministry to Persecuted
People." *The Army Chaplaincy*, Winter–Spring 2000, 36–37.
Wikipedia contributors. "History of Kosovo." *Wikipedia, The Free Encyclopedia,*
www.en.wikipedia.org/wiki/ history_of_kosovo.

Books

Albright, Madeline. *Madam Secretary: A Memoir.* New York: Miramax Books,
2003.
Auty, Phyllis. *Tito: A Biography.* New York: McGraw-Hill Book Company, 1970.
Boot, Max. *The Savage Wars of Peace: Small Wars and the Rise of American
Power.* New York: Perseus Books, 2002.
Clark, Wesley. *Waging Modern War: Bosnia, Kosovo, and the Future of Conflict.*
New York: PublicAffairs Books, 2001.
Clinton, Bill. *My Life.* New York: Alfred A. Knopf Publisher, 2005.
Cobb, Ronald L. *Memories of Bosnia: The 35th Division's SFOR 13 NATO
Peacekeeping Mission.* Bloomington, IN: AuthorHouse Publishers, 2004.
Columbus, Frank, ed. *Kosovo-Serbia: A Just War?* Commack, NY: Nova Science
Publishers, 1999.
Curtis, Glenn E., ed. *Yugoslavia: A Country Study.* Washington, DC: GPO for the
Library of Congress, 1992.
Donia, Robert J. and John V.A. Fine, Jr. *Bosnia and Herzegovina: A Tradition
Betrayed.* New York: Columbia University Press, 1994.
Dragnich, Alek N. *Serbs and Croats: The Struggle for Yugoslavia.* San Diego:
Harvest Books, 1992.
Friedman, Francine. *The Bosnian Muslims*, Boulder, CO: Westview Press, 1996.
Gerolymatos, Andre. *The Balkan Wars.* New York: Basic Books, 2002.
Gresham, Stella. *The Bosnia Files: An Intimate Portrait of Life Behind the Lines.*
Bristol, IN: Wyndham Hall Press, 1996.
Hartzog, William W. *American Military Heritage.* Washington, DC: Center of
Military History, 2001.
Honig, Jan W. and Norbert Both. *Srebrenica: Record of a War Crime.* New York:
Penguin Books, 1997.
Judah, Tim. *Kosovo: War and Revenge.* New Haven: Yale University Press, 2000.
_____. *The Serbs: History, Myth, and the Destruction of Yugoslavia.* New
London: Yale University Press, 2000.

Kindross, Lord. *The Ottoman Centuries: The Rise and Fall of the Turkish Empire.* New York: HarperCollins Publishers, 2002.

Korbel, Josef. *Tito's Communism.* Denver: University of Denver Press, 1951.

Lawson, Kenneth. *AGC Chaplains in Operations Other Than War.* Taylors, SC: Associated Gospel Churches, 1998.

Lembke, Chaplain Michael. *Greetings from Bosnia, Family and Friends.* Self-published, 2001.

Malcolm, Noel. *Kosovo: A Short History.* New York: New York University Press, 1998.

Mertus, Julie A. *Kosovo: How Myths and Truths Started a War.* Berkeley: University of California Press, 1999.

Sells, Michael A. *The Bridge Betrayed: Religion and Genocide in Bosnia.* Berkeley: University of California Press, 1998.

Smart, Ninian, ed. *Atlas of the World's Religions.* Oxford: Oxford University Press, 1999.

US Army Field Manual (FM) 41-10, *Civil Affairs Operations.* Washington, DC: US Government Printing Office, 1993.

Warren, Michael A. *The United States Army Reserve in Operation Joint Endeavor: Mobilization and Deployment.* Atlanta: US Army Reserve Command Historian, June 1996.

Wheatcroft, Andrew. *Infidels: A History of the Conflict Between Christendom and Islam.* New York: Random House Publishers, 2003.

Zickel, Raymond and Walter R. Iwaskiw, eds. *Albania: A Country Study.* Washington, DC: GPO for the Library of Congress, 1992.

Questionnaires, Interviews, and Correspondence
Questionnaires

Allen, Chaplain (CPT) Stanley. Questionnaire. 1 November 2005.

Appleget, Chaplain (CPT) Patrick. Questionnaire. 16 August 2005.

Baumann, Chaplain (CPT) Brad. Questionnaire. 25 July 2005.

Belz, Chaplain Keith. Questionnaire. 6 August 1999.

Bennett, Chaplain (CPT) Alva R. Questionnaire. 20 May 2005.

Blay, Chaplain (CPT) Joseph. Questionnaire. 5 August 2004.

Brown, Chaplain (CPT) Richard E. Questionnaire. 24 July 2004.

Cantrell, Chaplain (CPT) Steven E. Questionnaire. 31 January 2005.

Causey, Chaplain (CPT) Brent. Questionnaire. 13 April 2005.

Chandler, Chaplain (CPT) Vernon. Questionnaire. 29 July 2004.

Coatie, SGT De-Angelo. Questionnaire. 8 August 2005.

Cooper, Chaplain (CPT) Ronald. Questionnaire. 19 May 2005.

Crary, Chaplain (MAJ) David. Questionnaire. 9 June 2004.

Firtko, Chaplain (CPT) Steven. Questionnaire. 15 August 1999.

Flowers, SFC Lucinda. Questionnaire. 29 July 2004.

Gardner, SFC Craig. Questionnaire. 25 March 2005.

Guadiz, Chaplain (1LT) Christopher. Questionnaire. 5 November 2005.

Hartranft, Chaplain (MAJ) Jay. Questionnaire. 10 August 2000.

Hendel, Chaplain (LTC) Lawrence. Questionnaire. 25 October 2005.

Horton, Chaplain (CPT) William. Questionnaire. 5 August 2004.

Hubbs, Chaplain Kenneth. Questionnaire. 10 July 2004.

Huisjen, Chaplain (CPT) Matthew. Questionnaire. 1 November 2003.

Jackson, SFC Elbert. Questionnaire. 20 September 2004.

Jackson, SSG Yolanda. Questionnaire. 15 June 2004.

Johnson, SSG James. Questionnaire. 22 October 2004.

Jones, Chaplain (CPT) Scott. Questionnaire. 9 August 2005.

Kendrick, Chaplain (CPT) Martin. Questionnaire. 31 January 2005.

Kesling, Chaplain (CPT) Terrance. Questionnaire. 11 February 2005.

Khan, Chaplain (CPT) Mohammad. Questionnaire. 25 July 2005.

Lee, SSG Dae J. Questionnaire. 27 January 2005.

Lee, SGT David. Questionnaire. 5 August 2005.

Locke, Chaplain (CPT) Lonnie L., III. Questionnaire. 25 July 2004.

Loveless, SFC Wyman. Questionnaire. 13 October 2004.

Luckie, Chaplain (CPT) Marvin. Questionnaire 13 April 2005.

McLain, Chaplain (CPT) John. Questionnaire. 10 July 2004.

Metcalf, Chaplain (MAJ) Michael. Questionnaire. 13 April 2005.

Neal, SGM Pamela. Questionnaire. 15 and 16 June 2004.

Nelson, SSG James. Questionnaire. 16 August 2005.

Patterson, MSG Chris. Questionnaire. 16 August 2004.

Peek, SFC Deborah. Questionnaire. 20 May 2005.

Peterson, Chaplain Timothy. Questionnaire. 13 April 2005.

Powers, Chaplain (CPT) Darin. Questionnaire. 11 August 2005.

Roberts, Chaplain (CPT) Oran. Questionnaire. 26 October 2004.

Shrum, Chaplain (MAJ) Alvin. Questionnaire. 9 September 2004.

Simpson, Chaplain (CPT) Steven. Questionnaire. 4 November 2004.

Smiley, Chaplain (CPT) Philip. Questionnaire. 10 June 2004.

Stang, Chaplain William J. Questionnaire. 2 February 2005.

Sterling, Chaplain (CPT) Scott. Questionnaire. 15 March 2005.

Tsai, SSG Frank. Questionnaire. 29 October 2005.

Wead, Chaplain (CPT) Sean. Questionnaire. 20 July 2005.

Wehlage, Chaplain (CPT) William. Questionnaire. 25 July 2005.

Wismer, Chaplain (LTC) Frank. Questionnaire. 4 October 2004.

Yates, SGT Jasmine. Questionnaire. 27 October 2005.

Yoon, Chaplain Paul. Questionnaire. 19 July 2004.

Interviews

Baktis, Chaplain Peter, interview by Dr. John Brinsfield, 11 December 2003.

Baktis, Chaplain Peter, interview by author, 13 August 2004.

Brown, Chaplain (CPT) David, interview by author, 27 July 2005.

Chandler, Chaplain (LTC) Vernon, interview by author, 29 July 2004.

Giannola, Chaplain (CPT) Jeff, interview by author, 5 August 1997.

Hartranft, Chaplain (MAJ) Jay, interview by author, 6 August 1997.

Hicks, Chaplain David, and Chaplain Phil Hill interview by Dr. John Brinsfield, 3 March 2004.

Horton, Chaplain (COL) Janet, interview by Dr. John Brinsfield, 3 March 2004.

Howell, Chaplain Charles, interview by Dr. John Brinsfield, 10 December 2003.

Jones, Chaplain (CPT) Steven Mark, interview by author, 21 June 2004.

Kopec, Chaplain Rajmund, interview by Dr. John Brinsfield, 9 December 2003.

Kovach, Chaplain (MAJ) Allen, interview by author, 17 August 2005.

Land, Chaplain (MAJ) Robert, interview by author, 9 July 2004.

Lanious, Chaplain (MAJ) Chet, interview by author, 27 July 2005.

McChrystal, Chaplain (LTC) Scott, interview by Dr. John Brinsfield, 3 March 2004.

Moates, Chaplain (MAJ) Jerry, interview by author, 14 June 2004.

Steinhilber, Chaplain Hank, interview by Dr. John Brinsfield, 9 December 2003.

Szasz, Chaplain Steve, interview by author, 29 August 2005.

Wake, Chaplain (COL) Henry (Retired), interview by Dr. John Brinsfield, 4 March 2004.

Zalis, Chaplain (BG) David, interview by author, 4 May 2005.

Correspondence

Baktis, Chaplain Peter, correspondence with author, 4 October 2005.

Compton, Chaplain Douglas, correspondence with author, 3 November 2005.

Drew, Chaplain Gregg, correspondence with author, 19 December 2002; 16 March 2003.

Hartranft, Chaplain Jay, correspondence with author, 7 June 2004.

Hendel, Chaplain Lawrence, correspondence with author, 3 November 2005.

Holdridge, Chaplain Donald, correspondence with author, 4 October 2005.

Howell, Chaplain Charles, correspondence with author, 7 June 2004.

Hudson, Chaplain F. Douglas, correspondence with Chaplain Gregg Drew, 16 March 2003.

Overturf, SPC Kelli, correspondence with author, 6 December 2002.

Rambert, SGT Darnell, correspondence with author, 2 February 2003.

Stepp, Chaplain John, correspondence with author, 4 October 2005.

Appendix

US Army Deaths and Serious Injuries in the Balkans

From 1995 through 2005 in the Balkans there were several hundred incidents of injured US soldiers; only the most serious of these injuries were reported.* Officially, there were 113 serious injuries to US soldiers reported to the US Army Combat Readiness Center. The huge majority of these injuries were from transportation accidents. A combination of austere weather, poor quality roads, and aggressive civilian drivers all contributed to the high number of US military traffic accidents and related injuries. The next major factors causing injuries to US troops were related to the operation and maintenance of military equipment. There were also numerous accidents caused by land mines, carelessness with firearms, horseplay, athletic injuries, or malfunctioning equipment.

Nine US Army soldiers died while stationed somewhere in the Balkans: five were from ground accidents and four were from aviation accidents. The five ground fatalities were the 1 August 1999 death by electrocution, the 30 December 2000 death by the accidental discharge of a weapon, the 1 June 2001 death in a traffic accident, the 29 July 2003 death in a traffic collision, and the 20 September 2003 death by a heart attack while exercising. The four Army aviation fatalities include the 5 May 1999 aircraft accident that killed two Army pilots in Albania and the 8 June 2003 helicopter wire strike, causing the aircraft to crash, that killed two Army pilots in Serbia. These figures do not take into account the few civilian American contractors who were injured or killed in the Balkans.

The worst incident that caused fatalities in the Balkans was the 1 April 2005 crash of an Air Force C-130 that resulted in the deaths of nine Air Force personnel. Although Army chaplains supported the Air Force chaplain in this mission, the fatalities were from the Air Force and do not show up on statistics from the US Army Combat Readiness Center. The US Army does not maintain statistics on Navy, Marine, or Air Force personnel that were injured or killed between 1995 and 2005.

---

*Statistics are from the US Army Combat Readiness Center.

Index of Chaplains and Chaplain Assistants

Chaplains

Chaplain Assistants

G P O U.S. GOVERNMENT PRINTING OFFICE: 2006–553–572